Taking in Sail

It is time to be old,
To take in sail.

                R. W. Emerson, Terminus

Taking in Sail

Patrick Medd O.B.E., Q.C.

Panama Hat

Published by
Panama Hat
9 Kent Road, Harrogate
North Yorkshire, HG1 2LE

Published 1996

© Patrick Medd

ISBN 0 952877 80 5

Produced for the publisher by
Robert Boyd
PRINTING & PUBLISHING SERVICES
260 Colwell Drive, Witney
Oxfordshire OX8 7LW

Contents

	Foreword	vii
	Acknowledgements	viii
1	Background and Beginnings	1
2	Chertsey and Abberley	7
3	Uppingham	13
4	Apprentice Shipbuilder	19
5	Cambridge	22
6	The 'Grand' Tour	27
7	Phoney War	36
8	Pioneer	39
9	Infantryman	46
10	Gunner	55
11	Madagascar	61
12	Palestine and Ceylon	69
13	Introduction to Burma	76
14	Monsoon Victory	83
15	War's End and Marriage	93
16	New Life Begins	99
17	Early Struggles	114
18	I.C.C.U.S.	118
19	Hopeful Politician	126
20	County Council and Failed Politician	131
21	Odd Cases and Coal Miners	139
22	Taxman's Counsel	149

CONTENTS

23	Queen's Counsel	154
24	Some Odd Jobs and a Little Ambition	167
25	More Cases	172
26	Last years as a Barrister	184
27	Circuit Judge	192
28	Tax Judge	201
29	Final Assessment	211
	Index	214

Foreword

On the 22 May, 1559, almost exactly three hundred and sixty years before I was born, Benvenuto Cellini wrote at the start of his autobiography

"All men, whatever be their condition, who have done anything of merit, or which verily has a semblance of merit, if so be they are men of truth and good repute, should write the tale of their life with their own hand. Yet it would be best if they should not set out on so fine an enterprise till they have passed their fortieth year. And now this very thing occurs to me, when I am fifty eight years old and more, here in Florence, where I was born. Many are the adversities I can look back on such as fall to the lot of man; yet I am freer from the same than I have ever been till now. In truth it seems to me I have greater content of mind and health of body than at any time in the past. Some pleasant happenings I recall, and, again, some unspeakable misfortunes, which, when I remember, strike terror into me and wonder that I have, indeed, come to this age of fifty eight, from which by God's Grace, I am now going on my way rejoicing".

I take up my pen as this very thing occurs to me when I am fifty seven years old, under St Helen's spire here in Abingdon the town where my father met my mother and fell in love with her, and where I have worked and lived for many happy years. The merits of Abingdon are insignificant compared with those of Florence and any thing of merit that I have done is, of course, equally, or more, insignificant compared with the wonders of craftsmanship and art created by Benvenuto Cellini. But my fifty seven years have seen much change and many excitements and I recall some pleasant happenings and a few misfortunes and so I have decided to follow Cellini's invocation and write the tale of my life with my own hand. Perhaps it will tell my daughters, for whom I do it, something that they did not know of their father and something of the days they never saw.

★★★★★★★★★★

I wrote the above when I was in hospital recovering from a broken ankle, the result of falling from a tall ladder trying to mend a curtain rod in the hall of our home at 52 East St Helen Street in Abingdon. In hospital, I was bored with nothing to do. So I began to write this. I did not get very far before my ankle was mended and I was able to return to work and normal life. When I retired some seventeen years later, I took my pen up again and continued the story. While doing this, I have made some amendments to what I wrote earlier and have, I hope, thereby, eliminated any inconsistencies as to dates that might have otherwise appeared.

Acknowledgements

During the last years of his life our father, Patrick Medd, wrote this memoir, and during his last months we spent many happy hours sorting out photographs with him, and putting the manuscript in order. It is in memory of his life, and as a tribute to the father we loved, that, as Panama Hat, we have arranged for the publication of *Taking in Sail.*

In this endeavour we have been helped by many people. His sister, our aunt, Betty Dean, and his cousin Joy Robinson, have been tireless supports, reading the manuscript, checking proofs, and advising on design. Janice Corden typed several versions of the manuscript. David Chaffin read the proofs. Nigel Bentley has wrestled with the final proofs, and Amy Bentley has proved the best of clerical assistants. Bob Boyd of Robert Boyd Printing and Publishing Services, has given us the benefit of his sympathetic and experienced eye. We would like to thank them all.

Jane Bentley and Drusilla Modjeska

CHAPTER ONE

Background and Beginnings

I was born in Epsom on May 26, 1919. The following week the Derby was to be run — the first in peace time for five years. I was later told by my mother that the weather was of that perfect type that only England can produce when the gods smile on her in May and June. The Downs must have been a lovely sight and the crowds that gathered that year must have been more than ordinarily happy. A baby born into such a world could hardly fail to absorb the hopefulness and happiness around him and one born to such kind and gentle parents as mine was lucky indeed. I think I have always tended to be of a happy disposition and this I attribute to the good fortune that surrounded me when I was born.

My father was one of eight children of a country parson, Canon Peter Goldsmith Medd, and his wife, Louisa. The Medds came from North Yorkshire. Canon Medd was himself the son of a surgeon in Stockport who had married a Miss Goldsmith whose father lived in Leyburn Hall in Wensleydale. My father lived throughout his boyhood with his parents in the rectory at North Cerney in Gloucestershire. The rectory, a well proportioned William and Mary house under a roof of Cotswold stone tiles, lies alongside the little church in a fold in the hills bordering the River Churn, a few hundred yards from the old road from Cirencester to Cheltenham. Even now this is a part of England that has not been seriously disturbed by the motor car and it remains a beautiful and homely part of our countryside.

The living at North Cerney belonged to University College, Oxford, of which my grandfather had been a fellow. He left Oxford having failed to achieve his ambition which was to become master of his college. He was defeated in the contest by Dr Plumptre, a former suitor of Jane Austen's niece, Fanny Knight. At the time that the mastership became vacant there were six fellows entitled to vote in the election of a new master and of those six, three were Medds. The fact that even with such family connections he failed to get himself elected suggests that my grandfather had few gifts for political intrigue or management. They are qualities that I was to discover as I grew older that I too lacked conspicuously.

I never knew my grandfather who died some ten years before I was born, but he seems to have been a conscientious parson well liked by his flock and a loyal upholder of the Church of England. A high churchman and a prominent tractarian he played a considerable part in the foundation of Keble College, Oxford.

My grandfather was a strong Tory and a great admirer of Lord Salisbury. The pictures that remain of him show him as a stern and portly man, none show him smiling, and he must, I think, have been a rather frightening person. I suspect he lacked humour. When he was at Oxford and living in college there was an occasion when an undergraduate thought that the gaiety of nations would be well served if the outer door of his room was nailed up when he was inside. However my grandfather heard the noise of his would be captor hammering and managed to escape. He chased the culprit and, having caught him in the quad, administered peremptory chastisement. This incident was recorded for history by a college artist.

I remember my father telling me that he once went on a trip with my grandfather to the Scilly Isles, and as, before embarking, they were standing on the quay at Penzance news arrived from London that Lord Salisbury had died. This was received by everyone, and by none more than my grandfather, as a most solemn event. One of the pillars upon which the British Empire was supported had turned to dust. He was a Church of England parson of the old school.

My grandmother on my father's side was the only grandparent I knew. She was younger than my grandfather by some twenty years and survived him by about as much. I remember her as a very small and delicate old lady dressed in black with a bonnet and much lace. But though small I judge that she was a lady of strong character. I believe that she persuaded my grandfather to refuse the offer of appointment to the Bishopric of Worcester on the grounds that she would not live in so cold and uncomfortable a residence as Hartlebury Castle, the Bishop's official home. It is certain that she played the greater part in the upbringing of the large family in the rectory. She was a Nesbitt, a family that was settled in Staffordshire and had made some money from brewing. Her father, Alexander Nesbitt, lived at Tixal Lodge near Stafford where she spent her childhood. Though the family had been well off, by the time she grew up much of their wealth had been dissipated and she brought no great fortune to her husband. So it was that my grandparents had little money beyond my grandfather's stipend and bringing up a large family can have been no easy undertaking. A country parson at the end of the nineteenth century who had a reasonably good living was not however, relatively, as poor as the present day clergymen. A large house was useful for a large family. There was no such thing as central heating. You had big fires in the drawing room and the library and wore thick clothes. The glebe land provided pasture for two cows, which with pigs and poultry helped feed the household. Education for the children was possible with the help of clergy charities, and children did not feel deprived because they could not afford to pay for entertainment enjoyed by others. They found their own entertainment in the countryside around them. My father and his favourite brother, my Uncle Robin, walked and bicycled all over the area, they played cricket with their brothers and with the boys in the village, and occasionally shot rabbits or rooks. My father always used to bicycle to his school at Oxford, a distance of about thirty miles, at the beginning and end of term. He had a large suitcase tied to the carrier of his bicycle.

It has often been remarked how the children of country rectories do well in later life. In my father's family this was certainly true in that they all grew up to be well adjusted and contented. Though none became famous they all, save one, achieved a tolerable success in their various callings. The exception was Uncle Fred. He went into business, joining a firm which imported skins and traded for the most part with Russia. The First Great War brought difficulties which somehow Uncle Fred never surmounted. He was a keen rowing man, large and rubicund. He once rowed in the final of the Stewards Cup at Henley but did not win. He spent much of his later years in the bar of the London Rowing Club talking about rowing (as it had been in the good old days) while drinking beer (that likewise was not as good as it had been). He was always short of money.

Uncle Alfred, who was the third eldest, was killed at the very end of the war. I don't know much about him except that for a short time in his early youth he taught English to officers in the Russian navy at Vigo and, later, set up in business running a laundry at Shipton Bellenger. The others I got to know as I grew older and each one had qualities that I found delightful and admirable. They all regarded Cerney as their home and returned to it whenever opportunity offered. It must have been a very happy childhood, though tough by present day standards.

My grandmother, the mother of this large family, lived when I knew her in the first nine years of my life, in a cottage at Fetcham which was in those days a small village near Leatherhead. To me it seemed rural and remote. Now the village has been submerged under the bricks and mortar and tarmac that have advanced from the town. The last time I was in those parts I was unable to find her cottage or the little church surrounded, as I remember it, by a wall of soft coloured brick that seemed in summertime to give off a warm drowsiness.

For a short while after I was born my parents rented a cottage in Fetcham but then they moved to a flat in Battersea, facing the park, and we used to visit Fetcham at the weekends. My memories of those visits are hazy but I remember the joy of having a garden in which to play. My eldest sister, Marjorie, and I used to make houses in the lavender bushes and spent long hours talking to Mr Budd the gardener who must have been a very patient man. When we were good, which was not often, we were allowed to water the vegetables. The smell of trimmed box hedges reminds me of the garden to this day.

Life in our flat at Battersea was happy. My mother was necessarily the prevailing influence in our lives at that age and it was her innocent and gentle nature that fostered the happy atmosphere. The earliest memory of her that I am able to isolate of this period is of lying in my darkened bedroom when she came in to say 'good night' before she and my father went out to dinner with friends. I can still picture her as she came through the door and the light from the passage outside lit up her dark green evening dress of what seemed indescribable loveliness. As she stooped to kiss me her auburn hair shone with a silky smoothness.

While my father's forebears, descended, family research has revealed, from a Yorkshire farmer, Thomas Medd, who at the end of the seventeenth century lived in an isolated farmhouse named Esklets high in the Cleveland hills above Westerdale, were truly English, my mother, born Agnes Parsons, was descended on her father's side from an Irish family. She could be sure of her ancestry back to one Richard Parsons of Carrifogawill in County Limerick, and it is possible, but there is no real confirmation beyond a family tradition, that this side was connected with the Earls of Rosse of Parsonstown (now named Birr) in Offaly (one of whose relations, Sir Charles Parsons, invented the steam turbine). Another family tradition was that Richard Parsons was a direct descendant of Sir William Parsons who was sent to Ireland as Chief Justice in the reign of Queen Elizabeth I. The descendants of Richard Parsons seem to have been respectable Irish citizens marrying into families that served in India, in the Church and even in the Irish House of Commons.

On her mother's side my mother came from a family who for many generations practised as doctors in East Anglia. They were descended from a number of families, the Bests, de Hornes and Romillys, that were all of Huguenot stock. She could trace her origins back on this side to Oliver and Jocaminca de Horne who left the Netherlands in 1597 in order to escape from the persecution of the protestants by Alva. They settled in Norwich and later became Quakers. Their descendants lived for some generations in Stanway Hall near Colchester.

My mother's father left England at the age of twenty three for Calcutta where he remained for thirty nine years engaged in the jute trade. He was a strong churchman and helped the Bishops of Calcutta to build up the Church in Bengal, and his particular interest was the mission to the Eurasians. On 28 December, 1881, he married the first matron of a large hospital that had been started in Calcutta and in due course they had a family. The eldest child was my Uncle Richard Parsons later Bishop of Middleton, Southwark and Hereford, and a close friend of Archbishop Temple. There were in addition two daughters – my mother and my Aunt Muriel. Misfortune struck the family when my mother was only eight years old, as her mother then died from an obscure form of paralysis and at much the same time my grandfather's firm, of which he had just become a partner, had to cease business because of the sudden death of another partner. He, therefore, was compelled to look for other employment and returned to India to become Secretary of the Bengal Chamber of Commerce. This was, in financial terms, a substantial set back. The three young children were left in England in the care of maiden aunts who brought them up in a small semi-detached house at Swinton on the edge of Manchester. My mother's youth must have been one of comparative poverty and lacking in parental love and affection. When finally my grandfather retired from India he went to live in Abingdon where my mother kept house for him and here it was that she met my father whose mother had also come to live in the town on the death of her husband.

My parents were never well off, but both of them were by nature frugal and we always managed. I suspect that there were many periods when they were gnawed by financial worry, but neither of them shewed this to us. My father, undemonstrative and quiet, was the kindest of men. My mother thought of nothing but her husband and children and asked nothing for herself. Having been brought up with no mother herself she made for her children a home where her love and warm affection spread to every corner. And so it is that my memory of our childhood at the flat in Battersea is one of rosy contentment.

Though my mother's influence was paramount in the lives of my young sister and myself we spent much of our time with Kathleen who seemed to us old and wise, though I suspect she was no more than twenty. She was employed to help my mother. To call her a nanny would be to create a false impression. She must have been an early example of the mother's help. She was our firm friend and took us for walks in the park, to visit the owl house and to watch the deer that, in those days, were to be found there. She it was who told us about the mysteries of the outside world that were not quite the sort of things about which one could talk to one's mother or father. She seemed to think it was very important to have a young man and she talked a lot about that. When Marjorie tried to turn the conversation on to animals, especially ponies, which seemed to her the important things of life, she had only modest success. I had none when I tried to discuss steam engines or steam ships. So we always came back to the important things. But Kathleen had a brother who had been to the Nautical College at Pangbourne and had emerged as an officer in the Merchant Navy. Once his ship came into the docks at Tilbury so I was taken by Kathleen to see him on board. The ship was the 'Gascon' a small ship of the Union Castle line of about 6,000 tons, but to me she seemed as splendid as the Queen Elizabeth or any great Atlantic liner. The excitement of going up the gang plank on to the deck that seemed to dominate the quay side was intense. The hull was painted a light blue grey and a vast red and black chimney stack towered above the top deck. The engine room smelling of hot oil and the dining saloon filled, it seemed, with hundreds and hundreds of chairs and tables were what made the deepest impression on me. What wonderful things grown men could do. I came away determined to be a Merchant Navy officer and to wear the blue uniform with gold stripes that Kathleen's brother wore on that never to be forgotten day.

I first went to school when I was six. Close to the river at the south end of Chelsea Bridge there was a small kindergarten run by a Mrs Spencer. Each morning my mother used to escort me across the park to school and used the occasions to try and drive into my head the multiplication tables. Although I was later to be a fair mathematician the tables were always a terrible burden and no amount of coaxing and questioning had any effect so I remained unable to multiply without continuous use of all the fingers of both hands. One of my clear recollections of those walks to school was during the General Strike of 1926. Immediately opposite Mrs Spencer's school was the entrance to a large flour mill used by Hovis, and I remember the pickets standing at the gates. My mother thought they were dreadful people and clasped my hand more tightly as we hurried by. They looked ordinary enough men to me, but seemed very bored.

Once a year the school was thrown open to the parents who were invited to a concert which was an opportunity for them to hear their children playing elementary pieces on the piano, singing and acting. On one of these occasions we put on a performance of a scene from Julius Caesar. I was struck by one of the parents, a very lovely lady whose vivacity and liveliness set her apart. She was showing great interest in every line that was uttered by Caesar, being played by one of the oldest children in the school, a girl called Anne Casson. Little did I realise that the spectator was Sybil Thorndyke, already a famous actress and Anne's mother.

Saturday afternoons at Battersea were particularly enjoyable because my father, who was a solicitor, came back from work after lunch and took us out in the afternoon. In the winter evenings we would return home as the sun was going down and the gas lamps in the street were lit. The bell of the muffin man could be heard down the road and we would scamper upstairs and wait before the sitting room fire until my mother brought in a plate of the muffins toasted and soaked in runny butter. Then games and reading until bedtime. There was no television in those days and we did not have a wireless, but I think the way we spent the spare time in the evenings was more likely to stimulate a modest form of mental activity than long hours watching television which seems to be the modern way of keeping children occupied. My bedroom faced the street and I can remember lying awake watching the light and shadows cast on the ceiling by the lamps of passing vehicles. I could not understand why it was that when a carriage was going from left to right the light on the ceiling moved from right to left. By the time we left Battersea the car was becoming common, but there were still plenty of horse drawn vehicles about, and a number of lorries powered by steam engines. They did not, however, last long and soon their distinctive noises — the peaceful clipperty-clop of the cart horse and a sort of combination of clanking sounds produced by the revolving machinery and the hiss of steam escaping — became things of the past.

By 1927 our parents began to find the flat too small. In 1924 my second sister, Betty, was born and by the age of three she had grown beyond the stage when she could be confined to a cot or pram. Three children sprawling, crawling and getting in the way must have tried my mother sorely. But she never complained. The situation was eased a bit when in 1927, at the age of eight, I was sent away to prep school, and a year later we moved away from London to Surrey. My father first rented and later bought a house in Chertsey. There my parents lived for the rest of their lives. The house, Curfew House, was built in 1725 by a local worthy, Sir William Perkins, as the headmaster's house for a school that was accommodated in two buildings flanking it on either side. It is thought that the architect was one of Hawksmoor's assistants. Many years later the school was moved to new and larger buildings in another part of the town and Curfew House was occupied by a succession of tradesmen and later by doctors. When we went to Chertsey the front of the house was covered by virginia creeper which gradually became a nuisance by encroaching on the window frames and gutters so my father had it cut back. When this was done a stone plaque was revealed at the top of the house upon which had been carved

Founded by Sir Wm. Perkins, Knt,

For fifty children clothed and taught

Go and do likewise, 1725.

CHAPTER TWO

Chertsey and Abberley

The visitor to Chertsey in 1928 found a place very different from the one that some seventy years later his modern successor discovers. In 1928 it was a town, not far from London it is true, which had its own identity. It had not yet become a part of the great wen that as the years have passed has consumed nearly all the green that formerly divided one town or village from the next. In 1928 a ten minute walk in any direction from our home and you were in fields, and the noises and smells of the countryside were all around. From Curfew House it was but 400 yards to the lane which led past the site of the old abbey and over a mill stream, dug by the monks, to the ferry path, which then crossed the water meadows to the Thames. There, at the river's edge was a small cottage in which lived the man who would for a penny row you across to Laleham on the Middlesex bank. In another direction a quarter of a mile brought you to the fields and a path that led along the side of little streams, alive with minnows and gudgeon and, in summer months, bright with hovering dragon flies, to Thorpe, a quiet village built round a small fifteenth century church and shaded by many trees, elms and chestnuts, which always seemed to me to be unusually large and protective. Of course the change had started. Thorpe, even then, was no longer a country village ruled by squire and parson. The big house had already been given over to a nunnery and one or two of the smaller ones were occupied by families whose bread winner worked in London. But it was mostly locally employed people that lived in the cottages.

How different Chertsey and its surrounding countryside are today as I write. The town itself is no longer compact and recognisable. On all sides houses, monotonous and for the most part architecturally undistinguished, have been built so that a ten minute walk from the centre no longer brings you to open fields. It is difficult to find a reasonable sized bit of green within the distance one can walk in an afternoon. The houses on the roads that fan out from Chertsey have for the most part met up with those advancing from the towns and villages to which the roads lead. The planners have tried to keep a 'green belt' but the belt has become so thin and worn that it seems more like a bit of frayed string. The meadows on the walk to the ferry are bisected by an embanked motor way. Two separate strips of field are left, both dominated by the whizzing traffic. The path across the fields to Thorpe, and even the fields themselves, have disappeared. Part of them is now covered by a housing estate, the rest has become a vast pit, now filled with water, from which the gravel has been extracted, all surrounded by strips of wasteland. Here too along the side there is a new dual carriageway and a complex of access roads cross and recross the land that was formerly meadows. The local authority has now turned the gravel pit into a recreational lake known as Thorpe Park. It has, I believe, proved to be a success and is very popular. But I doubt whether children playing there will enjoy themselves as much as Marjorie and I and our friends did when we chased butterflies over the fields or swam in the streams.

We children were happy at Curfew House. The garden though not large had many odd corners that with the help of a little imagination made it easy to invent exciting games. The potting shed, the place below ground and known to us as the froghouse, where the boiler for the greenhouse was and the shrubbery and bushes became palaces or dungeons, forests or railway stations according to the necessity of the moment. My absorbing interests were steam railway engines and ships. I longed for a large model railway that I could lay out round the garden. A 'Castle' class steam engine, driven by me, would draw a line of small wagons, containing my obedient sisters and their friends, hissing and clanking and would pass through stations such as 'Froghouseton' or 'Backgateville'. I started to save up for this but soon learnt that tuppence a week was insufficient to provide in the foreseeable future the capital equipment that such a venture required. I can remember begging my parents to help and feeling I was being badly treated in comparison with the boys at school whose parents were better off. But, happily I was, I think, always conscious that my father was not well off and I hope I was not psychologically scarred by this deprivation. There was, however, one occasion when my childhood innocence did receive a mild scratch as a result, it seemed to me, of the monstrous unkindness of grown ups. Not long after we moved to Chertsey my mother became pregnant. For reasons which I have never understood, I did not notice the slightest difference in her shape (and, because in those days the facts of life were not divulged to small boys of ten, I would not, of course, have known what it signified if I had noticed). The only fact of which I was aware was that there came a time when a maiden aunt, my Aunt Sally, arrived to look after us, and my mother disappeared. Aunt Sally was a very friendly and approachable person and I had no difficulty in confiding in her my burning desire for a 'Castle' class steam engine, and she was, therefore, fully aware of my yearning. Then one morning she came into my bedroom to get me up and announced with great excitement that a wonderful present had arrived for me in the night. Something, she said, that I had always longed for. How marvellous, I thought, the steam engine has arrived. My only worry was what scale was it built to, was it big enough to pull carriages carrying people round the garden or would I have to be content with one that ran round the nursery floor. I had not dared to voice these fears before she told me that I had a lovely little sister. I had never longed for another sister — after all I had two already and that, surely, was enough for any one. My misery was happily, however, short lived because I discovered later that this new sister, Jo she was called being short for Jocelyn, was, though different, as delightful a companion as my other two sisters.

My other great interest, boats and ships, was more easily satisfied. Very near Curfew House ran a little backwater of the Thames, the mill stream cut for the Abbey which I have already mentioned. My boyhood friend Micky Gardner lived in the Abbey House which bordered this stream and he and I built canoes by stretching calico over wooden frames and painting it with many coats of thick paint. This enabled us to explore the stream and even occasionally to venture into the Thames itself. Ever since I have, at intervals, felt the urge to build a boat, a craving to which on several occasions I have given way. The result has been that my family has been compelled from time to time to venture forth in an assortment of canoes, dinghies and other craft of varying degrees of stability and seaworthiness, and not unnaturally they have always viewed with some horror any new manifestation of this instinct.

My prep school was in Worcestershire. Looking back I am amazed at the good fortune which ensured that I was sent there. Abberley Hall was started by a remarkable man, Gilbert Ashton, with the help of two friends, Leonard Greenwood and Mike Carr, shortly after the end of the First World War in which they had all served with distinction. It was to become and indeed I believe still is one of the foremost prep schools in the country and must have been very expensive. It would certainly have been too expensive for my parents had it not been for chance.

As I have already mentioned my mother's father spent most of his working life in India and his prospects of making a fortune were upset by mischance. However he achieved a modest distinction in commercial circles in that part of India. While he was there a young man called Ashton, Gilbert's father, came out to make his living and my grandfather did him some small service that helped to set him on his way. In due course this Ashton flourished, made a substantial fortune and ultimately returned to England where he bought a small estate at Ingatestone in Essex. It was when he was well established that my mother was born in India and the two families became friends. When later my mother was left motherless and put into the care of the Manchester aunts, the Ashtons shewed her much kindness, and she frequently stayed with them. The boys of the Ashton family, Claude, Hubert and Gilbert were all destined to become great cricketers; each played for Cambridge and for county sides. Hubert played for England. My mother attributed this remarkable family's skill at the game to the fact that when as a girl she used to stay at Ingatestone she was made to play with them. I am prepared to believe that if a person learned to handle my mother's fierce underhand sneaks bowled across the cobbled stable yard he would be able to deal effectively with any more orthodox bowler met later. This friendship resulted subsequently in Gilbert Ashton out of kindness to my mother and father accepting me at his prep school at substantially below the normal fees.

Abberley Hall had been built by some rich Birmingham merchant in the pleasant hilly country not far from Tenbury. It was bought by the school in the nineteen twenties and its rambling buildings and ample grounds provided a good setting in which young boys could be segregated from the world in an attempt to set them on the road of life firmly pointed in the direction indicated by a sound classical education. Gilbert Ashton and Leonard Greenwood were both Wykehamists and they built up a connection with the college with the result that the grounding in the classics and maths given to the pupils at Abberley was aimed at the stern standards set there. The very clever boys were groomed for Winchester Scholarships and the less clever for Winchester Common Entrance, and when, as happened in most years, the school managed to win one or two Winchester Scholarships there was great rejoicing. I remember one year, when we bagged three, the whole school was taken for an outing in a steamer on the River Avon to Stratford. To achieve a scholarship to one of the other public schools was regarded as a respectable attainment, but nothing very particular. I was not interested in Latin and Greek and so I never got far beyond the elementary in those subjects, a fact which I have always regretted. Now that I have travelled in Italy and the Mediterranean and have absorbed some of the atmosphere of that history steeped part of the world I wish I had tried harder. How much greater my enjoyment of the Italian countryside would be if I had read and understood Horace. Maths on the other hand I found easy. I liked the clean logical step by step approach to problems and found that I was interested. But, of course, to small boys it was not academic studies but games that were important, and here I was at something of a disadvantage. Ever since I was very young I have suffered from shortsight. This was discovered by my mother when once she was taking me for a walk and I drew her attention to the lovely red colour of the dress that a lady on the other side of the street was wearing. My mother looked in the direction I was pointing and saw no living soul, only a bright red pillar box. From that time onwards I have worn spectacles which, until I reached my twenties, gradually became thicker and thicker. Only very rarely have I met people who wore spectacles as thick as mine. Small boys who wear spectacles start several points down with their colleagues at school. Round horn rimmed glasses on a boy of seven look soppy and invite attack, but the fear of losing his specs in the fight does not foster in the soppy one the fierce spirit of counter attack that puts off other aggressors and if, in fact, the spectacles fly from his face then defence becomes difficult and the blind groping that becomes necessary in order to find them again makes him an even greater object of ridicule.

For games like rugger and soccer I had to take my glasses off and so I never became proficient. Cricket should have been easier, but for this I seemed to lack any aptitude though I was very keen. So keen indeed that I gave up piano classes as an extra because it involved lessons out of normal school hours and thus reduced the time available for cricket practice. There have been few decisions that I have taken in life that I have regretted so much. The ability to enjoy music is one of my greatest pleasures and I am sure that my ability to enjoy it would have been greatly increased if I had kept up my studies and attained even the slightest skill with an instrument. In the event the only thing I learned as a result of my decision to abandon the piano was that no amount of practice or keenness or anything else would ever enable me to bowl balls straight at other people's wickets or to hit balls coming straight for my own.

As years pass one's memory of details becomes, of course, blurred, but impressions remain, impressions formed presumably by detailed events and happenings that having made their mark passed into oblivion. The impression that remains of my earlier years at the school is that of a feeling of inferiority. I suppose it would nowadays be called an inferiority complex. I felt unhappy because I wanted to be good at the things that boys admired you for. Games, fighting, saying funny things about masters when their backs were turned. But I was hopeless at all these things, partly because of the limitations imposed by shortsight and partly because I had no natural ability in any of these directions anyway. It was no help being good at maths because no boy thought a whit the better of you for that. This consciousness of inferiority in those things which was brought home to me in those early years has had an effect on me that I have never been able to get over. I still feel terribly small when first I meet one of those fine hearty fellows who play games well or who are skilled at some other nationally admired activity or whose natural wit and repartee leave me with a feeling that I don't know what to say next.

But I owe a great deal to Abberley. Not only was I provided with a solid grounding in the basic subjects more thoroughly and less painfully than at most other comparable schools, but, thanks to Mike Carr the third of the triumvirate that founded the school, I developed an abiding interest in and love for painting and for the country life. Mike Carr was quite unlike any ordinary schoolmaster. He seemed to go his own way pursuing his own interests in a way which made those interests seem, even to barbaric little boys, worthwhile. With him I found that painting was exciting. He managed somehow to make me see colours and shades and patterns in ordinary everyday things that I would never have noticed if I had just looked at them by myself. I remember him making me look at the surface of the lake in the school grounds and tell him what the colours were that I really saw. Only then did I realize that all water surfaces are not blue. I always think of him when I see for the first time each year spring sunlight slanting through woodland trees and I wonder at the loveliness of the translucent green of young beech leaves. A colour that Constable loved and so few artists can successfully reproduce.

Mike Carr also ran the scouts and this too he did in his own distinctive way. Walks on the Worcestershire hills around Abberley and through the woods though ostensibly to teach you tracking or one or other of the skills for which one acquired badges as a scout were in truth occasions when one began to see the countryside as he saw it, something beautiful and interesting and, because he seemed to get pleasure from walking with us boys we got pleasure too.

The time came when it was necessary to consider what I was to do when I left Abberley. A Winchester Scholarship was out of the question and I suspect that the masters doubted if I was up to a scholarship at any school. But I was aware of my parents straitened circumstances and I felt that if I could get a scholarship anywhere it would help them so I determined to try. One of my friends at Abberley was a small boy, Harry Fawcus, whose father was the headmaster of a prep school near Rugby and one day Harry took me over to his home for lunch and tea. I remember Harry's father saying to me "Why don't you try for Uppingham? Harry's going there and it's a good school." That seemed sufficient commendation and so it was that I was entered for a scholarship at Uppingham and in due course travelled across country from Worcestershire to Rutland in order to sit the exam. The papers lasted for, I think, three days and ended with an interview on Saturday morning after which the candidates were dispatched back whence they came. I set off with another small boy whose school was in Malvern on the rail journey which involved several changes and should have resulted in us arriving at Worcester in the late afternoon. After one change we boarded a train which we hoped would take us to Birmingham in about half an hour. But after half an hour we were still racing through green fields. It soon became plain that something was wrong and after an hour and a half we were still travelling. Finally the train slowed and drew up — at Crewe. It was past six in the evening. We got out and walked along the drab platform to inquire the time of the next train to Birmingham and Worcester only to find that there was no train that would get us to Worcester before midnight. We were filled with horror for to return so late would surely be regarded as a grave offence. We phoned through to our respective schools and told them what had happened and then killed the two hours or so before the train left by walking round the town which seemed to consist of endless streets of extreme dullness made up of houses built of a peculiarly ugly red brick. We also bought, in my case for the first time, fish and chips wrapped in newspaper. When finally I got back to Abberley long after midnight I expected to be reprimanded by someone whose irritation at having to wait up for me would add venom to his perhaps justifiable anger at my stupidity. As I approached the school, however, I could see to my surprise lights shining from many upstairs windows and could hear much chattering and merriment. On entering I was greeted by a master, who I later realized had had a little too much to drink, shaking me by the hand and congratulating me warmly. At first I did not understand, but then I realized that news had preceded me from Uppingham that I had got a scholarship. I was taken upstairs to the matron's room where a party was in progress and a glass of champagne was thrust into my hand. I was, of course, very gratified, but not a little mystified. Even a returning successful Winchester scholar did not receive such treatment. His success was announced after prayers and we all clapped dutifully. But then I saw Miss Rowlatt, the under matron, who I had always considered to be very beautiful. This night she was flushed with happiness and she came across and told me that she had become engaged to Leonard Greenwood and was very happy. This, of course, explained everything, but it remained for me nevertheless a memorable occasion and I have never forgotten my first glass of champagne.

One Sunday shortly before the end of the term the Headmaster asked me to meet him after Chapel and he walked with me round the cricket ground. He asked me if my parents had explained to me the facts of life and I told him that they had not. I was then quite ignorant though I had begun to wonder how these things were arranged. Gilbert Ashton was a thoroughly pleasant person and he explained a bit about it using the simile of a flower being fertilized. He told me that the woman had a pretty rough time while the seed was being fertilized and for that reason one should always treat women with courtesy and respect. Although after my talk with him I remained in the dark on a number of important aspects of this business I have always been grateful to him for giving me this logical explanation of the need for chivalry.

CHAPTER THREE

Uppingham

The little town of Uppingham grew up round the cross roads made by the intersection of the main Leicester to Stamford road with the lesser road from Rockingham to Oakham. The Leicester to Stamford road runs more or less due east along a ridge and the main part of the town is spread out along it. The school buildings, chapel and hall, mostly built of the local stone that is a feature of the country round Stamford, occupy much of the south side of the street. The other lesser road running south towards Rockingham leaves the town from the Market Place and the church to descend from the ridge down a steep hill, Scale Hill, and then climbs up another, Red Hill, then down and up again in a series of undulations like a switch back. On the top of the ridge where this road crosses Red Hill were three of the school's boarding houses. These were known as the country houses in contradistinction to the town houses which were all reasonably close to the centre of the school. The boys in the country houses were not only further from the centre, but to get to or from school they had to go down and up these steep hills. They regarded the town house boys with their short walk along the flat to school as soft. I was allotted to Redgate one of the country houses. A few winter weeks of scrambling down Red Hill and up Scale Hill in the half dark in order to be on time for early morning school and then a walk back for breakfast, made me feel that if the town house boys were not soft we were certainly tough.

Life at Redgate was, I think, even for those days, tough. The housemaster was the Rev Fergus McNeile, known to all as Fergie. He had a certain glamour in our eyes as he was the cousin of 'Sapper' the author of the immensely exciting series of stories about Bulldog Drummond which were best selling thrillers at the time. Fergie must have been about sixty when I went to the house. Tall and very upright he was believed to have a cold bath every morning and he gave an impression of having always led an ascetic life. His brisk way of walking and his clear pink complexion confirmed this. Over thirty years later I visited him in Wales where he ended his days. He was then ninety six and looked exactly as he had done when I first knew him. Even then his memory of the boys that had passed through his hands was encyclopaedic and his comments on my contemporaries were shrewd and shewed that little that happened in the house had passed him unnoticed. But he left the running of the house largely to the pollys (as prefects were called at Uppingham; the word stems, I believe, from the classical 'poliurbis') who had power to administer canings in order to enforce discipline and they did not shrink from their duty.

I had never at that time been inside a prison and so I was not struck, as I would have been had I done so, by the resemblance that the boys' part of the house bore to a small gaol. The centre of the house was a courtyard roofed over with glass. Round the court were galleries off which doors led to small cell like rooms. Each boy was allotted one of these as his study in pursuance of a policy started by Edward Thring, the great headmaster in Victorian times, who had changed the school from a small grammar school for twenty five scholars into a large fee paying public school with three hundred boys. His decision that every boy should have a study of his own must have been blessed by many a small boy at Redgate. The study was a sanctuary. As fags, in which category one remained for two years, one was not allowed to loiter in the central hall, instead one had to run whenever one was in any of the public parts of the house. The only places where boys could congregate were the senior and junior changing rooms, where one changed for games and washed. The junior changing room was a dark dismal room and for me soon became a place to be avoided as much as possible. There a tough and brutal boy from Birmingham was the uncrowned king. When there was nothing else to do he and his cronies indulged in the sport of bullying the 'wets'. I was a wet and so was my friend Edward Raeburn. We never knew what reception we would get when we came in, but quite frequently one or both of us would be stripped and set upon by this lout. When it was my turn I did my best to hold him off, but usually before long I lost my spectacles and then I became helpless. The only way to avoid this sort of treatment was to stay in my study as much as possible, only venturing into the changing room when there was little time left before games and everyone would be busy changing. Poor Edward was slow and he had a much worse time than I did. But I do not think this treatment did me much damage, indeed it may even have had some advantages of an indirect sort. It meant that I read much more in my study than I otherwise would have done and it gave me a sympathy for the weaker person who is set upon by violent thugs which has never left me. From time to time since I have had young men in the dock before me whose behaviour bore a resemblance to that of the young man from Birmingham. I hope I have never let my dislike of him colour my judgement, but I have never believed in treating such people leniently.

During my first year at Uppingham the headmaster was Reggie Owen a straightforward God fearing clergyman who at the beginning and end of term delivered a sermon in the school chapel designed to make us realise the importance of clean living and of always doing one's best even if, as was the case with the majority of his audience, you were pretty stupid and your best would not be very good. "Freedom" he used to say "consists in doing what you ought when you ought, whether you like it or not". It was a good way of saying that freedom embraces the power to do right and to do wrong, "but you, boys, must do right". Self discipline, too, he preached and for him there was no middle course, no grey shades. Life as he put it before us was black or white.

Nowadays to express such views would, I suspect, be regarded as absurdly old fashioned, but they had their effect on me and I have never felt much sympathy with those modern intellectuals who say that there is nothing so awful as the stupid man who tries hard and does his best. But Reggie Owen left Uppingham a year or so after I arrived to become a fellow of Brasenose College. Later after a spell as chaplain in the navy he was chosen to be Archbishop of New Zealand. I was very sorry to see him go. He may not have been immensely clever but he made me feel that to lead a good life was important and in his presence one felt in the presence of a good man. That gives small boys a sense of example which helps to provide a target to aim at in life.

Reggie Owen was succeeded by John Wolfenden who was then, I believe, the youngest man, at 26, ever to be appointed headmaster of a public school. He was, we were all told when he arrived, a philosopher and very clever. He was as we would now say a whiz kid of humble origin who came to us from Oxford. He had arrived in Oxford from Yorkshire and had quickly taken the University by storm. We believed he had taken elocution lessons for the removal of his Yorkshire accent. This was, I am sure, an erroneous view based on no evidence more substantial than the fact that when he read the lesson or spoke to us formally he had a very clipped and precise diction. That he was clever there was no doubt. By the time he arrived I was in the science sixth and he made it his practice to take each of the sixth forms once a week for a sort of general discussion period. The first time he took us he came into the room and said to one boy "Well Smith what is a kettle?" Smith said nothing and the conversation never got off the ground. The reason for this was, however, not that Smith had no idea what a kettle was but that we had all heard that the same thing had happened a day or two before to the classical sixth (who were all much cleverer than us) and when the surprised boy who had been asked this unexpected question had answered something to the effect that it was a vessel made of tin for boiling water he had been taken up and led into a deep philosophical discussion on the nature of matter. We of the science sixth felt that if this happened to us we would only make fools of ourselves so we decided to take no chances. John Wolfenden later went to Shrewsbury as headmaster, became vice-chancellor of Reading University, headed a Royal Commission on Homosexuality, became Chairman of the British Museum and of the University Grants Committee and became a peer. He obviously was a great man but somehow he did not seem able to get across to me.

It is, I suppose, trite to say that anyone is lucky if he can say that more than one or two of the teachers through whose hands he passed in youth made a deep impression on him which lit a flame that thereafter illuminated some aspect of learning or life. But in this too I was fortunate. At Uppingham there were two masters each of whom made their subject come alive to me. Indeed they did more than that. Each, in his own particular way impressed his character and personality on me in such a way that the values that he respected and of which I became aware as he taught formed in time an integral part of my own philosophy.

Toby Belk was employed to teach English, but he did much more. His method was to gossip and so to start the class talking. Only after the talking had been going for a quarter of an hour or so did we realise that his amusing conversation was putting valuable ideas into a number of ordinarily unreceptive heads. He loved English prose at its best and I owe to him the stimulus to read the great prose writers. I am sure that if I had to read Conrad or Macaulay or Hardy as a matter of duty I would never have read them again voluntarily. As it was when he had casually let slip that the end of Tess of the d'Urbervilles was the most gripping and tragic piece of writing I found myself going off to the library and taking it out. I spent all night reading it under the bedclothes in the light of a torch. The next day I went back to the library for more Hardy. Toby Belk in his droll way taught me to enjoy our incomparable language and made me realise that conversation is a civilised way of learning and understanding; a fact that became clear when I reached Cambridge. He was the most tolerant of men.

V.T. Saunders, who taught physics, was very different. He gave the impression of furious intolerance. Many small boys were terrified of him because if he chose to reprimand you he did so with a scathing sarcasm that left you cowed and hardly daring to open your mouth again. But most reprimands ended with the injunction "Think, boy, think. Science is about thinking. Think, boy, think". When this had happened to me a few times I found that as the problems were posed I began to approach them in a different way. Then all of a sudden something happened and my mind began to work. We will probably never know what the thinking process really is, but I am eternally grateful to V.T. Saunders for somehow acting as the mental midwife to my infant mind and smacking it furiously to make it start to breathe.

Since then I have always thought that the most satisfying mental exercises are to be found in the study of mathematics and science. I found no difficulty in working hard in these subjects and managed to pass examinations with reasonable ease. At an early stage of my career at Uppingham I resolved to become a naval architect. In this way I would, I thought, be able to use my modest ability in maths and physics, would be able to indulge my love of boats and would not be tripped up by subjects such as Latin and divinity which I always found very difficult.

In those days naval architecture was taught as a university degree subject at only two universities, one of which was Glasgow. Thus, the decision taken, my last three years at Uppingham were spent in the science sixth where I studied the necessary subjects to enable me to achieve a place at that centre of learning. But during that period of three years in the sixth form a lot happened to change my future. Much of my time was spent in the school library rather than the classroom and I was free to read what I fancied. I soon found that there was little in the library for a boy with a consuming interest in boats so I began to look on other shelves. It was pure chance what I picked up, and it has often struck me since how different things might have been had I dipped into other books than the ones I did. I might have developed a taste for theology or butterflies or almost anything. As it was I picked up two books which set me off on a course that I had never suspected would interest me. I read the lives of H.H. Asquith and of Grey of Fallodon and that started an abiding interest in politics that has never left me. Asquith had been a man from a modest middle class background who, through the medium of the Bar, achieved a position of respect and ultimately became Prime Minister. It seemed that one could learn a lesson from his life. Grey was very different. He came of an old family that had historic ties with the Liberal and Whig parties. He was a man with a keen sense of duty and a deep love of the countryside. In their different ways these two Liberal statesmen seemed to me men worthy of emulation. So I became interested in politics. I read much biography, and slowly history, which hitherto had meant little to me, began to open up. It was an interesting time to be living too. To a young man who knew little of the world but who was beginning to take an interest in what was going on around him the period of the nineteen thirties was exciting. Labour was struggling to achieve respectability as a political party without at the same time losing its revolutionary ardour. Strange growths in Italy and Germany were becoming apparent. To me it seemed that there must be something wrong with a society that resulted in, on the one hand, ostentatious wealth in the hands of many who lacked any sense of responsibility as to how it should be used and, on the other hand, the terrible poverty and lack of hope that resulted from large scale unemployment. To many of us growing up at that time it seemed that Labour, because it pointed these things out, must be right when it said that they all stemmed from capitalism. Conservatives must be wrong because they with the Liberals had presided over the development of the society in which these evils had manifested themselves. My instincts were in favour of the liberalism of Asquith and Grey, but in the 1930's that seemed a philosophy that had little hope of revival. So I became a supporter of Labour. Labour seemed to have ideals and to be aiming for a better society.

All this had an effect on my later days at Uppingham. I found that I made more friends from those I met in the debating society than I did from the mathematicians and scientists by whom I was surrounded in class. When, towards the end of my time I was made a school prefect I found I was capable of a much closer rapport with those on the arts side than those on my own. It was at that time too that I first began to take an interest in buildings and architecture, an interest that has remained with me ever since.

During the summer term two days were devoted to expeditions. The school divided into groups and each group was taken on an excursion to see something of interest such as a factory, Stratford-upon-Avon or Lincoln Cathedral. I soon discovered that nearly all these expeditions involved long bus journeys and I used to feel (and sometimes was) horribly sick. When in addition to a bus journey I was expected to go round a factory which smelt of rubber or where there was an ear-splitting noise I soon tried to find an expedition that involved none of these things. Happily there had just joined the staff a new master, 'Cud' Wright we called him. He wore thick tweed knickerbockers and had sad black handle bar moustachios. I think he, too, disliked factories. He began to organise excursions on bicycles to nearby castles or big houses and other buildings of interest. I first went on one of these expeditions to avoid being sick in a bus. But I was soon bicycling over the undulating midland country enthusiastically and learned much from Cud Wright that I value greatly and that has added colour to my later life. The charm of English domestic and church architecture and the beauty of English gardens has been an unending source of pleasure.

I was at Uppingham for five years, and looking back over them they were for the most part happy years. The years that a boy is at his public school between roughly the ages of thirteen and eighteen are formative years. As he approaches manhood inner forces begin to make themselves felt and many educationists now feel that the spartan regime of the public school as it was in the thirties did not create the best environment into which these forces could emerge. But though I began to wonder about sex at that time it did not trouble me very seriously. I began to realise during the holidays that there was something alluring about some of my sisters' girl friends. But knowing little of the facts of life until I was well into my time at Uppingham I did not feel repressed and I do not think I suffered. I had, as I have said, been told the facts of life by Gilbert Ashton while he walked me round the cricket ground at Abberley. But it had been a simple explanation largely in the form of parables about flowers and pollen. I did not realise for some time afterwards that a child is begotten by conscious acts of its father and mother and I well remember the ribald laughter of some of the Uppingham boys when I asked whether the sex act took place in one's sleep. But though many laughed I remember one little boy telling me later that he had been glad I had asked as he too had wondered. So I began to learn about sex. But it was a much slower business in those days than it has been for our children who seem to understand all these things at a very early age.

Alcohol, too, was a mystery to me. My parents never drank except perhaps a formal glass of sherry after a bridge party. But many of the boys at Uppingham came from homes where drink was something with which they had become familiar. I well remember a friend, Ken Ferguson, a charming and delightful boy who was head of the house a year before me. When it was known that I was to succeed him in that office when he left for Cambridge he thought it right that my innocence on this subject should be dispelled. I was therefore invited to his study where he gave me a glass of lime juice into which be poured from a Brylcreem bottle a liberal portion of a liquid that looked like water. It was, of course, gin and the shock of the unpleasant taste was enough to put me off that particular form of alcohol for life, a result I have always regarded as fortunate.

In 1937 I left Uppingham for Glasgow to learn how to build ships.

CHAPTER FOUR

Apprentice Shipbuilder

The plan was that I should do what used to be known as a sandwich course. Six months practical experience in a shipyard, followed by six months reading naval architecture at the University. My parents came to Glasgow with me to see me settled in. I remember travelling up in the Royal Scot and being given an expensive lunch on the train as we raced through the English countryside on a hot and brilliant August day. I was to stay in Kelvinside in a hostel, run by the University, known as the Maclay Hall. When we reached it we found that it was presided over by a warden, a dull and sombre man who introduced himself to us as Mr Urquhart. He said that he hoped I would like it in the Hall. I do not think I ever saw him again. After I had taken my bags up to my room my father and mother and I set out to see a bit of Glasgow before they caught the night train back to London. We took a steamer from the bridge in the city down to Rothesay at the mouth of the Clyde. It was a fascinating journey, and I had little difficulty in understanding why Glaswegians have always regarded a trip 'doon the watter' as a splendid way to spend a day. As we left the city we passed the wharves where the cattle boats from Ulster and tramps from all over the world unloaded their cargoes, then reached that part of the Clyde that was concerned with the real business of the river — shipbuilding and marine engineering. Forests of cranes and scaffolding encircled great rusty hulls in all stages of construction. Some, just laid down, were shapeless masses of steel plates with frames stretching upwards like huge recumbent skeletons, others, nearly finished, were freshly painted ready for launching. Everywhere an intense bustle and a never ending clanking of cranes as iron bars or metal sheets rattled down into place. The staccato hammering of the riveters and the occasional blue flame of a welder accompanied the activity in the foreground. Away from the river and behind the shipyards green hills rose into the background until, nearer the mouth of the river, they merged into blue mountains around Loch Lomond. As we passed Clydebank the huge, but beautiful, hull of the Queen Elizabeth, the second of the great Cunarders, dominated its surroundings. She was nearly ready to slide into the water. Finally before turning back we landed at Rothesay on the Isle of Bute and walked on the front, had a cup of tea, ate an ice and re-embarked.

That evening I said goodbye to my parents as they set off again for England. It seemed a long way back to suburban Chertsey, but my sight of the river had made me feel that I was going to enjoy building ships.

A day or two later I began work as an apprentice shipwright in Fairfields yard at Govan. I was put in the charge of a 'mate' who was to be responsible for teaching me the art. He was an Ulsterman from Londonderry called Joe Gasser. Short and portly, he carried a considerable stomach before him. He was a good natured person and took endless trouble introducing me to the tricks of the trade, like drawing straight lines on the deck with a string and french chalk. He had worked in shipyards all his life except for the period of the depression when he had been out of work for three years. He was getting on for sixty when I joined him and he said that the slump had been bad for him but far worse for his children who, when they reached the age when they should have been able to earn money, could find no work. They had talked about going to America or some other part of the world but did not want to break up the family. Besides they might find themselves little better off when they got there. In the end two sons joined the army. I do not know what happened to them when war came.

We started work in the yard each day at 8 in the morning. I came across Glasgow to Govan in the underground. The memory of the smell of those trains packed tight with men in dirty and greasy overalls, many smoking rough tobacco, will remain with me always. It was a smell I have never met anywhere else. At Govan we streamed up into the open air, across the street to the yard gates and clocked in. Joe and I would collect our plans and set off to the ship we were to work on. Once there Joe would sit down for a few minutes to chat with his friends while I was dispatched to clear the area where we were to work. The shipwrights' job is largely concerned with making marks on parts of the ship where other people are later going to cut holes or fit things to the fabric of the ship. This meant that one had to read a plan accurately, measuring off the distance, for instance, from a cross frame to a point on the deck where a hatch was to go through. Then it had to be marked out so that when the platers and riveters came along they could see where to cut the holes and fit the angle bars and so on. This was considered to be skilled work and the shipwrights considered themselves a cut above the riveters and platers and simple labourers. Their rate of pay was higher, too, though not princely even so. When I first went to the yard as an apprentice shipwright I was paid ten shillings (50p) a week. Happily not long after my appearance (though not, I hope, because of it) the apprentices all came out on strike and after a week of idleness were given a 40% increase. Thereafter I got fourteen shillings a week (in modern terms 70p). In those days, of course, a young apprentice would live with his parents and he was not expected to live on his fourteen shillings. It was pocket money though most of my apprentice friends gave their mother at least five shillings a week for their keep. I think Joe Gasser was earning about £4 per week and he was a very skilled shipwright.

We worked sometimes in the dark bowels of the ship, between the rusty plates that encased the water tanks at the bottom of the hull, sometimes on the deck or in some cabin. Joe did not believe in working too energetically and every half hour or so he would knock off for a little break and smoke half a Woodbine. I would be sent on some errand to get a tool or a drawing so that, if approached by the 'Gaffer', he would have the necessary excuse that he could not get on without me to hold the end of the chalking line. The 'Gaffer' was the man who in England we would call the foreman. In the yard gaffers always wore bowler hats and I remember once asking Joe why that was. It was, he said, to protect them from red hot rivets. If one is on the deck of a ship high up on a slipway one is very high indeed and there is a tendency to look over the rail and watch people coming and going on the ground beneath you. If you see someone you do not like there is an awful temptation to drop something, accidentally of course, to see if it lands on his head. If it is a red hot rivet, and, there were plenty of them about, it would bounce off a bowler hat and do no damage. It might be otherwise if the target was wearing nothing on his head, or just a 'bonnet' (a cap as we in England would say). Foremen, who were regarded rather like the Gestapo, were always wise to wear bowler hats.

At lunch time the clatter of the yard stopped and for a short spell blessed silence took over. If the weather was good I took my sandwiches up on to the deck of the ship on which I was working and sat at the stern which jutted out high above the waters of the Clyde. Gulls wheeled and called and dived for crumbs of bread thrown to them over the stern rail. After half an hour the sirens screamed and once more the noise began as work was recommenced. We worked on through the afternoon until about twenty minutes before the time for clocking off arrived. Then all work stopped and we left our place of work, put away our tools and moved towards the gates where we waited with many hundreds of others until the siren went again, the gates opened and we streamed across the road to the underground and so home. It was always a problem for the authorities to ensure that work was continued up to the end of the working day, but no amount of negotiation with the unions or persuasion by the managers on the shop floor would stop us moving towards a vantage point from which we could escape from the yard the moment 'time' sounded, and this necessarily meant that we downed tools a good quarter of an hour too soon so that we could cross the great yard. I had not been in the yard long before I realised that I was only too ready to leave the ship I was working on and move away towards the gates. I found that as the day progressed the noise, the banging and clattering of steel plate on steel plate, the staccato rat-a-tat-tat of the riveting, all magnified by the confined space where we worked in the great hulls, had the effect of giving me a fierce head ache. Every day I ended my work feeling drained of all energy and suffering from something very closely resembling a migraine. This led me to wonder if a life of work in shipyards was really what I wanted. Much as I was interested at the thought of designing ships and the fascination of directing the construction of a beautiful engineering production, I did not feel that I could face the prospect of always having to work in shipyards cursed by the debilitating noise of riveting. Had I realised it the days of riveting were nearly passed. The practice of welding the plates together was beginning to replace the old fashioned and expensive process of riveting. The worst part of the noise of the shipyard was to be removed within a few years and had I realised this trend I would probably have stayed on and made my career with ships. How different my later life would have been. However I did not foresee that change, and after a while I told my father that I could not bear it any longer and that I wanted to leave. It was decided that I should read mechanical sciences at Cambridge. It was August, 1938, and I had to move quickly to be accepted by a college. Fortunately I had done well enough in my exams at Uppingham and Glasgow to be allowed to join the course starting in the autumn. My uncle, who was at that time the Bishop of Southwark, was a friend of the Master of Selwyn College which happily still had a few places vacant so I was entered for that establishment to which I duly reported in October.

CHAPTER FIVE

Cambridge

In 1938 I was nineteen and like many others of my age I found the summer and autumn of that year very depressing. It seemed that we were about to embark on a war with Hitler's Germany. Though my generation could not remember the 1914-18 War we had read and heard much about it. As a young man growing up it seemed to me that the stories of the huge numbers of men killed in the muddy trenches of the western front were so horrific that they could only be explained by wickedness in high places. To me, and I think to many like me, it seemed that the war had led to a criminal waste of life, that it had been mishandled by the old men in charge at the time, and that the massive slaughtering that had occurred in Flanders was typical of modern warfare. If a new war came such horrors would be repeated, but they would be likely to be much worse as the aeroplane would introduce a grisly new feature of its own. Bombing attacks on civilians in our crowded towns by large numbers of bombers would be impossible to stop and would lead to unimaginable carnage. It seemed to me that no one could be justified in allowing such a catastrophe to start. I did not realise then that if one takes that view and follows it to its logical conclusion one reaches the position that a wicked man determined to bring the world, or a part of it, under his subjection cannot be stopped if he controls his country's army and if he is determined. I think that it seemed to many of us young men at the time that there was little hope. I was far from clear what we would be fighting for if we were to go to war. I certainly did not then understand the wickedness of Hitler.

In 1938 Hitler still seemed to be a man who had pulled Germany together, provided employment for its millions of unemployed and set it on a course that would lead to prosperity. It was hard to believe that anyone could be so uncivilised as to behave in the manner that was attributed to him. So many of us were reluctant to believe what we were told, and thought that the stories must be exaggerated by people with reason for wishing to discredit him. Had war come in 1938 as a result of the Czech crisis I think that many people like me would have had doubts as to the righteousness of our cause. But, happily, war did not come and we went to Cambridge shortly after the Munich crisis. During that year at Cambridge we lived under the ever darkening cloud and slowly, but surely, we had to face up to the prospect that war would come. My views changed as day by day the true nature of Hitler and his colleagues was made clear by unfolding events. Until Munich it had seemed possible to make out a case for justifying his various actions, but after Munich that was impossible any longer. That meant that we who had taken the near pacifist view based on the wickedness of so acting as to cause a holocaust had to think again. Slowly I came to the conclusion that a war was justifiable if it was fought to protect innocent people from being wrongly assaulted, or to defend one's own country from invasion. Chamberlain has been heavily criticised for the Munich agreement. Those who have sought to defend him have done so on the ground that by gaining a year he enabled our armed forces and equipment to be brought more nearly up to what was needed. I do not know what weight can be given to that argument, but I am sure that during the twelve months after Munich and before the outbreak of war in September, 1939, a very large number of young men who at the beginning of that period would have felt that England was wrong to fight had changed their minds and were convinced that England had to fight to save her own life and to try to save the life of the oppressed states in Europe. Chamberlain should be given credit, perhaps, for having gained time for this change to take place, because thereafter it was a much more united and much less doubting young population that was led to battle.

But I have jumped ahead. It was under the depressing gloom of the advancing clouds of war that I went up to Selwyn in 1938, and the clouds certainly overshadowed the whole year, but they did not prevent it being for me a happy year.

Selwyn College was founded in the nineteenth century to commemorate Bishop Selwyn. It was the intention of the founders of the college that it should enable the sons of poor people to obtain a university education. There was to be no extravagance. A spartan frugal regime was to pervade the place. The majority of the undergraduates were, in those days, destined for holy orders in the Church of England, and there was only a handful of young men reading subjects other than divinity. A few reading medicine, English and law provided, however, a little leaven and the atmosphere was not as austere or solemn as the composition of the membership of the college might have at first suggested. I made friends with many of the embryo clerics and found them entertaining. Jack Barker, who had spent his childhood in Kobe in Japan where his father had been a doctor, was perhaps the person to whom I became closest. He was a cultured man with a whimsical sense of humour and a certain reserve which perhaps came from his upbringing. He liked good food and drink and was, in some ways, a very untypical Selwyn man — no muscular Christianity for him. We used often to dine at the restaurant at the Arts Theatre after watching the performance, and I found myself acquiring a taste for the theatre and, like him, for good food and wine. At that time Maynard Keynes had built up the Arts Theatre into a flourishing concern and excellent performances were regularly given there. He was married to Lydia Lopokova who had danced with Diaghilev's Russian Ballet Company and it was, no doubt, through her influence that the young Sadlers Wells Ballet Company paid frequent visits to Cambridge. I used to go, night after night, to watch Margot Fonteyn, then coming to the fore as the prima ballerina, and Robert Helpmann in Les Sylphides, Facade, Petrushka and the Three Cornered Hat and the other early ballets of that company. Occasionally Keynes would ask a few undergraduates back to meet the performers in his rooms in Kings. These were occasions not to be forgotten. I have always been grateful to Jack Barker for introducing me to the theatre and, indeed, to some of the other good things of life, though I have always been conscious that it was an introduction which caused me to ask my father for more money to keep me at Cambridge than probably he could afford. He was a very kind father and never complained.

Another interest that developed quickly at Cambridge was politics. I had already in my Glasgow days begun to feel strongly the fascination of politics. Even though when I had been in Glasgow the unemployment was much less than it had been in the years of acute depression in the early thirties there was still sufficient unemployment to make me realise what a dreadful experience it was. Working in the shipyard I talked to many men who had spent several years out of work and it needed little imagination to realise how demoralising such an experience would be to a decent man who wanted no more than to be able to support his wife and children in a modest way. With this background I was drawn towards the Labour Party. But I soon found I did not agree with all the views expressed by its protagonists. So I did not commit myself to a party at that stage. I did, however, attend debates in the Union and after a little while plucked up my courage to speak. This was an important step forward because, up to that time, I had been very nervous of speaking at all, not only in public but even in ordinary conversation, for fear of being thought stupid. But once I had driven myself to speak I realised that there was nothing so conducive to thought as the necessity of having to express myself clearly and of having to think on my feet.

At that time the President of the Union was Paddy Butler (later to become His Honour Judge Lord Dunboyne) who had been at Abberley Hall with me. After I had been intervening in debates for some time he asked me to make a paper speech. This meant that I had to make one of the initial speeches in order to start the debate off. The practice was that there should be a paper speech from one undergraduate and one distinguished visitor on each side, for and against the motion, and then the debate was open to all present. On this occasion the motion was about Colonial policy and one of the guests was Kingsley Martin the famous editor of the New Statesman. The other undergraduate speaker was David Bosanquet who had also been at Abberley Hall. So it was an all Abberley occasion with two speakers and the President all from there. I was the first to speak and as I stood up, trembling, to embark on my first 'big' speech in the Union I looked up at the public gallery which was directly in front of me and saw, to my horror, in the centre of the front row my old Abberley Hall Headmaster, Gilbert Ashton. Paddy Butler had invited him to watch the products of his prep school disporting themselves in this arena. Never have words so nearly failed me totally. Though I am still unable to overcome the feeling of fear and worry that besets me before I make any speech in public, never on any subsequent occasion has the effect been so paralysing as it was on that evening in the Union some fifty years ago. However when finally I started to speak, the words — somewhat to my surprise — came, and all went well. My speech was deemed a moderate success and I encouraged by others to persevere and it was not long before it was suggested to me that I should try to become President of the Union in due course. Unhappily that was an aspiration that did not survive for long because the war came and my Cambridge career ended abruptly. During the time that I took part in Union affairs the presidents, apart from Paddy Dunboyne, were two very remarkable men. Kumarangalam was a tall, lean aristocratic and strikingly handsome Indian who was later to have a distinguished career as a Minister in the Government of India after independence, but who was tragically killed in an air crash on the borders of India and China. Pieter Keuneman was from Ceylon. His father had been a High Court judge and was of Portuguese Burgher stock. Pieter was a Communist and on his return to Colombo after the start of the war was imprisoned for his political views and was still incarcerated when I visited Ceylon later in the war. He too was an impressive man and spoke with great charm and persuasiveness. I believe that he has in recent years lived a life of nearly total self denial and has devoted himself to helping the poor of Colombo. His extreme political views have kept him out of the centre of affairs. My activities in the Union and the friendships I made with these and other people of like interests made me determined to try and enter politics if the opportunity offered. But, here again, my plans were, for the time being, upset by the onset of the war.

During my first year at Cambridge from reading mechanical sciences I changed to reading law. I had soon discovered that I was not really interested in any aspect of engineering other than shipbuilding, so I embarked on a law degree. By working hard from Easter until June in 1939 I was able to scrape through Part I and during the term that I remained at Cambridge after the outbreak of war I was able to do enough of Part II to enable the authorities to give me a degree after only four terms work. But though my instruction was slight I was lucky in my instructors and one day in their courts was, as the psalmist said, better than a thousand. R.M. Jackson of Johns was for a time my supervisor and later I was put under Professor Ziegler of Pembroke. Two men more different in their approach one could never meet. Jackson, a socialist with strong views which came out in his classes, was a most invigorating influence. He made the history of the legal system more interesting than I would have thought possible, and somehow communicated a sense of vocation that made one feel one was pursuing a worthwhile study. Ziegler was an old man when I knew him. He was very deaf and used a hearing aid which took the form of a pair of headphones connected to a box that stood on the table before him and upon which there was a knob by which the volume could be controlled. When three or four of us came into his room for a supervision we would all start by speaking very softly and he would turn the knob so that with maximum volume he could hear us. We then all spoke very loudly and shouted whereupon he was overwhelmed with the cacophony and groped desperately for the knob to reduce the row. Young men can be very cruel to the elderly. But we all loved and respected him. He was of the old school. His favourite subject was Roman law and the disciplined intellectual approach to this subject that he instilled was perhaps the most valuable bit of legal learning to which I was ever subjected.

Ziegler was, I believe, of German extraction though he had lived in England all his life. He was a bachelor and very attached to the children of his brothers and sisters. During the war, shortly after the battle of Dunkirk, I was passing through Cambridge and called upon him. I found him very dejected because he had two nephews, one was fighting for the British and one for the Germans, and he was afraid they had both been killed. I never saw him again.

By the summer of 1939 it had become clear that Hitler's eyes were fixed on Poland. He seemed to be busy creating a situation which would enable him to invade that country on the pretext of rescuing the German population in Danzig. That city was separated from the main body of Germany by the strip of land running south from Gdynia on the Baltic, and known as the Polish corridor, which had been given to Poland after the first war in order that she might have access to the sea. By the end of the summer term at Cambridge Poland was very much in the news.

It was an agricultural country peopled largely by peasants and dominated by an aristocratic upper class the majority of whom seemed to have the title of count. Throughout its history it had suffered invasions across its borders and had, as a result, been partitioned and occupied by foreign countries many times. This history had bred in its people a fierce patriotism and a determination to preserve the integrity of their motherland. In those days before universal air travel it seemed remote and little known but Hitler's activities had given it a sort of glamour. Two of my Cambridge friends and I was drawn by this romantic country and decided to visit it in the summer vacation. As none of our parents were well off it was no grand tour that we planned. Each of our fathers put £40 into the central kitty and with that we bought for £20 a 1927 open touring Armstrong-Siddeley. The remaining £100 met all our other expenses for a period of over two months – crossing the Channel, driving through France and Germany to Poland, the length of Poland from north to south and then across Slovakia, Hungary, Yugoslavia and Italy and back through France to England. That it should have been possible to survive for so long on such a sum seems incredible in these days, when we have experienced periods of inflation as a result of which the value of money has fallen by a fifth or so in a year. In order to make the available funds stretch as far as possible we evolved a plan. The parents of each of us had a few friends scattered about Europe and we decided that our route should so far as possible take us past where they lived. We would then beg a bed for a night or two, have a good meal and a bath and then drive on. Between these havens we would camp. We built a large wooden box and fixed it to the luggage grid of the car and filled it with a tent, camping kit and food. Thus equipped we were able to go for many days with little need to spend money.

CHAPTER SIX

The 'Grand' Tour

We set out in early June, crossing the Channel from Newhaven to Dieppe in the car ferry. In those days car ferries were not the purpose built drive on drive off ships to which the summer tourist has since become accustomed. It was much more exciting. Your car was lifted and swung by crane from the quayside to the deck where it was chained down together with ten or so other cars. Part of the rest of the ship was given over to cargo as well as passengers and I had a feeling of adventure as we set out in one of these cross Channel 'tramps'. On arriving in Dieppe we lunched off fish and wine and then took the road to Bruges where we arrived in the early evening. Having no address to go to in Bruges we were looking for somewhere to camp when we came upon an abbey. Frank Tindal, one of my companions, who planned to be ordained, suggested we should go in there. We found vespers in progress and I can remember standing at the west end of the vast nave, facing up the length of the tall empty semi dark church and listening to the beautiful plainsong drifting down from the choir stalls at the far end where rows of monks could just be seen lit by candles. I wondered then, as I have done ever since, at the strange holy voice that calls a man to be a monk.

We were told we could stay in the guest house and when we had been shown our cells where we were to spend the night we were taken to have supper in the refectory. A plain meal in delightful company, made memorable by the fact that the Abbot, a most entertaining and civilised man, joined us because he wanted to practise his skill at English, of which he was very proud. The following day, having explored the town and its canals we drove on towards Rheims where we had an invitation to stay with friends of Frank's parents. During the First Great War Frank's father and mother had housed in their home in England Charles Heidsieck and his wife who had left Rheims during part of the fighting and they had invited us to call in as we passed. When we stayed with them Charles was presiding over the family's great champagne business but that did not prevent him from acting as a generous host to the three young and unimportant visitors from England. His family was large and ranged from a girl who was then, I suppose, about twenty and of surpassing beauty, down to a small boy of about four who was, I think, number seven. They shewed us all the sights and took us into the vast subterranean 'caves', dug out of the chalk hills, it is said, by the Romans, where the champagne is stored while it matures. Old men spent their time turning the bottles through a few degrees so that the wine is never still for long. Why this should be necessary I did not discover but it was apparently a vital step in the production of the famous drink. The Heidsiecks are, not surprisingly, very proud of their family's business and we were given much instruction in its mysteries. Every country had, we were told, its preference for a particular quality of wine. The Americans drank the sweetest, the English chose the driest, while for the French was reserved the medium dry, which was what a civilised man would drink. I remember on our first morning we came down to breakfast expecting, and rather hoping for, the traditional French petit dejeuner of rolls and coffee, but found to our surprise bowls of corn flakes which had obviously been specially provided as a concession to English taste. It was, however, washed down with champagne drunk from the tall narrow glasses that were customary there. I was surprised at how pleasant the unexpected combination tasted.

When a few days later we came to leave we were all in the street with the car loaded and were saying our farewells when Charles spoke to me. He said that the next year neither Frank Tindal, who would by then have embarked on his training for holy orders, nor my other companion who was engaged to be married, would wish to spend six weeks in France, but he wondered if I might like to do so. I said I could think of few things I would like more. He then told me that he was for that year president of some association of French wine growers and that they had a scholarship which was awarded by the president to a student. The scholarship involved spending six weeks in a wine growing district of France where one would be put up and given the opportunity of learning something of the wine of the area and how it was grown and made. In return one had to write an essay of six thousand words on the experience which, if they wished, they were at liberty to publish. When I said that I would indeed be interested in being considered for such a scholarship Charles said that he would see what he could do. We then set off. When I returned to England three months later and the war was on us I found a letter waiting for me informing me that I had been awarded the scholarship — for 1940.

It was our intention to drive from Rheims eastward across Germany quickly so that we could spend as much time as possible in Poland, the country we had really come to see. Soon after leaving Rheims we passed through the Maginot line, the great system of static fortification built by the French along the border of Germany. Nothing was visible above ground where we drove and one was not permitted to stop, so I was not greatly impressed by this allegedly impenetrable line of defence. The rolling countryside, not unlike the Hampshire Downs near Winchester, stretched as far as one could see. There was a winding line of rusty anti tank spikes curling over the hills, but otherwise it was a very peaceful scene. We crossed the Moselle near Wasserbillig and drove through the little Duchy of Luxembourg. I remember seeing for the first time carts being pulled by oxen. The sight made one feel that one was back in the Middle Ages.

Once in Germany we travelled fast on the autobahns that were the progenitors of the modern motorway. Italy and Germany alone, at that time, had built them and their routes made clear that their purpose was primarily a military one. We were however very impressed and sped from the western frontier to the centre of Berlin. There we had the address of a man who my mother had met when, as a young girl, she had spent a little while in Austria. When we tracked him down in a comfortable flat near Unten den Linden we were surprised to discover that he was a senior civil servant in Goebbels' Ministry of Information. He put us up in comfort and was very generous, but I well remember my amazement that a grown man could be so obsessed with a political idea. He spent all the time we were with him telling us of the wonders of Nazism. He did not encourage our wish to see galleries and the more orthodox sights of Berlin. Instead he insisted on sending us in a large car to see Hitler's great sports stadium, the Chancellery and other examples of modern Nazi architecture. His peculiar inability to consider any view except that which he was, I suppose, paid to propagate gave me an odd feeling and I began to sense the unpleasantness of a society ruled by a dictator. We had one experience that reinforced that feeling. We were in one of the main streets which was full of crowds and we soon gathered that a funeral procession was about to pass by. It was the funeral of a general and as the cortege approached to the martial music of an accompanying military band the crowds stood and raised their arms in the Nazi salute. "Sieg Heil, Sieg Heil" they shouted. This was an activity in which we took no part, not through any wish to seem unfriendly but because, as far as I was concerned, it seemed a foolish gesture and anyway I did not feel very sure of my pronunciation. When some young men standing near us realised that we were not joining in the salutation they approached us in a very threatening manner and for a few moments I thought we were about to be lynched. Happily, however, the moment passed.

We drove on towards Poland, passing through Stettin and thence to Gdynia. As we covered the last twenty miles to the frontier it became clear that there was much military activity. Soldiers, tanks, guns and military equipment were on both sides of the road, moving steadily up towards the border. The scale of the activity was larger than anything I had ever seen at home. The mechanised nature of it was what struck me forcibly — lorries, motor cycles, staff cars, guns and tanks as well as infantry seemed to fill the road. In the O.T.C. at Uppingham I had never seen anything more powerful than a Lee Enfield rifle and even in camp at Aldershot nothing to compare with such obvious military strength had come our way. Eventually with some relief we reached the customs point on the frontier. There we were greeted by a cheerful Polish official. He asked if we had seen much military movement as we approached. When we replied that we had, he told us his country was ready and that there were equally effective forces between us and Gdynia massing to oppose the Germans. After a few minutes genial chat we moved on. The wide tarmac road that had brought us from Stettin gave way to a narrow, unmetalled track through the flat Polish countryside. The only signs of military activity we saw as we drove the few miles that separated the frontier from the important Baltic port was a horse drawn cart moving slowly in the direction from which we had come. In it sprawled three Polish soldiers. They appeared to be drunk. So much, we thought, for the troops massing to oppose the Germans.

Gdynia, which we reached at lunch time, was a modern town built round the port. It had risen from nothing in the twenty years that had elapsed since the signing of the peace treaty that gave Poland the narrow corridor to the Baltic. We were hungry so we went into a small restaurant for some lunch, but were nonplussed when faced with a menu written in Polish and with none but Polish speaking waiters. In an effort to find an interpreter I asked people at other tables if they spoke English, French or German. Fortunately there was one young man who turned out to be a pilot from the sea plane base that could be seen at the end of the headland forming the westerly end of Gdynia bay. He was a delightful, charming and handsome man who spoke perfect English. He joined us for lunch and was soon telling us all that we needed to know. He took us bathing in the afternoon and later showed us the nightlife of the city. When we left next morning on our way to Warsaw he bade us farewell and insisted that in Warsaw we looked up his brother. When later we reached Warsaw we discovered that our friend's brother was the director of the State Opera House. He lived in a splendid flat that was formed out of one wing of a handsome building that had, we were told, once been the home of a Russian duke during the period when Eastern Poland was occupied by the Russians.

But it took several days to reach Warsaw. Our old Armstrong-Siddeley bounced along the rough track that passed for the main road. A cloud of white dust arose behind the car and much of the grime got into our skin and hair. In the evenings we camped, by a river, if possible, so that we could swim and clean ourselves. One such evening we found a delightful green space by the Vistula and while we were bathing, before we had an evening meal, children came from a nearby village and stood open- mouthed watching us. They climbed over the car and examined all our kit minutely. They finally left clearly of the opinion that we were mad.

The journey to Warsaw was unremarkable. The countryside was for the most part featureless and flat. Torun, an old walled town with some fine buildings, was the only place of interest on the way.

At Warsaw we called on the brother of our pilot friend and were received with what we soon learned was typical Polish hospitality. His comfortable apartment was put at our disposal and he gave us tickets for the opera. He took us round the city and fed us in restaurants where we acquired a taste for beetroot soup. Much of this great city was destroyed during the latter stages of the war and I daresay that little now remains of the fine town houses of the nobility or of the public buildings that together created the centre of the city. But certain it is that the part of the old town that made the greatest impression on me has vanished. The ghetto, where, later, fierce fighting took place as the gallant Poles struggled to hold off the German armies, while the Russian forces held back and refused them aid, was unlike anything I had ever seen. Narrow streets, with strange smells and a bustle of mercantile activity, seemed to be inhabited by a different race. Bearded merchants in black caps stood by their shop doorways encouraging the passerby to enter. The unfamiliar dress of the Jews and their serious devotion to trade was strange enough, but it was the overcrowding that surprised me. It seemed that many teeming thousands of these energetic people were confined within a few acres of intersecting streets of old and dilapidated houses.

One incident of our stay in Warsaw sticks in my memory. Because it had seemed likely that a war might break out when we were abroad we had promised our parents that we would call on the British Consul in each large city we visited in order to make sure it was safe to go on. At Warsaw the Consul was a man called Savery and when we went to see him he received us in great style. He was not very well and was in his bedroom sitting in an armchair by the window. He was dressed in a flamboyant silk dressing gown and wore exotic embroidered slippers with turned up toes. On his head was a Turkish fez. It turned out that he had been at Uppingham and he seemed pleased to talk to young men one of whom at least had a school in common with him. When we enquired of the political situation and whether it was wise to go on he told us not to worry about things like that. If a war came we would probably be interned but would have many adventures which we would never regret. He said that at the outbreak of the First World War he had been travelling in Germany and managed to get to Switzerland where he had spent four idyllic years. Though we were not sure that if we were caught in the south of Poland things would be quite as pleasant for us, it seemed good advice and anyway having come so far it would be soft to turn back. So on we went.

From Warsaw we drove on to Cracow, the fine cathedral city in the south west of Poland. Our host in Warsaw gave us a letter introducing us to a friend of his who was a professor at the university and so, once again, we were assured of a warm welcome. The journey to Cracow was, like that to Warsaw, through mile after mile of flat country planted with wheat. No hedges broke the monotony and only here and there a cluster of small houses and a few trees, dark blue green, and the onion top of a church indicated a village. One evening as we were looking for a good place to camp we saw a cloud of dust approaching from the opposite direction. As we came closer it turned out to be a small carriage pulled by a spirited bay pony. The driver was a handsome Pole whose face was given a sad expression by a pair of wispy drooping moustachios. As he approached he drew up and engaged us in conversation. We stopped and as soon as he realised we were English he became very excited. The English were heroes who would save Poland from her enemies, he told us in broken English. Was there not an understanding that the frontiers of Poland would be guaranteed? Where were we going to rest that night? "Camping, no, no, you must stay with me." We soon found ourselves following his carriage which turned round and returned along the road by which it had come. After a mile or so we turned off the main road and set off down a track through the corn. When we had been driving down this for a little while, we came to a clump of poplar trees in the middle of which stood an elegant white house. Stables and barns, cottages and sheds, were scattered around amongst the trees. Chickens and ducks scratched in the dust of the yard before the steps up to the front door. This little settlement centred on the house that belonged to our new acquaintance had a feudal air about it. We soon learned that everyone worked in or for the house and the driver of the carriage presided over all in an eccentric paternal way. We were quickly made at home. Flurries of women appeared and made up beds and brought hot water in buckets and prepared tubs for us to bathe in. A little while later we joined our host on the veranda much refreshed and a deal cleaner. We were entertained royally to a splendid dinner and much vodka and wine. I remember little of it except that as the evening proceeded the room began to spin around and I could no longer concentrate on his unending talk. But the end came and I fell into bed. Next day we continued our drive to Cracow.

My recollections of Cracow are vague. But I fell in love with the cathedral, a soft pink coloured building with a green copper covered cupola and towers. There was something hauntingly beautiful about the sound of the horn blown at sunset every evening from high up on its roof in remembrance of the brave man who sounded it when the Turkish hordes led by Süleyman were enveloping the city. The Wavel castle of the Kings of Poland and the buildings of the old university together gave me a strange feeling of being at the very edge of western civilisation. The oriental was not far away, but this ancient city remained an outpost of the Christian world. I also remember a visit to a night club where three young undergraduates sat, shyly, sipping vodka to the amusement of a similar number of blowsy tarts. We came away and walked back to our lodgings as the sun was rising and the birds were singing. We left Cracow and drove into the Tatra mountains that form the border between Poland and Slovakia. We stayed for a day or two in a log hut high in the hills at Zakopane, where in winter the Poles came to ski and enjoy winter sports. In summer it was nearly deserted. While there we were taken for a trip down the river that runs between steep banks along the frontier. The boat was an outrigger canoe carved from the trunk of a tree and the navigator was a peasant dressed in national costume, black jacket and white woollen trousers, both heavily embroidered in bright colours with traditional designs. As we were swept along in the current we passed groups of gypsies who sang folk songs to the accompaniment of fiddles. I suspect that if that country had not been swallowed up behind the Iron Curtain the fiddlers would have become a great tourist attraction.

Slovakia was a long narrow strip of mountainous country forming the southern end of Czechoslovakia. Its people were simple peasant folk, very different we were told from the more civilised and industrialised Czechs who inhabited the northern part of the country. There were no towns of importance on the road that crossed the country at this point and we soon emerged from the forest clad hills of Slovakia to enter Hungary at Debrecen. My recollection of Hungary is limited, and only a few incidents stand out in my memory. The first occurred just as we had crossed the customs barrier. Frank Tindal wandered away from us as we were having our passports checked and disappeared round the corner of a building that turned out to be the police station. When we had been cleared we took the car on in the direction in which he had gone. In a few moments we found ourselves in a long avenue lined with trees down the centre of which a body of soldiers was marching accompanied by a slow moving tank. Frank was busy photographing them. Suddenly he was surrounded by officials and police and wild gesticulations began to be exchanged. It was clear that neither side understood the other, but the Hungarians made their point by snatching Frank's camera and marching him off to the police station. There then ensued a period of several hours during which we tried to find someone who spoke English. Magyar was a language more unintelligible than any I had come across. Our attempts to explain that we were not spies, and to find out what they wanted of us in order that Frank should be released were wholly ineffective. There seemed no reason why they should ever let him go. The police and the officials to whom we spoke seemed totally unconcerned and merely shrugged their shoulders. In the end we were able to speak on the phone to the British Consul who came to our rescue. Frank was released and we were allowed to proceed on our way. It was an alarming moment.

The journey across Hungary to Budapest was uneventful and I recall hot dusty roads which passed villages where the houses were built end on to the road and were shaded by lines of broad branched trees. We lived, in the country districts, largely on water melons which were very cheap and, as I had never experienced them before, seemed exciting. However after two or three days with little else to vary the diet they palled. They were too, I suspect, lacking in any very great food value and so we looked forward to a solid orthodox meal. This we got when we reached Budapest. We found beds in a little pension on the hill behind the castle in Buda, the old city. After walking on the ramparts which overlook the Danube and the more modern part of the city in Pest on the other side, and after visiting the cathedral we descended to the fleshpots of the town. There we had, I remember, a huge meal of goulash at a rather expensive restaurant on an island in the middle of the river. As darkness came down and the lights were lit the whole place became festive. Bands and orchestras seemed to abound and music floated across the water from passing pleasure boats and from restaurants by the river's edge. The Hungarians seemed a happy race and I certainly thought that their dark haired girls were very attractive. We could not stay long, however, as it was expensive and our funds were running low. After two nights we drove to Lake Balaton which was the playground for Hungarians who, living in a landlocked country, had no sea coast to enjoy. One side of the lake is flat and has a fair amount of sandy beach where the locals disport themselves. The other side is hilly and far up on one ridge a fine monastery was visible. After we had had a swim and enjoyed an idle afternoon we crossed the lake in a ferry boat and explored the hilly side, looked at the monastery and ended the evening with a dinner eaten under a spreading vine in the paved forecourt of an inn overlooking the lake.

At that time Hungary was ruled by Admiral Horthy who was regarded by the people to whom we spoke as a dictator who would be likely to follow Hitler. We found it difficult to obtain genuine opinions. Everyone seemed fearful of talking politics. We were beginning to learn how a dictatorship quickly causes a blanket to descend on ordinary people inhibiting them from speaking their mind. They are friendly and hospitable but there is an underlying unease that, were you to live with it for long, would destroy happiness for anyone who had experienced normal unrestrained conversation.

From Hungary we aimed for the coast of the Adriatic at its northern end. We crossed Yugoslavia by way of Zagreb and reached the coast at a small fishing port called Senj. Zagreb is the capital of Croatia, a poor and mountainous country whose people have always been intensely nationalistic. They are peasant people of an independent turn of mind. At that time the leader of the Croats was, if I remember his name right, Machek. Somehow Frank Tindal managed to arrange for us to meet him when we reached Zagreb. We called on him one morning and I remember the surprise I felt when we were ushered into his room. I had expected someone who resembled politicians of whom I had experience at home: smooth gentlemen wearing black coats and striped trousers. He was not that sort at all. An old man, I think he was about sixty, with an unshaven appearance, he was wearing, and this was what particularly struck me, a shirt with no collar, open at the neck, a leather belt and old baggy trousers. I cannot remember what we talked about through the interpreter who accompanied us, but I remember well that he made a great impression on me. He seemed to be a simple but sincere man whose only aim was to lead his countrymen to independence. But it may be that I was over impressed by appearances. The experience made me realise however that the Croats were basically a peasant people scratching a meagre living from the rocky hills that formed the greater part of their homeland. When later we visited the Zagreb market we saw many of these simple people selling the produce which they had brought, on foot or perhaps on a donkey, from their holdings often many miles away.

The road from Zagreb to Senj is spectacular. It runs down towards the sea following the course of a stream which as it descends passes through a series of lakes. At one point it is possible to see several of these lakes one beneath the other, their colour varying with the changes in the strata of rock through which the stream passes. The lake at the upper end was a bright emerald green, the one at the bottom sapphire blue. We drove down the road on a wonderful cloudless day and fell in love with the country and its simple people. When we reached Senj we were once again captivated. A small town, once a Roman settlement, it lies round a harbour bright with many coloured fishing boats. Not far from the shore was an islet called San Marino to which we swam.

On my return after an afternoon sunbathing I was suddenly overcome with a terrible headache and earache. I lay in our tent where we were camped and became progressively worse. Before long I had convinced myself that I was going to die.

Finally Frank decided he would have to find a doctor, though how to do that in this small town, presented a considerable problem. At last a person who seemed to have some medical knowledge arrived. He diagnosed heatstroke and prescribed salt. This I took and was soon recovered. It was a very useful lesson which I bore in mind when later as a soldier I was in hot countries. I think I may have been very lucky because bad heatstroke unattended can have dire consequences.

From Senj we drove north along the coast until we reached Trieste on the Yugoslav Italian border. A busy harbour it had been the main outlet for Austria and Hungary to the sea. Mussolini was busy claiming that it ought to be included in Italy and there was a tenseness in the air as we passed through. But we did not pause and were soon driving over the bridge that spans the river forming the border between the two countries. We were on our way to Venice. There can be few people who are not immediately overwhelmed with the beauty of Venice. I was no exception as I had no idea what sort of a place it was. We parked our car at the end of the mole and set off on foot for the centre of the town realising at once the added charm of a city freed from the motor car. Gondolas, not yet power driven, glided along the canals. This was my first introduction to Italy and opened my eyes to the beauties of that lovely country. We spent three days enjoying the palaces and churches, squares and canals and occasionally swimming. We found a small restaurant under a bridge by one of the canals where we could sit overlooking the water and enjoying the excellent cheap food. Unhappily our stay was short as while we were there the danger of war breaking out in Europe was clearly increasing daily. We woke one day to learn that Russia and Germany had signed a pact of friendship. This meant that Germany could act in Poland as she wished without fear of interference from Russia. She would be free to fight England and France too. We feared that Mussolini would bring Italy in and join with Hitler. So we decided we should hurry across Italy and head for home. We called briefly at Verona and I remember visiting the little church where Juliet is supposed to be buried. I thought it was suitably romantic. As we drove on across northern Italy to Milan the price of petrol began to rise alarmingly. Our funds which we had thought would just about suffice to see us home were, we realised, inadequate. We had to wire our parents to send money to us in Nice. We hoped it would be waiting for us when we arrived there, but it was not. We were, therefore, compelled to wait there until it came. Thus it was that we spent three days in the resort where it seemed that all the visitors were immensely wealthy and we alone were paupers. Even with war fast approaching the holiday makers were plentiful and appeared to be oblivious of what might be coming. I did not like Nice. It was an early example of what has now become common place. A holiday resort built on a beautiful stretch of the Mediterranean coastline but ruined by the extent of the commercial development. Famagusta in Cyprus which I saw more than thirty years later gave me the same feeling.

When we had received more money, we decided to make all speed for home. War was very close and it was difficult to tell what would happen if we were out of England when it began. It felt better being in France, at least she was on the same side, but the series of lightning attacks made by Hitler on surrounding countries had made one feel that anything might happen. I hoped that there might be a chance of returning to Poland and helping there. But it was sensible to get home first — and fast. So we drove without stopping to Calais, taking it in turns to drive through the night and pausing only for meals. At last we reached the Channel and camped for the last time on the dunes looking towards the grey sea. Next morning we motored into Calais and the splendid old car was hoisted aboard a Channel boat and we returned to England. The war began a few days later.

CHAPTER SEVEN

Phoney War

Although I am writing more than fifty years after the events of early September, 1939, I can remember much of that time clearly. It had been apparent for some time that war was inevitable, but when at last it came I was overwhelmed with a feeling of horror. I imagined that it would not be long before the terrible slaughter that had taken place in Flanders from 1914 to 1918 was repeated. The only difference, it seemed, would be that aerial bombing would increase the horror and the carnage. But that the war was just I had no doubt, and that England could not honourably have stood aside I was certain. It was plain, therefore, that I should volunteer for service. I decided to apply to join the navy and I wrote off to the Admiralty offering my services. I can remember writing that letter. I was at the desk in the drawing room of Curfew House and when it was finished I showed it to my father. When he had read it he said war is a hateful thing. Sensible people act totally unreasonably and things are said and done which in ordinary times no one would consider saying or doing. I was not at the time altogether clear what was on his mind — he might have been thinking how absurd it was to imagine that I could be any use as a sailor or soldier — but as the days passed and as I began to understand the changed attitudes that war brought about, I realised how true his words were.

I soon heard that the navy could not make use of me, my eyesight was too bad. In those early days there was a rush by young men, like myself, to join up but so great were the numbers applying that the services were not able at once to absorb them. I had to wait until I was called for and in the meantime I was to continue with my studies at Cambridge. So, a few weeks later, I returned to Selwyn to work until I was called up. In the early days of the war Cambridge life was very different to what it had been the year before. Many had left for the army and those like myself who returned felt guilty if they indulged in the free and easy ways that had been so enjoyable in 1938. Part of the college was taken over by the military so that we had to share our rooms. My room had a bunk put over the bed and Freddy Vaughan Jones, a theological student whose ambition was to go as a missionary to the Christmas Islands in the Pacific, joined me. We became good friends but, unhappily, when we left less than a year later we went very different ways and I have heard nothing of him since. Perhaps he went to the Christmas Islands and is still there.

The first winter of the war was very cold. Deep snow covered Cambridge and the fenlands for several weeks. I felt sorry for those under canvas or in slit trenches, but was reasonably comfortable myself. I worked hard at the law, feeling that time was short and I should do all I could before being called into the army. When spring came the war was still in its 'phoney' stage, though it gradually became clear that it was not to continue in that condition for long. During the Easter holiday I went with several others from Cambridge to a forestry camp outside Tintern where we were employed in war work of a sort — cutting down young pine trees and then reducing them into suitable lengths to make pit props for use in the mines. I greatly enjoyed this short period. The hard physical labour in the beautiful woods on the hills above the Wye Valley, the smell of the felled pines and the evenings spent drinking cider and gossiping at the Cherry Tree Inn induced a feeling of well being. The war seemed remote — but it returned to overhang our lives as soon as we returned home after a few weeks.

I went back to Cambridge in the summer for what was to be my last term. I did not, as many of my contemporaries did, go back to Cambridge when the war was over for a third year. Fortunately I managed to get a reasonably good degree even though I switched from mechanical sciences to law after two terms and had therefore only four terms to do both parts of the tripos. I was very lucky because by virtue of the special regulations that applied during wartime I was exempt, when I returned from the army, from Part I of the Bar Examinations. The result was that I am I believe one of the least qualified people ever to have been allowed to practice at the Bar of England. Things are very different now and young men are subjected to a long and detailed training for the profession. I doubt if I would have survived such treatment.

In May and June, 1940, despite the war, Cambridge was as beautiful as it always is when spring comes. The daffodils bloomed along the Backs and the stone of the colleges shone gold and white in the sun of early summer. The bricks of the Tudor courts and St John's and Queen's glowed again with the warmth of England. The Cam flowed gently beneath the willows. The conditions were, unquestionably, created by God to beguile young men and I fell in love. Catherine Patch lived at Parkstone in Dorset and was introduced to me by John Barker, my Selwyn friend, who also came from there. She was at Bedford College, at that time a part of London University reserved for ladies only, and arrived in Cambridge when the college was evacuated from London. She was reading English and enjoyed the theatre and ballet, and so it was that, though I was working hard, the gloom of war did not altogether overshadow those days. There was time occasionally to go with her to the Arts Theatre and to watch the Sadlers Wells' Ballet. Thanks largely to Catherine ballet and music occupied more and more of my leisure time. But that was not the only pastime. With John Barker and other friends — I remember particularly George Bunton who was reading medicine — I would walk to Grantchester on a Sunday afternoon and, like Rupert Brooke, take tea. Edward Vere Hodge, who had been at Uppingham with me and was up at Emmanuel College, would sometimes descend on me in my rooms and take me to walk in the fenland countryside. He was deeply worried because he was a convinced pacifist and was tortured by his conscience. I can still see his furrowed face beneath an unruly shock of carroty red hair as he strode across the Cambridgeshire fields and debated endlessly whether he should register as a conscientious objector or should smother his convictions and join up with the rest of us. It was for him an agonising decision. In the end he joined the British Council and was able to do valuable work in Africa — where I later met him again — and in Turkey and the Middle East. But he was altogether too sensitive a person and could not reconcile living in the world where he saw so much that he regarded as evil with his high ideals. He died tragically by his own hand some years after the war just when it seemed to his friends that, perhaps, at last he had found a way of life that brought him contentment.

The summer term soon passed and I sat my examinations. Before I left for home there were to be a few happy days of idleness and a final incident that I remember because of an odd coincidence. To celebrate the end of work Jack Barker and Catherine and I and a few others took a picnic lunch, hired a punt and set off to Byron's Pool, a backwater not far up the river. When we reached it we found that the water was running very fast and try as we would we could not make any progress against the flood using the orthodox method of propulsion with a pole. The boat kept swinging round and setting off backwards. I noticed, however, that the water though flowing fast was shallow so I decided to jump out of the punt and wade. In that way I could push it up the rapids. But unhappily I did not look carefully enough before I went over the side with the result that my foot landed on a broken beer bottle lying in the bed of the river. In seconds the water was red with blood. I had clearly cut an artery in the base of my foot. Someone applied a tourniquet round my knee and it was decided that I should be taken across the fields to a house that could be seen a few hundred yards away. The house turned out to be a mill house and when we reached it the front door was open but the place seemed deserted. The stillness of the summer pervaded the sleepy afternoon. Eventually, however, a young man appeared who said he would drive me into Addenbrookes Hospital. He had a rather sporting M.G. and told me he painted. At the hospital I was quickly stitched up and bandaged and told I could go. I then found the kind man who had driven me in was still waiting and he drove me back to college. Only then I asked him his name. He was Peter Scott, son of the great explorer, and himself, even then, a well known artist.

CHAPTER EIGHT

Pioneer

Not long after I had returned to Chertsey I received my call up papers telling me to report to the Pioneer Corps at Clacton-on-Sea. The Pioneer Corps was the unit into which all those who for one reason or another were medically unfit for the front line infantry were drafted. The corps had taken over Butlin's holiday camp as a place for training its new recruits. We were an unimpressive lot of men. Some, like me, short sighted and wearing thick spectacles. Others with disabilities ranging from deafness to mere stupidity or an inability to co-ordinate their limbs so as to march in step. We were not material from which a smart unit of well trained fighting men could readily be created. But the unfortunate officers and N.C.O.s who were given the thankless task of training us did their best. We were paraded on the football ground and made to march up and down. We were taught how to handle a rifle and to do arms drill. The Sergeant Major struck terror into all of us. A small man with sandy hair he shouted at us, but despaired of ever making any progress. Nothing he could do would teach the splay footed, hobbling and half blind assortment of young men to march in step or to shoulder arms together. We bore a marked resemblance to that body of men whose military adventures and mishaps later became famous when recorded on television in the programme 'Dad's Army'. Four of us slept in one small room and, thrown together accidentally, became good friends. When parades were over and we were allowed to leave the camp we went together to sample the pleasures of Clacton-on-Sea. They were not numerous. The civilian population of the town had been evacuated and the streets gave the impression of a ghost town — row upon row of empty houses and silent boarded up shops. We normally repaired to the Marine Hotel, an establishment that had remained open and was presided over by a jolly blonde barmaid called 'Mumsy'. We might have been incompetent military material but my three friends and I quickly became experts at darts and shove halfpenny. Jerry Hart had a glass eye and was the most skilled darts player of the four of us. He had been training to become a solicitor and was the only one I met again after the war was over. We occasionally bumped into each other in Fleet Street. The other two also were delightful companions. One, called Meekings, whose steel rimmed spectacles, balding head and faraway expression caused him to be renamed 'the professor' was older than the rest of us and had worked in the Record Office in peace time. The other one was hoping to be an accountant. I have forgotten his name. Back in our billet after our evenings at the Marine Hotel or at the cinema we settled down to try and sleep on the concrete floor of our bare room. Even on the straw palliasse or mattress that the Army provided I found this the most uncomfortable part of the experience. Somehow my hip was always in the way and painful on the hard floor, and sleep did not come easily.

After our short period of initial training we were formed into battalions of pioneers, whose task it was to provide manpower to help with the manifold labouring jobs that have to be done by the army. My unit was billeted in a fine modern building, St Monica's School for Girls. But once again I had to sleep on a concrete floor. Two incidents from this period have stuck in my memory. The east coast in the vicinity of Clacton was thought to be a possible area for a German invasion force to land and so we were engaged in work designed to make invasion more difficult — erecting barbed wire entanglements, helping to build concrete pill boxes and jobs of that sort. One day we were sent to Walton on the Naze with a group of engineers and ordered to blow up a section of the pier so that German ships could not use it for landing. During the night, shortly after this had been done, we saw rocket signals being fired out at sea. They were being put up by a ship in distress. Next morning we were ordered to return to Walton on the Naze to build a wooden bridge over the gap in the pier we had so carefully blown up a day or two before. No one had noticed that the lifeboat was housed at the end of the pier and its crew had been unable to go to the aid of those in trouble.

The other incident I remember occurred on a sunny Sunday. I was on guard duty and was standing in the guardroom which was the showroom of a commandeered garage. I was looking out through the large plate glass window towards the camp, the entrance gates of which were on the other side of the road. The sky was cloudless. Suddenly I saw two objects high up descending through the air in a perfect parabola. I quickly realised that they were large bombs, but they appeared apparently from nowhere. There was no visible aeroplane that could have dropped them. They descended and landed with a deafening thump in the sand of the beach on the far side of the camp. They did no damage whatever. It was sometime before I realised that the aeroplane that released them must have approached from behind me and immediately it had dropped them turned to go back across the sea, so that I never saw or heard it.

Not long after this incident I was promoted to the rank of lance corporal and sent on a course to learn about gas warfare. The course took place at a training school near to St Austell in Cornwall. Once again the camp was what had in peace time been a holiday camp on the coast, but it was much smaller than Butlin's camp at Clacton. This one consisted of a large stone house surrounded by considerable grounds in which a number of small chalets had been built. We were accommodated in tents on what had once been a tennis lawn. The course was a short one, I think it lasted just over a week, and I remember very little about it except for one strange incident. We had turned in one night and I was sleeping soundly in my tent when suddenly a sergeant put his head in and shouted to us all to get on parade outside as fast as possible with all our kit on our backs. In the semi-dark we struggled into our battle dress and pulled on our knapsacks and equipment and, still half asleep, formed up in ranks outside. We were then divided into platoons and finally each platoon was marched to one of the line of buses which had appeared out of the night and were drawn up in the drive. When our platoon of some twenty men was embarked our bus set off — we had no idea whither. Soon after we had started an elderly and stout lieutenant who wore a line of medals from the 1914—18 war stood up in the front of the bus and addressed the bewildered group of men that had been piled into the seats facing him. We were going, he told us, to a position on the coast where we were going to be allotted a length of cliff top which we would have to defend if the Germans arrived. He said it was reported that a German invasion force was on its way. He spoke with patriotic fervour about our duty to defend our homeland with our lives and to the last round. I remember feeling that there was something vaguely ridiculous about the old boy. It was all very alarming — but there was nothing we could do about it. Eventually we were deposited in a muddy lane and led by a guide to a field overlooking a path that came up from a small cove to the cliff top. Here we were allotted positions and told to dig in. So, still with little idea of what was going on, we spent the rest of the night digging slit trenches and trying to place ourselves so that we could cover with fire from our rifles the path from the beach. Then we waited. The elderly lieutenant had disappeared and we had no idea where any other troops were. Indeed we had no idea where we were ourselves. It was, I remember, very cold even though it was late summer. Eventually dawn broke and we hoped that someone would bring us information about what was happening. Fortunately there was no sign of any ships on the sea so the Germans had not arrived yet. The day wore on and still no one came and no message reached us. By midday we began to feel hungry and one of our number, a delightful cockney, disappeared into some bushes and a few minutes later returned. Somehow he had managed to kill a rabbit. So we lit a fire and made a sort of stew. Late in the afternoon the lieutenant reappeared and told us that it was all a false alarm and that a bus would soon arrive to take us back. We learned later that someone in Whitehall had sent out the codeword 'Cromwell' and all round the coast of Britain the alert was sounded and the troops stood to. On the whole I think it was fortunate that the Germans did not come. I have a feeling that they would somehow have managed to get ashore if they had arrived at our cove — though I hope we would have put up some sort of a show.

One day not long after this when I had returned to Clacton I was summoned to see the Commanding Officer. I assumed I had done something wrong and was going to be reprimanded, so I was more than a little surprised when he asked me whether I would like to become an officer. I had had a particularly sleepless night on the concrete floor of my billet and my immediate reaction was that as an officer I would probably not generally have to sleep in such uncomfortable conditions and so I said "Yes". A day or two later I was again summoned to the headquarters office and told I was to be appointed a second lieutenant in a Pioneer unit in Shropshire. I was given a week's leave in which to acquire the necessary uniform and then made my way to Shrewsbury where I reached the headquarters of the unit to which I had been posted. The adjutant who received me had his office in the upstairs part of one of the numerous public houses in that city. It was in this way that I first became acquainted with Shropshire, the county which, for scenic beauty and for simple unadorned countryside and villages and perhaps above all for charming country folk, I have ever since regarded as the most delectable corner of England. It was the start of an acquaintance that developed into a lifelong friendship and attachment. The adjutant of the unit was a Captain Sainsbury, who I soon came to know as 'the skipper', a wise and most civilised man. He had served on the western front in the first world war with the West Yorkshire Regiment and gained the M.C. In peace time he ran a family business which made expensive chocolates and retailed them from a small shop in Bond Street. When the war was over I once visited the shop and saw the skipper in his civilian incarnation. He was serving the rich ladies and the elegant young men who frequent those parts. The former, I imagine, bought the chocolates to eat themselves, the latter bought them to give to their girlfriends when, later in the evening, they went to the theatre. But it was clear that the skipper had found a profitable outlet for his charm and efficiency. Whether they were old ladies or young men about town they usually bought a large box rather than a small one when the skipper had been chatting to them for a few minutes. But this was not the impression he gave me when he received me in the room over the public house that day in 1941. He was welcoming, friendly and efficient. Having explained that the unit was responsible for managing a large ammunition dump which was spread over an area of some hundred square miles of Shropshire, he gave me a railway warrant and despatched me to a company that was centred in Craven Arms, a market town between Church Stretton and Ludlow. The officers' mess was in the Craven Arms Hotel, a small country hotel on the corner where a minor road joined the main Shrewsbury to Ludlow road. There were four of us, the Company Commander, the medical officer, myself and one other newly created subaltern, Norman Miller, who was to become a lifelong friend. Within a few days the company commander left and was replaced by the skipper who was promoted from adjutant to major. The troops for whom we were responsible were some two hundred pioneers billeted in the larger buildings in the town.

The daily work of the unit of which I had now become a part was to move ammunition to and from the railway sidings at Craven Arms. Each day goods trains arrived bringing from the factories ammunition of every type, from the huge shells for heavy and medium artillery to the small tracer bullets for anti-aircraft guns. Other empty wagons were filled to make up trains that departed with the ammunition destined for the troops in England or abroad. On arrival the ammunition had to be dispersed. It was, therefore, loaded into lorries which were driven off into the countryside. Spread at intervals along the many miles of the small roads that criss-cross the area between Bishops Castle and Clun in the north and Ludlow in the south and between the little villages that are tucked away in that delightful bit of England, there were corrugated iron shelters placed under trees and concealed in various ways from the view of aeroplanes. In these the ammunition was stored until it was required. My job was to supervise my men as they carried out this task of loading and unloading. It involved driving and walking for miles between the little villages and farms in that part of the world. It is without doubt one of the most purely rural and attractive parts of our island. I came to know it well. The many beautiful houses and farms and churches scattered over the valleys that lie between the wooded hills came for me places of happy exploration. Walcot Hall, near Lydbury North, once the home of Clive of India, was the headquarters of the Ordnance Corps and I often had business there but was inclined to be diverted to watch the many varieties of wild duck that were kept on the lakes by the house. Further north, under the west side of the Long Mynd, was Plowden Hall, still owned by the great Catholic family of that name. It was another place in the grounds of which ammunition was concealed. It was from this same house that Edmund Plowden, who was responsible for the building of the fine Elizabethan Hall of the Middle Temple, came. A marble bust of him now stands at one end of the Hall and all Middle Templars regard him as the true father of our Inn. When I dine in this magnificent place I often think of the little village on the edge of Wales which he must have known so well and wonder what he would have thought had he known that his fields and woodlands were being used to store vast quantities of lethal ammunition. Further south was Stokesay Castle, a gaunt medieval house standing in the middle of fields in a wide valley. And, of course, Ludlow, a small town of lovely black and white gabled houses and stone buildings spread over a hill overlooking the River Teme and guarded by the vast ruins of its castle.

The skipper and the doctor were keen bridge players. Norman Miller and I were less keen, but after dinner almost every evening we were persuaded to join the other two for a few rubbers before we retired for the night. One Saturday after we had been pressed into these games for many consecutive evenings, Norman and I decided we would make a rapid get away at the end of dinner, before the others had time to ask us to play bridge, and entertain ourselves in some other way. Immediately dinner was over we left and went into the saloon bar of the hotel. While in there, planning what to do for the rest of the evening, the door burst open and a group of pretty girls in the charge of an attractive lady of about forty flooded into the room. This sort of thing did not happen often in my experience and it was too much to expect that two young subalterns wondering how to spend a Saturday evening should not attempt to get into conversation with the two best looking of the bunch. It turned out that they were all students at a secretarial college that had been evacuated to a village called Hopton Heath some mile away on the border of Wales. They had been invited to a dance at the R.A.S.C. camp near Ludlow and were being taken there by the lady who proved to be the mother of one of the girls — the one I had regarded as the most beautiful and with whom I managed to strike up conversation. They had called in at the hotel to break the journey. It was not long before we had been persuaded (in no way against our will) to join them and go to the dance. It was in this way that I met my first wife.

Jeananne Powell was known to everyone as 'Pookie'. Her father and mother had taken a small cottage at Bedstone when they had to leave their home at Nayland in Essex which was a bit too near the vulnerable east coast for comfort. Pookie's two brothers were at Shrewsbury School and so it was convenient for the family to move to Shropshire. In the short period before I was moved from Craven Arms I contrived to visit this family in the little cottage at Bedstone frequently and came to know them well. Pookie's father and mother were both remarkable people — but very different and, unhappily, ill-suited to each other. They both came from Cardiff. Jack Powell was a chartered surveyor whose father had been, I believe, an estate agent in South Wales. Jack was intensely ambitious and was something of a snob. Toto was the grand-daughter of the Richard Thomas who had made a considerable fortune in Glamorgan as a steel master and had founded the great company of steel makers that became Richard Thomas and Baldwin. It was said that when he died he left a steel mill to each of his sons, but none of the sons were of the same quality and the mills were sold. The sons lived on the capital thus produced. They were moderately wealthy and were able to lead a comfortable life amongst the society of Cardiff and Glamorgan. Toto and her sister Ruby, with their two brothers, grew up in this provincial atmosphere amongst the children of the better off in South Wales. In the period immediately after the First World War they must have been some of the most lively and entertaining of the young people that made up this social set. I suspect that Jack Powell married Toto partly because he saw that by so doing he would gain entry into circles in

South Wales that would be helpful to him in his career. I suspect that she married him partly because she realised that he was a young man with great drive and determination to succeed. By the time that I came to know them they had been married some eighteen years and there was little love or affection between them. Toto was frivolous, full of fun and cared not what people thought of her. She was inclined to laugh at Jack who was so earnestly trying to impress and this wounded him and made the anger rise up so that they quarrelled furiously. On my first visit to Bedstone I arrived in the middle of one of these outbursts. They had both been drinking and abuse and unkind remarks were being exchanged so that one could see that each infuriated the other to such an extent that forgiveness seemed almost an impossibility. I had never experienced this sort of thing before. My own parents, so gentle and so loving, had never so far as I was aware quarrelled. I did not realise then that to have been brought up in a family where one never heard a cross word spoken by one parent to another was a rare privilege. I felt sorry for Pookie who was caught up in this unhappy atmosphere. She seemed innocent and unable to protect herself from the fury of the parents which, at times, was directed at her.

But my stay at Craven Arms soon came to an end. After a few weeks I was sent with a platoon of Pioneers into the middle of Wales. Lake Vyrnwy is an artificial lake made as a reservoir to provide water for the city of Liverpool. The authorities feared that German planes might drop poison into it which would be taken into the city's supply, or that sea planes might land on the lake and leave spies, or fifth columnists, whose task would be to operate as saboteurs and collectors of information. When I arrived with my small band of men I found that we were to take over the watching and guarding of the lake from a company of Royal Engineers and some machine gunners. An elderly captain greeted me and showed me the huts in which the equipment his units were leaving behind was stored. He handed me a bundle of papers and asked me to sign them. Then he hurried off leading the convoy of lorries into which all his men had been crammed. We were then alone in this remote and beautiful corner of Wales and settled down to enjoy the agreeable surroundings. All was very peaceable and no Germans appeared and after a few days I congratulated myself on my good fortune. Then one day a staff car arrived with a brigadier and the quartermaster from headquarters in Shrewsbury. I shewed them round our camp and explained how we were doing our work. The men had cleaned their equipment and were smart when inspected by the brigadier. I felt fairly confident that we would get good marks for our efficiency and competence. Then, as these senior officers were about to leave, the quartermaster said, "would you send the 500 pairs of wellington boots you took over from the engineers down to Shrewsbury when next a lorry is going that way?". I did not remember seeing so many boots but assumed that they must have been amongst the stores in the huts I had signed for on arrival. The Brigadier departed and I went to find the boots. But there were no boots anywhere. Stores of all kinds there were but absolutely no boots. There was nothing for it but to tell headquarters that I had not got them and this I did by letter. A week later the quartermaster was on the phone saying that I would be charged with the value of the boots. I had signed for them so they must have been there. The cost of the boots would be deducted from my pay. 500 pairs of wellington boots was an expensive item and I saw my pay of £3 per week stopping for weeks or even years. I was very worried. Happily a day or two later the quartermaster, a tough but pleasant Yorkshireman, arrived again, this time to check all the stores. He went through everything in the huts and checked it against the long list which so clearly bore my signature. It was only the boots that were missing. He did not seem surprised and after I had given him some lunch he departed back to Shrewsbury. As he got into his car he said "Perhaps we can arrange to have the boots written off — but don't forget in future to check your stores carefully when you take over a camp. Engineers like wellington boots — they are useful". I never heard any more about it. But I had learned one of the first rules of army life.

About that time I had a weekend's leave and went to Parkstone to stay with Catherine whose parents lived there. Her father was a retired general who had been on friendly terms with the Military Secretary. I felt that life in the Pioneers was not really the most exciting way to spend the war and told him I wished that I could be transferred to a line regiment that had some chance of seeing real active service. He said he would see what could be done. The skipper had told me that most people who tried to get transferred from the Pioneer Corps were unsuccessful and so I was not hopeful. It was therefore with some surprise that shortly after I had returned to Lake Vyrnwy I was told to report again to Craven Arms where the skipper shewed me an order that had arrived from the War Office posting me to the 5th Battalion of the South Staffordshire Regiment stationed at Prudhoe, a mining village on the Tyne, a few miles up river from Newcastle.

CHAPTER NINE

Infantryman

The 5th Battalion of the South Staffordshire regiment was a Territorial battalion drawn almost entirely from the area of Walsall. The men were for the most part from the mining community, while the officers were local professional or business men. All were volunteers. They had spent a considerable part of their free time during the last years of peace attending camps and learning the art of soldiering in the evenings. The skipper had told me, when I left the Pioneers, that the county regiments were often splendid units, very efficient and of the high morale which comes of a strong local patriotism. The 5th Battalion was certainly such a body. Sadly I was not with it for very long. When I joined it, it was training and after a short spell in the valley of the Tyne it was moved further north to the coast of Northumberland between Lindisfarne and Bamburgh. The headquarters of the battalion was in Belford Hall, a fine Palladian villa, which after the war became nearly derelict, but was later saved from demolition by being restored and converted into flats. The battalion was a part of the 59th (Staffordshire) Division which was allotted the task of defending the coastline at the same time as undergoing training for more offensive tasks that we all hoped would come later. After I had left the division it was part of the invasion force that landed in Normandy later in the war. In that great offensive it distinguished itself though ultimately it suffered dreadful casualties. The 5th Battalion was nearly wiped out.

In Northumberland our time was spent partly in manning defences that looked out across the greyness of the North Sea along that bleak but beautiful stretch of coast, and partly in exercises on the moors inland. Wild country that those who live there rightly regard as unrivalled in its austere loveliness. Long marches across the Cheviots and nights spent in the cold and wet of the hillsides were made endurable by the knowledge that from time to time the sun and rain, mists and morning and evening light would combine to create landscapes that made one yearn to be able to paint. The miners of my platoon did not see it that way. They longed to be back in the warmth of the homely pubs of Walsall and the slag heap industrial landscape of their native Black Country where the girls were more to their liking. That was the countryside and those were the people that moved their emotions.

Not long after I had joined the battalion I was sent off to the dales of Yorkshire on a course for young infantry officers. As I had not been to an officers' training unit I had much to learn about a subaltern's role in modern warfare. The course was held at Bellerby

Camp on the moors high above Leyburn, the small Yorkshire market town whence my father's family had come. The course lasted about a month and was intended to toughen us up and instil into us aggressive ideas about fighting. The training was based on the methods adopted to teach the newly formed commandos, small groups of men who were to be used to carry out raids behind the enemy lines and across the Channel into occupied territory. The idea was to create fierce fighting soldiers each one of whom was self reliant and capable of operating alone, or with only one or two others, to do damage and cause consternation to the enemy out of proportion to their small numbers. This concept was important because up to this point in the war — it was not long after the Battle of Dunkerque — it had been difficult for those of us, like myself, who were not natural soldiers and to whom world strategy meant little, to understand how we would win the war. We realised that the cause for which we fought was right, and that if we lost we would be overrun by Hitler's armies and become slaves in a state ruled by the repulsive principles of Nazism. But how to win? Until now the German military machine had seemed so big and so efficient as its huge armies and numerous armoured divisions, supported by waves of terrifying dive bombers, had rolled across one European country after another. Resistance by armies composed of ordinary infantry soldiers drawn largely from civil life — people like me — had seemed impossible. The commandos and the ideas that those who led them cultivated seemed to provide something of the answer for which we had all been looking, hitherto without success. Morale, certainly my morale, improved at once. One began to see how we could win — and if we could, we would, win.

The instructor who was in charge of the syndicate to which I was allotted on the course was a civilian soldier with a genius in putting over this new philosophy, and I admired him greatly. Later, after the war, when television came and our way of life was transformed by it, he was to become famous, indeed almost a household name, as a programme producer. Huw Weldon was then a young, and I thought rather handsome, officer in the Royal Welch Fusiliers, and he it was who, more than any one else, gave me the inspiration necessary to convince me that the war could be won. Many years later, by then Sir Huw, he came as a guest to a dinner in the Middle Temple and I had a few words with him. Middle age had made its mark. His good looks and his inspiring way of talking were no longer his prime attributes, but he was still able to make a subject interesting, as those who watched his talks on music, or painting, or Royal art collections will testify.

When I returned to my unit in Northumberland we embarked on intensive divisional training and took part in army manoeuvres all over the north of England and it soon became clear that before long we would be considered fit for war. We expected to be moved to somewhere in the real battle zone such as the Middle East, at that time the only place where British troops were in actual contact with German and Italian forces. The Eighth Army, soon to be christened the Desert Rats, was then beginning to show that we were at least the equals of the Germans when it came to a war of movement in the desert, where fast moving tanks could operate rather like ships at sea. But when the order to move came to us it was to Stranraer that we were sent, to embark on ships bound for Northern Ireland. This was a dreadful disappointment. Instead of the sun and desert of the southern Mediterranean coastline the drab greyness of the country south of Belfast was to be our lot. I found myself billeted in a gloomy building, the Slieve Donard Hotel, in Newcastle, County Down. It is there that, in the words of the romantic song, the Mountains of

Mourne sweep down to the sea. But we saw little romance in our position which suggested that we were destined to remain as garrison troops in an unexciting backwater. I was not, however, there for long because within a few weeks the battalion was called upon to produce a draft of troops to go as reinforcements overseas and I, and one or two others, as recently joined officers who had not been with the battalion in its territorial Staffordshire days were invited to 'volunteer' to go with them. So I was soon back in England on embarkation leave and fitted out with tropical kit — which included the traditional pith helmet designed to protect one's head and neck from the effects of the tropical sun. It is an odd fact that these strange items of kit, formerly so symbolical of the British in distant parts of the Empire, were still being issued to the troops going abroad, because when one got abroad one found that absolutely no one wore them. To wear one's pith helmet was a sure sign that you were fresh from England and knew no better.

I left the 5th Battalion with some regret because I was becoming attached to the men that made it up. The tough miners were a friendly lot and when they accepted someone, like myself, from outside their own circle they became delightful comrades. Had I stayed in the battalion I would, I have no doubt, have become a loyal Staffordshire man. But it was, perhaps, lucky for me that I left because, as I have said, the battalion was later decimated in Normandy, and few of them survived. Such, however, are the chances of war and one's survival may be dependent on just such a whim of fortune. There was later at least one other event in the war that turned me from a course that, had I continued on it, would almost certainly have led me to a death by drowning in the Indian Ocean. So I was lucky, but thoughts such as these have from time to time returned to haunt me in later life as I have wondered how different things might have been if the splendid young men I knew then had survived to the war's end.

But these thoughts were not in my mind when shortly afterwards I reported at the barracks in Worcester, where the draft to which I was allotted assembled. A few days were spent getting to know the troops with whom I was to travel overseas. I remember well our last day at Worcester. In order to fill in the empty hours, and, I suppose, to help keep us fit, we were sent on a route march. We marched from the barracks at Worcester to a point just beyond Pershore where the road to Evesham crosses a small river by an old and beautiful bridge. As we approached the bridge flakes of snow began to fall. The officer in charge decided that this gave us an excuse to turn round and retrace our steps over the seven or so miles back to barracks. This decision was greeted by vociferous cheering. Like a horse that will amble reluctantly when ridden away from its stable, but will gallop and canter joyfully when its head is turned homewards, the troops began to march with spirit and sang happily as they strode in the gathering storm along the road back to the barracks. From that insignificant episode I learned an important truth. The English Tommy will do anything that is asked of him but he will do it sulkily if he can see no purpose in what is required of him. As soon, however, as he can see an object in the orders he receives he will carry them out with a cheerfulness that is difficult to suppress. By the time we were half way back the snow had developed into a blizzard but the singing and joking continued.

The next day we were put into a troop train that took us to Liverpool where we embarked on one of the many ships that were to form a large convoy of ships full of troops and supplies for the Middle East.

R.M.S. Otranto, a liner of some 20,000 tons, was to be our home for the next six weeks. She had in peacetime been one of the fleet belonging to the Orient line that sailed from England to Australia. On the upper decks was accommodation for first class passengers, comparatively luxurious with comfortable cabins, bars and lounges and a large dining saloon. This part of the ship was occupied by the officers. Less comfortable cabins that had been for second class passengers in normal times were used by senior N.C.O.s, sergeants and upwards. The rest of the ship consisted of cargo holds fore and aft. Here the remaining troops were confined in makeshift quarters that had been hurriedly created when the need for a greatly increased number of troopships had arisen. The conditions in which the soldiers were accommodated were appalling and I felt very guilty as, each evening, I sat down to dinner in the officers' saloon to a well cooked dinner and was waited on by mess servants. The difference in the conditions was too extreme.

Long after the end of the war I learned that I was not alone in feeling that the difference in the conditions was inexcusable. Unknown to me there was amongst the troops abroad that ship an airman, John Colville, on his way to South Africa to continue his training as an RAF pilot. He had worked in 10 Downing Street and was later to become one of Churchill's most trusted helpers. He knew Mrs Churchill and when he got to Durban he wrote her a letter describing the appalling conditions in which the troops were compelled to travel and the strong and bitter political feeling to which it gave rise. When Mrs Churchill got the letter she shewed it to the Prime Minister who immediately ordered that the matter should be put right; which it was.

Soon after we left the Mersey and began to sail round the north of Ireland into the Atlantic the weather deteriorated and a powerful storm got up. The ship began to roll and pitch alarmingly. I quickly discovered that I could only avoid the horror of continuous seasickness if I remained on deck or lay flat on my back in my cabin. But from time to time I had to visit my soldiers in the hold where they were confined and, equally, prone to sea sickness. I think that hell for me will be a place where I am required to descend at frequent intervals to the bowels of a large liner to visit a sprawling mass of men many of whom are being uncontrollably sick as the hold is thrown about in an Atlantic storm. The smell and the obvious discomfort that the men were subjected to made me feel utterly miserable. Fortunately however the storm did not last for long. After three or four days we were clear of Ireland and were moving into calm waters. Thereafter our journey was through smooth seas that became progressively more and more blue as we sailed southwards. The convoy took six weeks to reach Durban, so there was much time to kill. Only two events took place that brought some variety into the life we led. When we were off Dakar, a port on the Coast of French West Africa which was occupied by the Germans, a German aeroplane was seen. As we had seen it the certainty was that it had spotted the convoy and it was assumed that it would not be long before German U-boats would have been told of our whereabouts and sent to hunt the convoy down. The result of this was that instead of sailing on southwards the convoy turned abruptly westwards and sailed nearly across the Atlantic on a zig-zag course designed to make it difficult for marauding U-boats to pick us up. While this diversionary exercise was being carried out I began to appreciate the remarkable skill the Royal Navy had acquired at running convoys. Our convoy consisted of about twenty ships ranging in size from large ocean liners, like the Otranto, of which there were three or four, now converted to troop carriers, down to small cargo ships and many intermediate sized craft. We steamed in four parallel lines, each made up of five or so ships. Escorting us was a battleship, I believe she was the Royal Oak, one of a class of heavy battleships built about the end of the First World War. She had eight fifteen inch guns as her major armament and a number of smaller guns. With her were two fast destroyers that circled the convoy rather like sheep dogs shepherding a flock of sheep on a Welsh mountain. By night the ships showed no navigation lights, and from time to time the whole convoy changed direction by 45 or 50 degrees so as to run on a zig-zag course. There was wireless silence between the ships so when in total darkness the whole convoy changed direction with the precision of a battalion of the guards, I realised the wonderful skill that was shown by the naval commanders and by the merchant navy officers in charge of the individual ships. Our course took us nearly to the coast of Mexico and then we doubled back and called at Freetown, a harbour on the West Coast of Africa, and capital city of Sierra Leone. We were not allowed ashore so for two days we remained anchored in the torrid heat of the tropics while the ships took on fuel and supplies of food. This was my first sight of Africa. The blue haze that hung over the hills behind the town and the sultry stillness of the air in the harbour gave me the impression that one was living through one of Conrad's stories. Canoes manned by nearly naked Africans plied between the ships selling coconuts and trinkets to the soldiers leaning over the rail high above them.

During the long days of those monotonous six weeks the problem was what to do. Efforts were made to provide some useful training for the troops, but limitations of space together with the fact that we had very little idea of the sort of warfare we would be engaged in, and the fact that no one on the ship had any experience of the only sort of campaign that seemed likely made this difficult. Every officer was stretched to provide lectures on any subject that might prove useful or interesting. But the English Tommies are not natural attenders at lecture halls, and it was difficult to hold their attention. There was little room for any other type of training except the occasional P.T. period for which the games deck was taken over by each unit in turn. The afternoon was spent by the troops sunbathing or taking a modest amount of exercise. Endless letters were written by all on board and much of my time was taken up in censoring the troops' mail. This was an unbelievably boring occupation. Soldiers, for the most part, are not lively letter writers. Particularly when they have nothing to write about more interesting that the daily round on a troopship. Occasionally, however, a shaft of light would come through the gloom. I remember well one letter in which a Black Country gunner described to his girl friend in Burslem a lecture I had given on my experience in Poland. He began by describing me as a young officer who looked as if he had never kissed a girl, and would not know what to do if he tried. He then made it clear that the addressee of his letter would have the good sense to rebuff any advances if made by such as me. He described the substance of what I had said in the lecture with some colourful additions from his own imagination and ended by making it clear that he did not believe that a young innocent like me could ever have been to Poland and had the experiences I had described and that in all probability everything I had said was invented.

In the evenings the officers played card games and drank beer in the great saloon provided for First Class passengers. There was a small contingent of W.A.A.F. officers, about twenty in all, who brought an element of feminine charm to the evenings. There was even a certain amount of courting, but the competition was very keen. It was the tall dark and handsome amongst us who made the running. One such was Richard Cross who was later to become a distinguished solicitor in the Customs and Excise. He eventually married one of the W.A.A.F. officers, a lovely redhead who caused the hearts of all who saw her to beat a little faster. Shortly after the journey was ended, and we realised Richard had pressed his suit to the point where an affirmative reply was likely, (the odds offered by the ship's bookie, an officer of the South Staffordshire Regiment, were 7:1 in favour of an engagement before we docked) she was suddenly taken very ill. She had been lying on the deck all the morning on a cloudy day but had become terribly sunburnt. In the tropics the fact that the sun is shrouded by cloud does not mean its rays do not reach your body. The poor girl was for several days in great pain and very ill. But all ended well. She recovered and she and Richard became engaged and, indeed, I believe they married in Durban. The bookie made his money and everyone was happy. Many years later when I was a silk I received a brief to appear for the Customs and Excise against the Church of Scientology and to my delight was instructed by Richard.

Eventually the long journey ended. We woke one morning to find that several of the ships in the convoy had left us during the night. They had 'peeled off' to land their cargoes at Capetown, while we sailed on towards Durban. The last evening before we docked was perfectly still and clear. The stars were diamond bright in the dark sky. The Southern Cross was clearly visible as we thrust northwards leaving a long phosphorescent trail behind us. The troops had a sing song. I remember looking down from the bridge deck on to the forward well which was thronged with Tommies half naked, or in their short sleeves, in the warm night air. They sang the army songs — 'Roll out the barrel', 'We'll hang out our washing on the Siegfried Line' and 'Lili Marlene'. Tears came to my eyes as I listened to those simple men singing. Many were to die and none knew what the future had in store for them, but now they sang with all the gusto they could command the songs which expressed in some way their inner thoughts. The determination to reduce Hitler and all his works to their proper scale of insignificance and the homesick dreams of the girls they had left behind. There is something about the tune of Lili Marlene that exactly captured the feeling of the soldier who had fleetingly seen and loved a pretty girl whom he had been compelled to leave behind. Even now when I hear the tune I am still almost moved to tears. Next morning we docked in Durban.

The Otranto was due to stay in Durban for three days, to refuel and take on stores and then it was to continue its voyage in a smaller convey to the Middle East. We were allowed shore leave each day and as we came ashore we saw that the quayside was packed with private cars and taxis each containing some kind South African who was prepared to offer hospitality to the soldiers from England. I was with a friend from the South Staffordshire Regiment, John Thompson, a peace time brewer and a very stolid Black Countryman. We were whisked away by a mother and two daughters to a pleasant house on the outskirts and treated to a delicious dinner, to hot baths and all the delights of a welcoming domestic life. On the last day before the Otranto was due to sail we decided we would return this family's hospitality by giving them dinner in the town. So John and I drew from the paymaster all that we were allowed to draw and took them out to the best meal we could afford. We ate lobster and danced with the daughters at a restaurant on the cliffs overlooking the Indian Ocean until it was time to rush back to the ship before she sailed at midnight. Almost as soon as we had returned we heard the ships loudspeakers making an announcement. At first we paid no attention and then suddenly we realised that our names were being called out. "Would Lieutenants Medd and Thompson and about a dozen other officers please report at once to the ship's adjutant?" In horror we went to the office fearing that perhaps we had committed some offence of which we were unaware. But as soon as we arrived we were told that we had ten minutes to pack our things and disembark. We were to leave the ship and report to a transit camp 20 miles from Durban where we would be given further instructions. The ship was all set to sail and continue with the rest of the convoy and we were to disembark before she cast off in a few minutes time. Rarely have I moved so fast. My last sight of the Otranto was as her great form silently pulled away from the quayside and moved into the channel to start the last leg of her journey to the Middle East. John Thompson and I were sitting on our kitbags on the quayside waiting for a truck to take us to the transit camp. We had not the remotest idea what was in store for us or where we were going.

Eventually we reached the camp; a collection of huts in the middle of a dusty plain. The only visible feature of significance was a railway siding with a few trucks on it. This as things turned out was to be our home for three weeks. It was the place our service people were sent who had arrived in South Africa and did not know where to go next. We discovered amongst those who had found their way here — Australian airmen, Indian soldiers, a few men from Mauritius and a New Zealand vet. They, like us, had been told to report here and that they would be told what to do. One thing, however, was clear and that was that no one knew what to do with any of us. It was here, I think, that I learned one of the truths about war. One always imagines an army consisting of regiments and battalions forming part of a coherent whole — the fighting force. But, at any one time, for every man that helps make up a fighting unit there are two men somewhere behind the front, in a transit camp or moving aimlessly from place to place up or down the lines of supply. We had now joined this straggling army. For a day or two we did not move out of the camp, but as we now had no troops for whom we were responsible, no job to do, nothing for which we could prepare, a prospect of unending tedium seemed to open up. We decided we must leave the camp if only for a day, but that was easier said than done. We had only ten shillings between us and there seemed no prospect of getting any more. The paymaster was only allowed to pay out to troops passing through the equivalent of one week's pay. This we had both already drawn to finance our party the week before. To obtain more it was necessary to get money sent out from our banks in England and this was bound to take a long time. With luck we would have moved on before it arrived. However, we decided better to be out of camp with no money than to be in camp and die of boredom. We managed to get a lift into Durban and on the way saw a notice announcing that there was a race meeting that afternoon. John was a keen racing man and determined we should go despite our meagre resources, and so we made our way to the course. Many service men were amongst the crowds and large numbers of white South Africans. John suspected that there was something of a bookmakers' conspiracy to take the money off the visiting troops and so for the first four races he would not bet even a single shilling on a favourite. But just before the last race was due to begin we were standing near a bookmaker who was only taking a limited number of bets but, from what we could hear, such bets as he accepted were large ones. Then as the horses were approaching the starting gate and the race was just about to begin, a large important looking Afrikaaner, smoking a cigar, went up and placed a bet. John told me afterwards he heard the name of the horse — it was 75:1 — and the amount of the bet which was a very large sum, £500 I think, and he surmised that the man must be the owner or someone else in the know. Before the bookie had time to change the odds John placed our ten shillings, our total liquid wealth, on that horse. Within seconds they were off. A few minutes later it romped in an easy winner. So we were suddenly rich. Over £37 was in those days enough to enable two young subalterns to live it up in Durban for several days. This fortunate investment transformed our stay at the transit camp which continued for a further fortnight at the end of which we once again received orders to embark. We boarded a French ship, the 'Compiegne', which was due to sail the next day. We asked where we were going but no one would tell us.

When we embarked we learned that we and ten other army officers were the only passengers on this small ship. The French speaking crew told us that they too were ignorant of our destination. We learned that the captain had received sealed orders which he was not allowed to open until the ship was on the high seas. Not long after we had set sail we were told that the first port of call was to be Mombasa and that we would leave the ship there. So we settled down to enjoy the gentle cruise up the east coast of Africa. This ship was no 'Otranto', she was very much smaller and, being French, was not kept clean and shipshape in the manner of British merchant ships. The galleys stank and rubbish and litter lay about in the passages and on the decks. The one redeeming feature was, however, the food, which in the French style was consistently delicious.

After a week steaming between the mainland and the west coast of Madagascar we finally reached Mombasa where we landed and were soon on a train bound for Nairobi. The building of the railway line from the coast of Mombasa to Nairobi was a considerable feat of engineering carried out in difficult and occasionally dangerous conditions. Man-eating lions had harassed the labour force that had been used to build the line some 40 years earlier. A fascinating book which I had read on my way from England 'The Man eaters of the Tzavo' tells the story graphically. As we travelled slowly across the great tawny plain there was little to see except the occasional cluster of huts that was an African village and here and there a dark green thorn tree. In the distance a line of blue hills. I found this journey, my first in Africa, exciting and it was not difficult to understand the attraction that the country had exercised over the early explorers and settlers. As we approached Nairobi the train climbed on to the uplands of Kenya where farms were scattered over the landscape, the more solid farmsteads standing in clumps of trees indicating the presence of the European.

My stay in Nairobi was short. A day or so after I had arrived I was sent for to the Headquarters of East Africa Command where I was interviewed by an elderly officer, the Military Secretary, who was responsible for directing officers newly arrived from England to the units that needed reinforcements. He asked me what experience I had and when he learned that at school I had been a mathematician and scientist he seemed pleased. Up to this time the native army in East Africa was composed almost entirely of infantry. There were several regular battalions of the K.A.R. (King's African Rifles) which had been raised before the war and somewhat expanded when hostilities against the Italians had begun in Abyssinia, but there was no artillery and it had apparently been decided to create an East

African Artillery. So far very few officers with artillery experience had come from England and so when it was learned that I boasted some mathematical ability I was told that I would be posted to the newly formed artillery base near Kijabe, a small village in the Rift Valley, some thirty miles from the capital. So my association with the South Staffordshire Regiment came to an end and I was no longer an infantryman. Thenceforth I remained a gunner.

A bumpy journey in the back of an army truck through the coffee growing area of Limuru brought me eventually to Larkhill, the camp, named after the artillery school on Salisbury Plain, where the few gunners that had been marshalled were to be found. The final approach to the camp was spectacular. As we drove along the dusty red earth road through the scrubland and forest that covered the undulating countryside beyond Limuru, we suddenly found ourselves at the top of a steep tree covered escarpment. Some two or three hundred feet below us was the bottom of the rift valley. As far as the eye could see there stretched a flat and arid plain with the occasional volcanic mountain breaking the monotony of the skyline. A very different landscape to the uplands round Nairobi. A strange flaw in the earth's crust must have resulted in a band of the world's surface, about 60 miles across, subsiding below the surrounding hills. The plain is sparsely inhabited, only the occasional herdsman of the primitive nomadic tribe, the Masai, was to be seen guarding his cattle. These men, tall and proud, were usually dressed in no more than a piece of sacking. They always carried a spear. As during the ensuing months I came to know the Rift Valley better I realised that this great dry plain was the home of a wide variety of game. Gazelle and buffalo, giraffe and lions, leopards, ostriches and innumerable other birds were to be seen. Eventually the truck descended into the valley by a series of terrifying hairpin bends and I was delivered at the door of a hut that served as an officers' mess. Around it were a few tents and a flagpole. It was here that I was to start on my career as a gunnery officer and to meet the men with whom I was to stay for the remaining three years of the war.

CHAPTER TEN

Gunner

The part of Kenya in which I found myself, and where I was to stay for some five months, was near the Equator. This simple fact had a marked effect on our way of life. Each day the sun rose at six o'clock in the morning and set at six in the evening. There was none of the lengthening and shortening of the days that one knows in England and which marks the seasonal changes that bring such variety to English life. Each day was like the day before and the day after. Bright clear skies all day followed by sudden cooling of the earth as the sun went down. Within a few minutes of six each evening one sat down with a glass of beer (bottled from South Africa) or a whisky and watched the red ball of the sun sink over the horizon. Then one talked and talked. My first night at this camp introduced me to the task that faced the small band of officers that I found there. I learned that the plan was to recruit enough African soldiers to man a regiment of artillery comprising three batteries. When I arrived sufficient men had been brought in from their villages for two batteries. Each of these batteries had a major to command it and a battery captain who was responsible for administration, making sure the men were fed, clothed and provided with the necessary ammunition and transport. I was the first junior officer to be allotted to 57 (Tanganyika) Field Battery East African Artillery.

The battery commander was Justin MacCarthy, a regular gunner from England, and the battery captain was Raymond Tubbs, a former district officer in the Colonial Civil Service. The latter had just returned from a journey into Tanganyika where he had recruited some two hundred young men from the villages round Mount Kilimanjaro. He had tried to recruit those in the villages who could read or write as it would be difficult, it was thought, to turn them into gunners if they could do neither of these things. But despite his efforts the majority of them were illiterate and many of them had hardly ever seen a white man. When I arrived the task of making soldiers and gunners of them was about to begin. The other battery was a little more experienced. That had been recruited in Kenya and was commanded by a small Scot, MacCrae, who had been a gunner in the First World War, since when he had been a coffee farmer in Limuru. He had begun to train his men who, having been soldiering for two months, regarded themselves as veterans. In command of all of us was another Kenya farmer, also a Scot, called Mackinley who had farmed in the highlands at Nakuru. He too had, I think, served in the First World War.

The job of introducing 200 men, who, for the most part, could not read or write to a science like gunnery which required at least a minimal knowledge of mathematics was, in itself, daunting, but when on top of that basic difficulty I could not myself speak a word of their language and did not myself have any appreciable knowledge of the subject the prospect became formidable indeed. But I need not have worried over much. Justin MacCarthy was not only a regular soldier of immense charm, he was also an admirable teacher and a very knowledgeable expert in his own field. So he taught me the rudiments of gunnery. Raymond Tubbs, a very different sort of person, was an equally good teacher of Swahili, a language he spoke perfectly having been in Tanganyika for several years before the war. He understood the simple African and liked him and so was very popular with our new raw soldiers. Raymond taught me Swahili, which, happily, is not a very difficult language to learn. It stems from Arabic and is spoken at its best by the Africans who live on or near the coast. It is a language which until the European came to East Africa had never been written down. Thus when, after the arrival of the English, people began to write it, it was written phonetically. This made it easy for me to learn. Thus it was that, having spent a wearisome two months on troopships and in transit camps doing nothing, I was suddenly plunged into a spell of furious activity. I would spend my day trying to teach the new soldiers the basic needs of a military life and passing on to them what I had learnt the night before of the art of gunnery. The evenings after dinner I would divide between trying to grasp Swahili in order better to be able the following day to teach the gunnery that I swotted up in the rest of the evening. In this way surprisingly rapid progress was made. The askaris (soldiers) were very happy. They were better fed and better paid than they had ever been before and they enjoyed the active military life. For the first few weeks we were primarily concerned with trying to teach them simple military skills. We were greatly helped by a number of regular K.A.R. (King's African Rifles) non-commissioned officers who were seconded to us. Just as the old Indian Army had produced a core of immensely smart, dedicated and efficient N.C.O.s who were the base on which discipline was built, so, in a smaller way, the pre-war K.A.R. in East Africa had acquired a fine cadre of African N.C.O.s without whose devoted help the vast expansion that took place in the war could never have been achieved.

Before many weeks had passed further reinforcements arrived from England and a number of subalterns trained in gunnery joined us. It was not long before we had reached a stage in the training which justified us in taking the troops out into the Rift Valley on simple exercises with the battery guns. Up to this time East Africa was very much a backwater, out of the main stream of the war, with the result that our equipment was old and out-of-date. Our guns were 3.7 inch howitzers, immortalised by Rudyard Kipling in his poem 'The Screw Gun'. They had been discarded by an Indian mountain regiment which had been re-equipped with the modern 25 pounder and sent to the Middle East. The true Indian mountain regiment was equipped with the screw gun, so called because the barrel was in two parts that unscrewed in the middle so that each half could be loaded on to a mule when the time came to move. It was a marvellous weapon for use with tribesmen on the North West Frontier where high angled firing over steep mountains was necessary. But their short range made them useless for desert warfare against an enemy with more powerful and longer ranged weapons. We used to set off across the scrub land, the eight guns drawn by a selection of elderly lorries and we would practice bringing the guns into action at speed and firing at targets way out in the bush, the guns being directed by one or other of the officers at a forward observation post on some slight rise or hill. At the end of a hard day's practice we would dig in and bivouac in the middle of the bush land. After the troops had been fed and the guns serviced the officers would sit round on camp stools each clutching his glass of whisky and watching the red sun sink in the west. Slowly the battery began to develop and the despair which had from time to time nearly overcome us lifted as we realised that we might make gunners of the Africans yet. When once they got hold of the idea they became remarkably accurate gunners.

The scrub land country over which we manoeuvred in those clear dry days of almost perpetual sunshine was the home of many species of big game as well as a multitude of different types of birds — from the macabre vultures and large eagles, down to beautiful and highly coloured little birds. Nowadays, some fifty years on, rich men from all over the world spend a great deal of money on expensive trips organised by operators on a safari (the Swahili word for journey) hunting and shooting the big game. But we were lucky. We had all the pleasure of seeing the wild animals in their natural surroundings and the trip was entirely paid for by His Majesty's Government. I can remember when we were on exercises near Narok in the middle of the Rift Valley seeing lion, elephant and rhinoceros in a matter of two or three days. All over the plain herds of gazelle and wildebeest were to be seen grazing. On one occasion when a troop of four guns was positioned in a clearing in the scrubland the African gunners suddenly started to scream and those near the officer, who was giving the orders to fire, took to their heels and ran into the bush. The reason for their sudden flight became apparent a moment later when a powerful wild boar, tusks bared and shoulders hunched, charged across the open space and made for the gun position officer. Phil Denby, the officer concerned, had, I believe played rugger in peace time and he had a good sidestep so happily the boar disappeared again into the surrounding scrub. At intervals along this part of the Rift Valley at Naivasha, Elmenteita Nakuru, there are substantial lakes. The latter two were salt and were favourite places for flamingoes. Once when we were doing an exercise near Elmenteita I was, at sunrise one morning, on a low hill that overlooked the lake. It was my task to direct the fire of the guns on to the sandy beaches at the edge of the lake where, for the purposes of our exercise some hypothetical enemy troops were supposed to have appeared. I ordered the first salvo to be fired. It landed considerably off the intended target and well out into the lake close to a flock of feeding flamingoes. The colour of the flock as it rose, a huge mass of pink flapping wings, into the slanting rays of the rising sun was something I would not have believed to be attainable had I not seen it. A painter who tried to reproduce it would certainly be accused of exaggeration.

Though the greater part of our time was taken up with our military tasks there were, of course, spells off duty and short weekends of leave when it was possible to see more of the country and its people. During the previous half century farmers from England had settled in many parts of the highlands of Kenya and had gradually converted the wild bush land into meadows and cultivated fields. It was a beautiful and fertile countryside and, as one climbed higher into parts where there was greater rainfall, it became more and more like England. Herds of cattle in well fenced fields covered the rolling hills. Here and there a red roofed homestead was to be seen nestling in a clump of trees. The families that had created these farms were generous and hospitable to the young soldiers that had suddenly descended on their country from the homeland. Few of us were without invitations to stay during our leave periods with these charming folk. I was particularly lucky to have been invited to spend a few days leave with a family called Allen who had a farm on the road from Gilgil to Thompson's Falls. When the Allens had first come out to Kenya shortly before the First World War, they had settled on a large expanse of bush land. They lived first in a tent, then in a grass hut and after a few years built a wooden bungalow. By the time I reached them this had been replaced by a comfortable house made of stone dug from a quarry they had started in a nearby hillside. The bush had been hacked down and grubbed out over about half of their holding, so that the land had become a series of fields, some down to grass and feeding a substantial herd of half bred cattle, local cattle crossed with English shorthorn; other fields were sown with pyrethrum or arable crops. I spent several weekends with these delightful people and enjoyed the company of their two lovely daughters. This family, who had started with little or no resources except the land granted to them by the Crown, had by dint of unremitting toil over a period of some 35 years changed the landscape from its natural, unproductive, state into a farm producing substantial quantities of food for export. Their experience was typical of the British settler in Kenya. Such people developed a love for the country of their adoption, and a paternal affection for the natives they employed to help them. Now that self-government has come to countries like Kenya it is easy, and regularly done, to regard the way such people treated the native Africans as if they were exploiting them. But nothing could be further from the truth. The Allens built houses for their employees far better than the mud huts in which they would otherwise have lived, gave them medical attention and education, as well as paying them a wage which, though low by current standards, was several times more than they could possibly have expected had they remained in their simple state. Mrs Allen spent much time looking after their health, ensuring the babies were properly fed and caring for the old workers who were no longer able to labour. The word paternalistic has now become a dirty word in this sort of context — but I do not believe the period of English influence in Kenya, largely exerted by these farmers, was other than good.

Much later and when the war was over I heard from the Allens again. They told me that they had decided to retire and sell their farm. They knew that I had said I would like to farm when the war was over and so they said they would let me have the part of their land which, so far, they had not been able to clear of scrub and which was still uncultivated, at no cost. They said they would get more than enough for their needs by selling the farm house and the land they had managed to cultivate. I did not take up this astonishingly generous offer as by then, as will appear later in this story, I had become very doubtful whether it would be possible to live in the country without fear of revolution and whether, if I married and had children, I could afford to send them home to England for their education. But such was the generosity of these splendid and considerate people. Sadly I later lost all touch with this family. I often wonder what became of them.

One other incident comes back to my memory from those days of weekend visits to the English who lived round about. Once very soon after I arrived in the country, I accepted an invitation to spend a weekend with a retired admiral and his wife who lived in a beautiful house on the edge of Lake Naivasha. Another young officer, a Scotsman, 'Jock', came with me. Our host and hostess were kindness itself. On arrival we were shewn to a small bungalow, a little distance from the main house, which was the guest house. Then we were given dinner, and what a dinner it was: deliciously cooked and made the more delicious by ample wine. The admiral was a very jovial and entertaining old boy and we sat up till the early morning while he regaled us with whisky and told stories of his early days. He was a keen big game hunter and told us that he loved the country he had chosen for his retirement because there he was surrounded by all sorts of game. One only had to walk down the garden to the lake's edge to see hippos wallowing in the muddy water, across the plain, towards Longenot, buffalo, leopard and lion were all to be found, and, if one was lucky, shot. He showed us proudly his big game rifle — a fearsome weapon with a thick rubber pad at the end of the butt intended to absorb the recoil when held to the shoulder. The tales went on until I began to feel drowsy under the influence of the whisky. Eventually he took us to the door and pointed out the direction to the guest hut, gave us a hurricane lamp and said "Off you go. If you see two red eyes looking at you in the darkness it will be a lion. Put the lamp on the ground and walk on. The lion will keep looking at the lamp. Good night". And he shut the door. Happily no lion interfered with our short walk to our sleeping quarters and so with some relief I lay down and quickly fell into a none too sober sleep. But my head had hardly touched the pillow, or so it seemed, when I was awakened again by a loud shouting and banging on the door. It was nearly dawn and a grey light was coming through the window. It was the admiral. "Get up boys, get up, we have cornered a lion on Longenot. Come and shoot him." Never had I felt less adventurous. My head ached and I lacked sleep — but to have turned over and slept on would have seemed cowardly or dishonourable. Jock was suffering even worse than I was, but we were soon dressed and blinking on the verandah. There we were each handed a weapon like the dreadful thing we had been shown the night before and some bullets which looked as if they were intended for use against tanks. We then set off behind the admiral, escorted and guided by the two Africans who had reported the 'cornering' of the lion. The volcanic mountain, Longenot, was a few miles away. We could just see it against the pale sky rising steep above the plain. As dawn broke and the colours of the night gave way to the heat and brightness of the day our little party strode across the bushland. An hour later we were struggling up the rough volcanic rocky side of the mountain. My head thumped and I wished I had given way to cowardice and dishonour. But we went on, up a small tree covered gully that ran down the side of the mountain. The top of Langenot is about ten thousand feet and we were climbing the last four thousand from the plain. At that altitude the inexperienced — particularly those suffering from a hangover — soon find themselves suffering from shortness of breath and exhaustion. So it was with Jock and me, but on we went up and up cursing our fate. After about an hour and when we were within a few hundred feet of the top we emerged from the trees into the bare side of the mountain and there waiting for us was a huge, nearly naked, African holding a spear and grinning happily. "Simba nakwenda, bwana" he said to the admiral. "The lion has gone, master." To have said that the lion was 'cornered' seemed to me an odd way of describing what, we felt, must have been the situation on this vast expanse of wild open country. We wondered whether, perhaps it had been a joke.

 The admiral swore and we began to retrace our steps. I was not sorry, as I had not liked the thought that I might be called upon to fire the huge rifle with which I had been provided. At last we reached the house again, hot, dusty and exhausted. But the admiral summoned us to breakfast and we were plied with eggs and bacon (four eggs each I recollect) and then, we thought, we could catch up on that sleep we had lost. Alas, no such luck. The admiral announced as we tucked into toast and marmalade (and other delicacies not seen in quantities in England for two years) that he had arranged for us to go to the 'Yacht club' for a day's sailing on the lake. There was a regatta he said. This mystified us because there was no sign of any yachts on the lake which stretched for several miles across the open plain with only here and there the trees that indicated another house along its fringe. However we were piled into the admiral's van and driven for two or three miles round the lake and eventually reached a grass hut beside a small wooden jetty to which were tied 4 or 5 twelve foot dinghies. This was the yacht club and its yachts. A few Europeans were by the boats chatting and apparently preparing to sail. The admiral asked if either of us had sailed before and I, remembering my Glasgow days, admitted to have done a little. "Good" said the admiral "you had better sail this boat for the first race. You must meet the crew". I was then introduced to a handsome and as I remember a rather saturnine man and his attractive wife. "Meet Prince Paul and Princess Olga of Yugoslavia" said the admiral. The prince and princess had fled from their country as Hitler and his armies overran it and had ended up here as refugees. And so it was that I spent a pleasant morning sailing a dingy with a royal princess (she was my crew) on a lake in the middle of Africa, slowly getting rid of an awful headache.

Not all days off duty were as eventful as that weekend, but we were very fortunate to be in so wonderful a country. The Indian Mountain Regiment with whose old guns we had been provided had been one of the last mounted units in the Indian Army. The officers had ridden on horses and the guns and stores were carried by mules. When the regiment was sent to join the Middle Eastern Desert Army it left its mounts behind and they were kept in our camp in the care of Somali syces. This was a bit of luck because we were allowed to ride them out on to the plain exploring the country round about. I learned a little about riding too.

But these happy and energetic days were not to last for long. It soon became clear that the powers that be had something in mind for the East African troops. Our battery was attached to a brigade of three battalions of infantry. One battalion from Nyasaland, one from Tanganyika and one from Uganda. Together with units of the other supporting services we were formed into a brigade group and we began intensive training together. Then we were moved to the coast at Mombasa and embarked again on troopships.

CHAPTER ELEVEN

Madagascar

Madagascar is a larger island than many people realise. From north to south it is over a thousand miles long and it is nearly 400 miles across at its widest point. Its area, therefore, is greater than that of England. Before the cutting of the Suez Canal its position gave it a strategic importance as it lay close to the route to India via the Cape of Good Hope. But with the opening of the Canal, its importance had waned and little was known about it by the average Englishman. The French had colonised it and it was said to have considerable mineral reserves in the mountains which form the backbone of the island. But when Italy entered the war the Germans were able to attack from the air our convoys going through the Mediterranean with the result that the passage to India and to the Middle East had once again to go round the Cape. Thus the strategic importance of Madagascar re-emerged. At its northern tip is a huge, nearly landlocked, harbour — Diego Suarez. If the Japanese were to capture that and base a fleet of submarines there they would hold a knife to our throat and our ability to supply the Middle East or India would be threatened. The Vichy French had a small force on the island and Churchill was very worried that it might be reinforced from Dakar where there were a considerable number of French troops and ships. There were fears that the Vichy French might allow the Japanese to occupy the island and use the harbour. To remove this threat an attack on the northern tip of the island was planned with the object of capturing the town of Diego Suarez and the port of Antsirane which lie on either side of the entrance to the great harbour. The attack was carried out by two British brigades and the 5th Commandos, all of which had been in a convoy bound for the Middle East and India, but were diverted, when they reached Durban, to carry out this operation. They landed at three points on bays on the East coast and marched across the 15 or so miles of the peninsula to Diego Suarez and Antsirane and captured both of those important points in just forty eight hours. A small but highly successful combined operation was carried out by a group of fifty Royal Marines from H.M.S. Ramillies who landed in the centre of the harbour and under cover of darkness created havoc in the port of Antsirane. Unbeknown to me then was a young major who led the small contingent, one squadron I believe, of tanks across the island. He was Jack Simon whom I had the great good fortune to get to know later at the Bar. His career in the law was brilliant and but for a tragic bit of bad luck I have no doubt that he would have been Lord Chancellor and would have been one of England's greatest. He was to have a profound influence on my life later — but we never met in Madagascar.

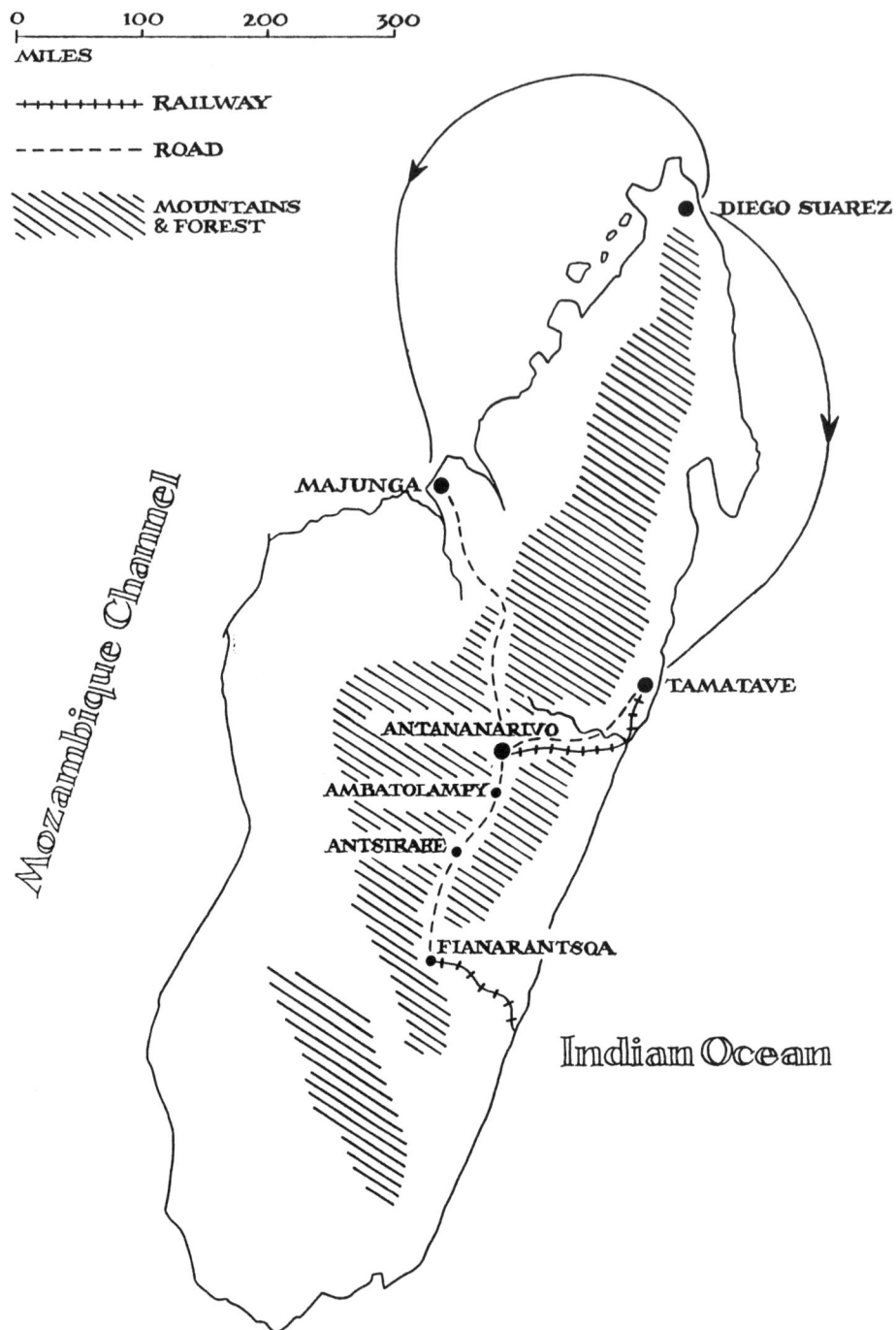

A sketch map of Madagascar.

The part allotted to the East African brigade in this minor skirmish of the war was itself a minor role and was to follow in the wake of the attacking forces and to be prepared to garrison the harbour area when the British troops re-embarked in their convoy and continued their interrupted journey to the Middle East and India. The French troops that had put up a mild resistance withdrew to the south of the island along the rough tracks through the mountainous and forest covered country that separates the northern part of the island from the capital Antananarivo. We embarked at Mombasa and after twenty four hours landed without any trouble and were soon deployed on the hills to the south of Antsirane. We were to stay here from May to September. Very shortly after our arrival I suffered a war injury. It was an inglorious incident. I was with a small body of askaris in scrub land when a sudden and quite unexpected explosion occurred in the bushes to our left. At first I thought it was a serious attack by some straggling group of French who had caught us quite unprepared. No one was hurt but I realised that I had gone deaf. A little blood came out of my left ear — which had been partially deaf since I had a mastoid operation when I was a little boy. There was a horrid singing noise in my head and when anyone spoke to me I could not make out what they said. When I spoke the noise in my head seemed to be worse. It turned out that a 75 mm French gun had been left behind by the retreating troops and as my little party passed it was fired at point blank range. Though the shell passed harmlessly over our heads and landed, doubtless in the bush several thousand yards away, we were directly under the blast from the barrel and this it was that damaged my ears. For two days I was totally deaf and I resigned myself to being thus afflicted for life. But God's mercy is infinite and after two days the hearing in my right ear returned, though I remained stone deaf on the left side. My right ear retained what the doctors called 'tinnitus'. This is a continuous singing in the ear on a very high note and has remained with me ever since. When eventually I was able to see an ear specialist he told me that it was nothing to worry about. It would never go but would not get worse, and either I would learn to live with it or I would go mad. I have never dared to ask my friends which of the two alternatives had materialised but I have persuaded myself that it was the former. This small mishap resulted in a change in my fortunes that resulted in me living to see the end of the war. Had it not occurred in all probability I would have gone down in the Indian Ocean off the Maldive Islands where a troopship, the Khedive Ishmail, was later sunk carrying 301 Regiment, E.A.A., to which my battery belonged. Of the total of about one thousand troops on board only 7 officers and a handful of men survived. As a result of the damage to my ear, however, the doctors said that I must no longer remain with the guns as there would be a real risk of becoming deaf in both ears from the sound of gunfire. So it was decreed that I should leave the Battery and join the staff. I became I.O.R.A., which, being interpreted, means Intelligence Officer, Royal Artillery. As more and more soldiers from the territories of East Africa were recruited and trained it was intended to form an East African division and I was allotted to the Headquarters staff of the divisional artillery. Ultimately the division had three regiments of field artillery and one regiment of anti tank artillery, but when I was first given my new job there was only the one regiment in Madagascar so the work of the Headquarters staff was not onerous. We spent the next few months on garrison duty and training. The country round Diego Suarez is not particularly attractive and the climate is horrid: very hot and sultry. The only consolation was the sea and bathing, but even that had to be carried out with care in places where there were shark barriers because there were a lot of sharks around. Indeed on one occasion an Askari swimming in the harbour was attacked and killed by a shark and I remember the horror of seeing the sea suddenly becoming red with blood. A few days after we arrived in Diego Suarez the Ramillies, one of the great Queen Elizabeth class battleships which had escorted the convoy bringing the attacking forces from Durban, was at anchor in the harbour when she was struck by torpedoes and crippled. Fortunately she did not sink, but she was put out of action for the time being. The attack was carried out by two Japanese officers in a miniature submarine. They carried out this daring and suicidal exploit and then, having jettisoned their submarine, managed to get ashore where they were promptly shot by a patrol that found them. But such excitements did not recur and our life soon sank into the dull routine of garrison troops. One strange incident I do however remember. A little way out into the country was a large lake said to contain a sacred crocodile. A friend and I decided one afternoon to visit it. On arriving we found some local natives and an old man who told us that for a small sum of money he would ask the maidens to dance on the strand and the crocodile would emerge. He placed a large bit of raw meat on the sandy edge of the water and three dusky young ladies danced a ritual dance near the meat. Slowly a huge and ugly crocodile came up out of the water, swallowed the meat and returned to his lair. I got the impression that the crocodile was more attracted by meat than by the beauties of the female form.

During the months that followed the taking of Diego Suarez it was hoped that the French rulers of Madagascar would abandon the Vichy Government and join the Free French. Had that happened it would not have been necessary to mount another small campaign to bring the rest of the island under the control of the allies. But the French Governor General remained adamant. So the second Madagascar operation had to take place. The plan was simple. On either side of the island, more or less half-way down the length of its coast line, is a port. On the east coast Tamatave and on the west Majunga. From each of these ports a road ran inland through the mountains to the capital Antananarivo, which was situated in the centre of the island at a height of about 6000 feet. A force was to land in the vicinity of each of these ports, capture the port and then march inland to Antananarivo subjecting the capital to a two-pronged attack. The East African Brigade with its supporting artillery was deputed to carry out the advance from Tamatave in the east and it was, therefore, to Tamatave that I was next sent. Tamatave was a pleasant spot, a small town bordering the sea with the facilities of a modest port having quays and cranes and warehouses sufficient for the needs of the inland population. A railway ran from Tamatave to Antananarivo and it was along the line of the railway that the troops advanced. The first fifty or so miles of the journey was along the coast south of Tamatave to the mouth of a great river, the Riva, which is crossed by a long bridge and after which the railway turns inland and drives into the mountains towards the capital city. The first troops to land set off hot foot towards the bridge to ensure that it was not destroyed by the French. Had the bridge been blown up the supply from the port of food and ammunition to the troops moving towards Antananarivo would have been very difficult. But happily the bridge was reached and secured undamaged and the advance continued against only slight resistance. During the first part of the advance I remained at Headquarters in a camp on the outskirts of Tamatave. Here we had little excitement except for one rather odd incident. The meteorological unit which was, I think, sent in by the R.A.F. introduced itself to us by issuing a warning, after we had been there only a day or two, that a cyclone was on its way across the Indian Ocean, and that its course suggested that it would hit the coast more or less exactly where we were. We were told that we must strike camp and move away from any trees or buildings. We therefore took down our tents and set off away from the houses and trees amongst which we had just settled down and moved into an open area where there seemed little risk of trees or building being thrown on to us. We lashed all the furled tents and other items of equipment like lorries and guns and pegged them to the ground. And then we waited for the cyclone to arrive. Three days passed but the weather remained bright and sunny and windless. Then we were told that we had been spared and so we put up our tents and resumed our former way of life. Within a very few days we received another warning and we went through the same procedure, and, yet again, nothing happened and yet again we eventually put up our tents once more. Shortly after this second warning I left to start the journey inland and was not to return to Tamatave for several weeks. When I did come back it was a strange sight of desolation that I saw, because shortly after I had left a third cyclone warning had come and this time the forecasters had been right. The cyclone had hit the town and had caused widespread destruction. Except for one or two modern reinforced concrete buildings at the harbour side almost every building in the place had been flattened and was a pile of wood and brick rubble. The tall palm trees that were a feature of the area had been stripped of their leaves and stood gaunt and naked like rows of bare poles. Almost every native hut had disappeared. Most extraordinary of all was the sight of a Royal Navy sloop that had been torn from its moorings and lifted bodily by the mountainous seas on to the quayside where it had come to rest high and dry out of the sea.

Our headquarters followed the advancing troops up the railway line which ascends along the valley of the river. It was a route of remarkable beauty. First across the coastal plain and then into the tropical forest that covered most of the mountains as the route approached Antananarivo. Every now and then a clearing by a village would appear and an area of cultivation, paddy fields and here and there other vegetables, would come into view. The local population gathered to meet these strange intruders and offered us jungle cocks and vegetables which were welcome and provided a pleasant change from our tinned rations of bully beef and M & V. There was little fighting and so it was a civilised advance and in the rear with Headquarters we could not be accused of doing anything gallant. When the leading troops reached Antananarivo the French forces withdrew down the road which runs south from the town and along the spine of the island, through Ambatolampy, one of the highest towns on the island, and on to Fianarantsoa where they eventually capitulated. Our Headquarters spent some time camped on the edge of Antananarivo. I have many recollections of that brief stay as that part of the island is truly one of the world's most idyllic places, peopled by a delightful race of happy and attractive folk. My first sight of the capital city whetted my appetite for what was to come. When the town had been taken the railway was quickly working and we travelled the last part of the journey on a train. We arrived at the approaches early one morning as the sun came up. The train stopped shortly after it emerged from a valley running through the hills. I remember looking out of the window and seeing a picture I have never forgotten. The sun shone crystalline bright in the chilly atmosphere. About a mile away on the far side of an emerald green expanse of paddy field the hills on which the city is built rose up. Its buildings stood out on the ridges and down the slopes towards us. Domes and towers of churches, pinnacles and turrets of large public buildings shone in the bright morning sun. The roofs were made of delicious warm red coloured tiles and many of the walls were smothered in bougainvillaea, then in full flower in blue and purple. At the bottom of one of the slopes the surface of a large lake reflected the colours, and the elegant lines of a tall column at one end of it. It was a truly breathtaking view.

One characteristic of the town that came as a pleasant surprise to me after my time in East Africa was the style in which the French had built. Whereas the majority of buildings put up by the British in Kenya were roofed with corrugated iron and were at best dull architecturally, the French had used local bricks and tiles, which, as I have said, were of a pleasant colour, and had built in the European way. The buildings were traditional in design and well proportioned so that the town seemed like an eighteenth or nineteenth century French provincial town transplanted to this island near the tropics. It compared, in my eyes, very favourably with the shanty town appearance of all that I had seen, even in the capital, in Kenya.

The people, too, surprised me. As Madagascar lay off the coast of East Africa I had imagined the native population to be similar to those I had seen there – negroid and curly haired. But the Malagasy are quite different, much more like the peoples of the East Indies. The girls had straight black hair which they wore long and collected together at the back of the head in the manner of Malaysians. They are a paler coloured race than the people of East Africa and have the grace and cheerfulness of nature characteristic of Polynesians. I have been told that the reason for this is that there was an emigration from the East Indies many centuries ago and having crossed the Indian Ocean the emigrants came to rest in Madagascar. It is a strange bit of history of which I should like to know more. These people mixed with the French and there was much intermarriage.

When we first arrived in Antananarivo the French in the town were frigid, indeed hostile, to the British troops. Fraternisation was not a possibility and the atmosphere was far from friendly. This was not altogether surprising as after the fall of France in 1940 there had been very little contact between the French in Madagascar and the outside world. Few or no imports arrived and no visitors to bring news of metropolitan France. I think that they had some difficulty in deciding on which side their bread was buttered. This state of affairs worried General Platt who had commanded our troops and who at the start was responsible for relations with the French. He determined to try and bridge the gap and get on to good terms with them. As a step in this policy he determined to give a ball to which the leading French families would be invited. All officers stationed in the town were asked to come and given strict instructions to be on their best behaviour. They were to be ambassadors for England. In due course we all assembled in the Town Hall and there were large numbers of French, many ladies with lovely daughters in their best evening dresses. But though most of them looked beautiful their faces wore sullen expressions. The General started the dancing by leading off with the wife of the Governor General. Slowly other pairs joined them on the dance floor and the orchestra struggled to liven things up – but to no avail. The French, like Queen Victoria, were not to be amused. I danced with a pretty girl who would only reply "oui" or "non" to my faltering French and no sign of a smile lit her face. The evening progressed in this lack lustre way for an hour or two and then the Governor General and General Platt's party left and the younger officers remained to carry on the entertainment. Only then did we realise that our guests had been under orders, because no sooner had the nobs departed than the ice melted and the gloom dispersed. It was not long before the young men and maidens were enjoying themselves as they always will in such circumstances and when the dance ended we felt our diplomatic mission had been achieved. From then onwards the French talked to us and treated us as friendly visitors.

Our stay in Antananarivo was short and we soon moved further south to Ambatolampy where I remained for the rest of my stay on the island. It was a delightful period, though brief. The French colonists of Madagascar have made many attractive townships in the island but none more pleasing than Ambatolampy. At nearly the highest point in the island, with, on all sides, views of blue hills and forests interspersed by fresh green valleys, and enjoying a mild and gentle climate it is situated in as pleasant a setting as it is possible to imagine. The small town, in this truly blessed spot, was built round a tree lined square containing as its main buildings, in proper French style, a Catholic church and a cafe restaurant. It was at the latter, two or three evenings a week, that we learned how the French lived. There would foregather the doctor, the curé and the District Commissioner (I have forgotten the latter's proper title, but he corresponded to the District Commissioner in charge of an area of one of our colonies). Other local worthies would occasionally join this nucleus. It was the District Commissioner who welcomed us into this friendly group as we had, perforce, to meet him to deal with the problems that inevitably arise when foreign troops come to live in an area. He was a delightful and amusing man with a great deal of quiet, rather cynical, wisdom. He told us that the difference between the British and the French way of treating the natives in their colonies was simple. The British treated them fairly and with consideration during the day and ignored them after dark and were hated. The French, on the other hand, treated them like dirt and often thrashed them during the day and slept with them after dark and were loved. He realised that to make friends in the evenings with these new intruders was the simplest way of ensuring that there was a minimum of friction between the African troops we commanded and the indigenous population for whose welfare he was responsible. His great interest in life was the management of a trout farm which he had established a few miles out of the town. He stocked local streams with the fish he bred and then he and his many French friends would angle for them on Sundays using as bait the small frogs which abounded in the marshy land of the valleys. When transfixed by a large hook these unfortunate animals wriggled furiously and were, evidently, a deadly lure. The more refined Anglo Saxon habit of fly fishing struck him as very odd.

Our evenings were full of merriment and I have no doubt did much to bring about Anglo-French accord in that small bit of the remote island. The curé and the doctor were good company too, and the English contingent was enlivened by the arrival at this time of a number of officers from England to staff our growing divisional headquarters. Of the new arrivals one in particular sticks in my memory. John Anderson was a regular gunner officer who was appointed to be B.M.R.A. (Brigade Major, Royal Artillery) to the division. As was so often the case with regular artillery officers he was a man of wide culture, well read, interested in the arts and a very amusing conversationalist. Our French friends at the cafe delighted in his company. He was, too, a most efficient soldier and administrator and did a great deal to teach the non regular amateur soldiers, such as myself, the way the army worked. When ultimately we got to Burma he was promoted to colonel and commanded one of the field regiments with distinction and skill throughout our campaign. Tragically he died quite shortly after the end of the war without reaching the higher echelons of the army for which he was so well suited. But he added greatly to the enjoyment of Ambatolampy. He it was, I suspect, who arranged that I should go up to the Middle East at this time to attend the Junior Staff College there and learn the trade of army administration properly. And so, sadly, the happy days at Ambatolampy were brought to an end.

CHAPTER TWELVE

Palestine and Ceylon

In the years before the war when the views of many people of my generation were moving more and more to the left it became common to disparage regular army officers. It was thought that they were for the most part those who could not have passed any exam necessary for a respectable profession, that they were stupid, old fashioned and out of touch with reality. The cartoonist's picture of Colonel Blimp was not thought to be seriously overdrawn. This attitude was, I think, partly caused by the feeling, that was widespread, that during the First World War the generals had been an incompetent and uninspired lot and that the appalling casualties had been a direct result. I had certainly absorbed my share of this intellectual arrogance but I was to be sharply disabused of it during the next stage of my army career. It was during my time at the Junior Staff College in the Middle East, that I learned how wrong my views had been. The commandant and instructors at this school were, without exception, men of outstanding ability and personality. They did a marvellous job.

The college was modelled on the Staff College at Camberley where regular officers in peace time were put through a rigorous course lasting, I believe, two years during which they learned how the army was organised, how it was supplied and moved about. They took part in manoeuvres and exercises designed to enable them to solve the many problems that can arise in administering an army in different kinds of warfare and in different parts of the world. War time courses were shorter and more intensely concentrated. For about two months we worked extremely hard, and I certainly learned a great deal that was to prove of value not only in the army but in later life. It was an enjoyable period too. As well as lectures from senior men concerned with all kinds of different aspects of the war effort we were made to take part in many and various exercises. Much of this work was done in the open moving about the different parts of Palestine, from the desert of Gaza in the south to Nazareth perched on its hill to the north. The college itself was at Sarafand on the plain, between the hills and the sea at Jaffa and Tel Aviv. It was in the centre of a considerable area of orange groves which had been created by the immigrant Jews out of the arid desert. Mile upon mile of little concrete channels divided the space into small squares each of which could, by blocking the appropriate channels and causing the water to spill over into the sandy ground, be supplied with water. In each small square were four or ten orange trees. In this simple way was the desert made to bloom. Not a drop of water was wasted. To see at first hand the energy of the Jews who had come to make their lives here was for me an eye opening experience.

Several of the young officers who were with me on this course were interesting companions. One, Robin Thorn, with whom I became friendly, had shortly before the outbreak of war entered the Colonial Service and was a keen walker. He knew his Bible history well and, wherever we went in the course of our military exercises, he always had a copy of the Old Testament in his pocket. On one occasion we walked up to the Musmus Pass which leads over the ridge that lies between Mount Carmel on the coast behind Haifa, and the range of hills which form the backbone running down the centre of the country. When we reached the top of the pass we sat down on a rock and looked to the north across the dry brown plain. It was a clear hot day and the plain of Esdraelon where much Old Testament history was enacted lay below us. Robin took out his bible and read me bits that were familiar — but which had, never before, had any real meaning for me. Suddenly I could picture the events and imagine the tribes of the Israelites with their flocks in the dusty arid land and could see in my mind's eye the camels and the shepherds and the tents of the armies. As we looked across to the hazy distance I realised how little that part of the country had changed since those days. The stories of the Bible became real in a way they had never done before and I shall always be grateful to Robin for enlightening me in this way. I lost touch with him after the war and was sad to learn, many years later, that when serving in Aden, he was the target of a terrorist attack and suffered nasty injuries in a bomb explosion.

Another interesting character who crossed my path during my stay in Palestine was Bernard Fergusson. He was later to become Lord Fergusson and Governor General of Australia. At the time I met him he had recently returned from Burma where he had been one of the column commanders under Brigadier Orde Wingate in his first expedition behind the Japanese lines. He gave us a talk on jungle warfare and his experiences in the forests of North Burma. He was later to write a book, 'The Wild Green Earth' in which he managed to capture the fascination of life in the jungle clad Chin hills. He was a good writer, indeed he was something of a poet, and had been ADC to Field Marshal Wavell (himself no mean poet) of whom he was a great admirer. I was one of the few on the course who was expecting to have to take part in the fighting in Burma rather than that in North Africa, so his talk was of particular interest to me. He had the gift, bestowed on but few, of being both an actor and an original thinker. His skill as an actor ensured that his thoughts were presented in the most attractive guise possible, with the result that, at any rate as far as I was concerned, they were absorbed with enthusiasm. I remember that he brought his lecture to an end with an amusing little trick. He was wearing battle dress, the standard khaki uniform of those days, which had a substantial breast pocket on each side of the jacket. Throughout his lecture he had in his right eye a monocle from which hung a trim black cord. When his talk was finished he raised his eyebrow and the monocle fell from his eye directly into the breast pocket. This little exhibition of the skill of the conjuror ensured that he was given an enthusiastic ovation.

Half-way through the course we had a short break which Robin Thorn and I with a few others spent on a tour round the more historic parts of the Holy Land. In Jerusalem we stayed with the Church of England chaplain, who had been a friend of John Wolfenden, in a hostel in one of the old buildings close under the city walls. He organised the tour and proved to be an entertaining and informative guide whose knowledge of biblical history was immense. With him we travelled north to Nazareth and beyond, and south to Bethlehem. The weather was fair and the flowers of the desert came out after a short spell of spring rain. We visited monasteries in the hills and many sites of biblical and later history, including a crusader castle and the old Arab town of Jaffa where we spent two days bathing and surf riding, a sport I greatly enjoyed. It was, however, all too short a rest and we were soon back at the college moving imaginary divisions and brigades about the country. When the course was over I was told that instead of rejoining the East African Division in Madagascar, where I had left it, I was to go to Ceylon and so, in due course I flew to Colombo. There I was to wait until the units of the Division arrived and I could join them. Part of the flight to Colombo was in a flying boat, a form of air travel that is now extinct but which I found most enjoyable. We landed on the Nile at Luxor and Khartoum and spent a night at each place. At Luxor there was sufficient time to explore some of the ruins of the ancient Egyptian kings. At Khartoum I spent an evening on the verandah of an hotel reading John Buchan's Essay on Gordon at Khartoum and imagining the final scenes enacted within a short distance of where I sat. Across the river as the sun went down I could see the desert, a reddish brown, where was fought the Battle of Omdurman, by which the death of Gordon was avenged.

When I arrived in Ceylon I found that the 11 (East African) Division was being concentrated there so that it could have a period of training for jungle warfare in the forest country to the north of the island before being sent on to Burma as part of the army that was destined to drive the Japanese from the borders of India out of Burma and South East Asia. The Divisional Headquarters was situated in the palm groves on the coast about 30 miles to the south east of Colombo at Bentota. Bentota at that time consisted of a few small shops, a Buddhist temple and a railway station. The railway ran along the coast from Colombo to the old Portuguese town and fortress at Galle. At Bentota the line was a few hundred yards from the sea. Our headquarters was housed in tents under the palm trees. It was a most pleasant camp site. The beach at this point is of the purest white sand and was for miles unspoiled by any serious impact of human beings. Here and there one could see a group of outrigger canoes where local fishermen had drawn their craft up out of the sea and occasionally a small house thatched with banana leaves, but otherwise there was no sign of any living thing except the sea birds, and, as I shall relate, the occasional turtle.

I revisited Sri Lanka, as the country is now called, in 1981, nearly forty years later and went again to Bentota. Now the lovely beaches are flanked by modern hotels and beneath multi-coloured umbrellas sun seeking westerners lounge and enjoy themselves by concrete swimming pools or in the breakers of the Indian Ocean. Fortunately the architects have not been allowed to build the hideous concrete slabs that have caused such horrid disfigurement to the Mediterranean and other coastlines in recent years. The buildings are restrained single storey construction and not unattractive.

The short time that I spent by the Indian Ocean at Bentota was a period disproportionately important in my life. We were assembling at the headquarters of a newly trained division and new faces appeared each day to take up posts in the organisation. So it was that in this very short period I came to meet for the first time many men who were to become lifelong friends, and others with whom I would have dearly liked to keep contact but from whom fate was to decree that I should be separated.

Dudley Murray Evans had just qualified as an architect when the war began and he found himself posted to Bentota as the intelligence officer for one of the other regiments of artillery that joined us. He was one of those rare beings who never allowed the crudities of service conditions or the petty jealousies of a confined army life to deflect him from his guiding star which was an ardent appreciation of the classical forms of beauty whether they were displayed in architecture or painting, music or even women. He had recently married a charming Russian girl — though I was not to meet her until some years later. Olga had been smuggled out of Russia by her father at the time of the revolution in 1917. She grew up in England but never lost a strange aura of the country of her origin. Her natural sweetness was made the more attractive by her voice which was trained for the singing of opera and was of a delicious quality such as I have never come across elsewhere. After the war Dudley returned to his practice as an architect and was kind enough to help me to restore three houses that I have at different times lived in: 52 East St Helen Street in Abingdon, was perhaps his best bit of work. Out of four derelict cottages he made two elegant houses that added distinction to one of the best old streets in England. The hall and staircase he created at 52 was a work of much beauty.

Alec Barnard was very different. He had all the qualities I associate with Friar Tuck. A large and comfortably covered body was surmounted by a small round and pink face. He was a bachelor and seemed always to be chuckling at the absurdity of some aspect of the military life that then confronted him. A most unmilitary soldier he was a highly efficient adjutant to one of the field regiments and later the same qualities enabled him to become Staff Captain. In peace time he was a solicitor at Luton and he lived with his mother in a lovely house near Dunstable. He was later to become godfather to my eldest daughter, Drusilla, and remained a good friend.

Martin Suter was a saintly man, destined for the Church, who came to be the Staff Officer responsible for intelligence in the division. He too was a most unmilitary figure and yet, as so often happened with civilians brought into the army for the duration of the war, he became a master of his particular aspect of military knowledge. He was, as we proceeded to Burma, to become the great expert on the Japanese army. He gradually acquired a complete mastery of the Japanese order of battle, both on our immediate front and in other remote parts of the Far East. Towards the end of our campaign he left us to go to Corps Headquarters and I was promoted to take over his job. I remember well my last interview with him before he left. He told me that he thought the war was nearly over and that the normal intelligence work would become of less importance while the aspect of the 'I' Staff's duties that was concerned with internal security in the Division would become more significant. He was worried about the emergence of small tribal secret societies in the various units of the division. He advised me to keep a close watch on that side of my work. I will tell later how wise he was. After the war he went into the Church as he had intended and for a time had a parish in a poor part of Acton. Later he moved, I believe to the Channel Islands and, alas, I lost touch with him. I suspect that he has continued quietly to work for others, the while presenting to the world a shining example of a true Christian at work.

Of John Anderson I have already spoken. He had joined us in Madagascar. He was a chubby man with a rather rubicund complexion and a disarming smile. He was a lively talker and enjoyed a leisurely dinner which would allow him to make the most of the conversation. When shortly after he arrived in Ceylon the Divisional Artillery was sent off to the East Coast for shooting practice we were camped for some time at Hambantota in the centre of an area of undulating scrub land bordering the sea. In the evenings we enjoyed driving into the wild country inland and going to a rest house by the side of a tank, (or reservoir) built by one of the early kings of Ceylon. It was surrounded by scrub and jungle but an area of grass separated the trees from the water. Here we sat on the verandah of the rest house and as the sun went down watched the game, mostly deer, come out of the trees to drink. I always wished I had a camera; I would not have believed how many animals came out from the cover of the woods to drink if I had not actually seen it happen. When darkness fell we dined on curry and drank bad wine or South African whisky, which was equally awful. The rest house was in the care of a delightful Sinhalese who cooked wonderful sloshy curries. They were so good that one hardly noticed how bad the wine was. Our stay at Hambantota was, alas, all too short and the whole division was then put through a period of intensive training intended to be its final preparation for active service in Burma.

These were some of the men who had joined us and who later became good friends. But I would have accumulated many more friends from those days had it not been for one tragic and ghastly disaster. My old regiment which I had left in Madagascar in order to go to the Staff College was embarked on an old Egyptian ship, the Khedive Ishmail, to bring it to Ceylon to join the rest of the division that was gradually concentrating there. It had an uneventful journey across the Indian Ocean until it reached the vicinity of the Maldive Islands during the afternoon of the day before it was due to dock in Colombo. It was a clear and perfect sunny day and normally the troops and officers would have been taking advantage of the weather on the open decks, but orders had been given that they should get their kit packed up and ready to disembark the next morning, so nearly all the 1000 men on board were below decks in their various quarters. At that moment and completely without warning the Khedive Ishmail was hit amidships by a torpedo fired from a Japanese submarine that no one had spotted. She was an old ship and more or less broke in half. She sank in a matter of minutes. In a very short time all that was visible where she had been was a patch of oil and a few bits of wreckage floating on the water and a ships lifeboat that had somehow managed to be released. There were less than 100 survivors from the thousand souls that the ship had been carrying: of these seven were officers. The whole of 301 Field Regiment had been wiped out at a single stroke. I was at Bentota when I heard the news next morning. I hurried immediately to the hospital just outside Colombo to visit the survivors. Three who had been saved were the commanding officer Lt Col Stevens, the adjutant Michael Blackwood and the regimental quartermaster, an old regular soldier from Yorkshire. Luckily they had been on the top deck where there was a small orderly room and so had not, as had almost everyone else, been trapped below decks. I remember the old quartermaster telling me in his robust north country accent of his experience. He had just come on to the top deck dressed only in his shorts intending to do a little sunbathing when suddenly the explosion occurred. The ship began to sink and he found himself being dragged down under the water. His shorts had somehow got caught on a bit of rigging and he felt himself being pulled down deeper and deeper. The water changed colour from green, becoming gradually darker, and he felt as if his lungs would burst. He realised his only hope was to free himself of his shorts and so he struggled out of them, and then he began to rise and the water again changed from darkness to green and light. Then he bumped his head hard on something and reached the surface spluttering — and naked. He had hit his head on the keel of the only lifeboat that had survived and so he struggled into that. The colonel was already in it. Apart from the other troopships that had been travelling with the Khedive, there was nothing to be seen except a few heads bobbing in the water and a British destroyer which was coming from a mile or so away to the scene and was soon dropping depth charges. The submarine moved to place itself under the survivors, but was eventually forced to the surface and duly sunk by the destroyer. The surviving troops were taken on to the destroyer and delivered safely in Colombo a few hours later.

The suddenness and the completeness of this loss affected me profoundly. So many good men I had known were snuffed out in a matter of minutes. Many of the officers were friends with whom I had served in East Africa and Madagascar. Many of the African gunners were simple men to whom I had become greatly attached. The full horror of it was brought home to me with ghastly vividness a week or two later when I received a letter from my best friend in the regiment, Henry Head, who had formerly been its adjutant. He had posted the letter before the ship sailed and it arrived after he had died. In his letter he spoke so cheerfully of his delight at being given the command of a battery, and how much he preferred dealing with the troops to his former largely administrative work as adjutant. He looked forward to our meeting again soon. Henry's loss was a grievous blow to me. Like me he had decided on the Bar as a career and we had much in common. Had he lived he would surely have achieved great things. He had been a King's Scholar at Eton, but was notwithstanding a modest and vivacious person. His father had been a County Court judge in Norfolk and Henry had been imbued with the traditions of the Law from his childhood. When in Kenya he had met and fallen in love with a beautiful girl, the daughter of a farmer in the Highlands. Many years after these sad events I met her when I was asked to dine with a judge at Norwich before whom I had been appearing in a case. She was there as the wife of the present judge in that part of Norfolk who was, in fact, Henry's brother Adrian. Adrian had polio as a small boy and had not been able to fight. After the war Adrian married Henry's loved one and he and his wife were then living in the same house that Henry's and Adrian's parents had formerly lived in.

The loss of one field regiment from the three allotted to the division was, of course, a severe blow, but it was not allowed to interfere with the divisional training which continued vigorously. Before being dispatched to the Burma front we took part in divisional exercises in the northern part of the island. Ceylon is an island roughly the shape of a pear and if one imagines a pear slit down the line of its core and then one half of it laid flat with the cut side downwards one gets a very good idea of the geography of the island. Colombo and the large centres of population are in the south, at the bottom of the bulbous part of the pear. Inland from the south the land rises through a series of ranges of hills to Adam's Peak the highest point in the island. In the highlands are the tea plantations and the centres of what in the past were the main English settlements. Kandy, the ancient capital, a fine city, is about half way up in the hills. North of the hilly part of the island, in the long thin part of the pear, above the bulbous bottom, the island is more or less flat and largely covered with dense scrub and jungle. It was in this part of the island that we were sent to do our final training because it was thought to bear some resemblance to the jungle covered hills of Burma. It was a tough training, in some ways tougher than the actual time in Burma. But my memory of this period is limited. I have a vivid recollection of marching 36 miles in one day up a jungle track in sweltering and damp heat. The forest through which we passed was interspersed with small areas of paddy fields where a few villagers had cultivated the flat ground and where water buffalo wallowed. But apart from that trees and scrub covered everything. The only relief was provided by a strange natural spectacle. Every now and then during this gruelling day we came upon a place where there had been a hatch of butterflies. As we marched along, the air around was full of thousands upon thousands of bright yellow and dainty little butterflies. The forest was hot and humid. Occasionally we heard the cry of a jungle cock. Hills rose up out of the surrounding forest at intervals and it was always necessary for the gunners to get to the top of them in order to find the best observation posts from which to be able to bring down fire from the artillery on any target. I was, therefore, continually climbing up and slipping down rough rocky paths on my way up and down these hills as I visited the officers controlling the shooting. It was as hot and exhausting exercise as I have ever indulged in. When I revisited the island again in 1981 and was driving across the island from Trincomalee to Colombo, I passed some of the sites that we had occupied during these exercises. It was an odd feeling to see the same hills, with their recognisable shapes and features, forty years later. They are still wild and remote.

After that final exercise we returned once more to the south of the island and I remained there for a few days more before I was sent on with a small advance party to Burma, but during that short time I had one unusual experience. I had a small tent pitched under some palm trees just above the beach at Bentota. It was a lovely setting. When I lay on my camp bed to sleep I looked out of the tent across the sand to the Indian Ocean. The gentle lapping of the waves was the only sound and when the moon came up I could see, framed by gracefully arched palm trees, the curve of the shore against the luminous sky. The most peaceful and idyllic scene and, as it seemed, no living thing in sight. One night having gone to sleep I was suddenly woken by a snuffling noise and when I opened my eyes it seemed as if there was something in the tent. My view was almost completely obscured by a huge dark form in the opening of the tent. When I had overcome my fright and put on my spectacles I realised that some very large creature was busy making a hole in the sand. I got out of bed and investigated, and discovered that my visitor was a turtle that had come up out of the sea to lay its eggs. Its head was towards the sea and with its two rear flippers it had made a considerable hole in the sand into which it had evidently laid its eggs. I watched it fill up the hole and then after about five or ten minutes it flopped its way back down the beach and into the sea where it suddenly became streamlined and swam away. My assessment was that it was about 8 feet from nose to tail and about 3 to 4 feet wide. It was certainly considerably larger than I had ever imagined a turtle could be.

A few days later I set off to Chittagong, a small port at the top of the Bay of Bengal, through which the part of the Army that formed the southern flank of the Burma Army was supplied.

CHAPTER THIRTEEN

Introduction to Burma

By our standards in England Burma is a large country, though it seems small when compared with its neighbours – India to the west and China to the East. It measures about 700 miles from north to south and 400 miles from east to west. When one studies a topographical map one realises that its natural formation is like a horse shoe with the open end pointing to the south. All round its fringe are mountains, in the north the vast Himalayas, to the east the Shan Hills which separate it from China and Siam and to the west the Chin Hills which run along the boundary with India. Enclosed by this horse shoe of mountains is a vast plain through which flow three great rivers, the Chindwin, the Irrawaddy and the Salween. The two former meet below Mandalay and reach the sea, after spreading into a huge delta, west of Rangoon. The Salween to the east of the plain finally reaches the Bay of Bengal, south of Rangoon at Moulmein. In peace time and under British rule Rangoon was the centre of Government and thither one went, usually by sea, when entering the country from the outside world. Once inside Burma the lines of communication ran more or less north and south following the rivers or the railway, which itself ran parallel to the Irrawaddy from Rangoon to Mandalay and on to Myitkyina. The great majority of British commerce and activity was centred round Rangoon, though forestry and oil drew a number of people into the more remote parts of the country. From Mandalay, a beautiful and ancient town situated on a bend of the Irrawaddy more or less in the centre of the country, a road ran north east across the mountains into China. Otherwise communications across the surrounding horse shoe of mountains were virtually non-existent. A few rough tracks ran from village to village but nearly all of them became impassable when the monsoon rains turned them into muddy channels.

On 7 December, 1941, the Japanese had carried out the sudden and devastating attack on Pearl Harbour in the Pacific and, in the few months that followed their armies swept round South East Asia, taking Java and Sumatra, Malaysia and Singapore. By March 1942 they were entering Burma from the south. Rangoon fell in the second week of March. This meant that the only escape for the British Army and the civilians was northwards up the river valleys and then westwards across the mountains into India. It was a journey of some 600 miles much of which was through jungle. The small British Army and many civilians who had administered the Government struck northwest from Mandalay and aimed for Kalewa on the Chindwin and thereafter struggled on to Imphal. Transport gradually became more and more scarce; petrol ran out, vehicles broke down and supplies could not be brought in. Eventually all transport, tanks and aeroplanes had gone and the straggling remnants completed the journey through the final mountainous area on foot. By 17 May the survivors under General Alexander reached Imphal where the army concentrated and again turned to face the enemy. Fortunately almost immediately the rains came and the monsoon ensured that the mountain tracks over which the British had recently retreated so painfully became nearly impassable so that, in their turn, the Japanese were held up and could advance no further.

When the retreat from Burma to India was completed the two sides settled down to face each other, neither having the capacity to advance decisively into the territory held by the other. Our forces were too weak and the prior needs of the war against Germany meant that they could not be substantially reinforced with the men or materials that would be needed if a successful counter attack was to retake Burma. Likewise the Japanese were at the end of extended lines of communication from their homeland and were forced to supply their troops across an immense tract of Asia. To have advanced into India would have involved them in fighting at the end of even longer lines of communication. So, for the time being, serious fighting subsided while the contestants licked their wounds and began to rebuild their strength. But soon the main points of contact between the rival armies became clear. There were three areas where the Allies were in contact with the Japanese. In the extreme north of the country General Stilwell commanded a force of American and Chinese troops who hoped in time to re-enter Burma and build behind them as they advanced a road from the railhead at Ledo. This road, it was hoped, would eventually join up with the existing road that ran from Mandalay across the Shan hills into China. As soon as this was effected China could once again be supplied by land from Western sources. At the other and southern end of the border with India there was a second point of contact near the western coastline of Burma. A British force kept contact with the enemy in the Arakan hills that run in a southerly direction between the Irrawaddy and the coast. There British troops were supplied from the port of Chittagong at the north end of the Bay of Bengal.

Between these two points of contact there was the third area where the two sides were pressing against each other. This was around Imphal. It was to this area that the East African Division to which I belonged was to be sent and in which I was to spend the last part of the war.

Imphal was the capital of Manipur state, a small and unimportant Indian native state which stretched for the most part over a wide area of thinly inhabited mountainous territory. The mountains were inhospitable and very little in the way of food could be obtained from them. The only part of the state which was agriculturally productive was the country immediately surrounding Imphal itself. The little town was in the centre of a plain some twenty miles long and rather less across through which ran the Manipur river. This flat area lay like a saucer surrounded on all sides by the mountains which stretched in a succession of blue ridges as far as the eye could see in whichever direction one looked. The whole plain was excellent rice growing land. By withdrawing on to it and then defending it General Alexander shewed great wisdom, because by denying the fertile plain to the Japanese he ensured that their armies operating in this sector of Burma were in country that could not support them with food. Had the Japanese been allowed to

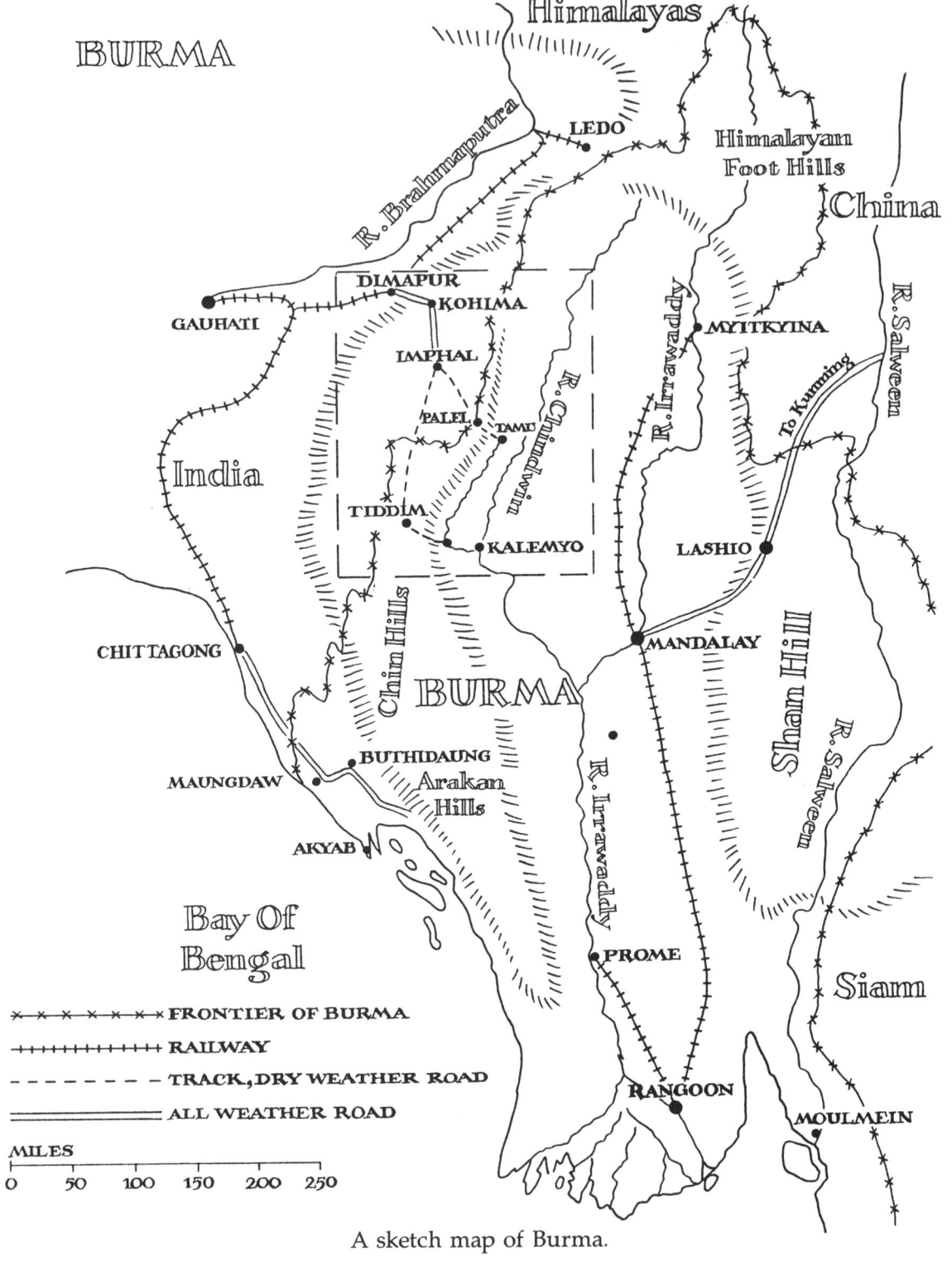

A sketch map of Burma.

advance and take Imphal they would have been provided with a source of rice sufficient to supply a large rice eating army and the task of invading India would have been made immeasurably easier.

Such was the position when the British retreat ended. Throughout the monsoon that followed and the period of dry weather in 1943 the Burma front remained quiescent. The only offensive operation was Wingate's first expedition with its long range columns operating many miles behind the enemy lines and well into the heart of the country. But this commando-like raid, though of immense value as a booster of morale and as showing that it was not the Japanese alone that could fight and survive in the jungle, was of no great strategic significance. Then the rains came again and both sides having rested and regained their strength planned to attack when the weather improved. The initial effort by the Allies was designed to re-open a land route to China and to this end Stilwell advanced towards Myitkyina in the north while Wingate, this time with a much larger force, was flown into the centre of the country. From there his columns fanned out, bent on creating as much havoc as possible to the Japanese road and rail communications running up the northern plain which supplied their forces facing Stilwell.

Shortly after these operations had begun the Japanese began to advance on both the other fronts. First in the Arakan a long outflanking march through the jungle was carried out by a whole Jap division with a view to cutting the supply route along the road from Chittagong to the two British divisions that held the front line. The Japanese hoped to take the port of Chittagong and thereafter to be able to move into India. Further north, on the Imphal front, they carried out a somewhat similar operation. Once again a wide outflanking movement through the jungle-clad hills enabled them to cut the road that was the route of supplies for our troops in Imphal. This road ran from the railway at Dimapur through the mountainous hills near Kohima and on to Imphal. Initially it must have seemed to the Japanese that both of these operations had been successful. In each case they were able to bypass our forward units and establish themselves across the road by which all those units were supplied. All experience from the past shewed that when one succeeded in cutting the forward troops off from their source of supply they were forced to retreat, particularly when, as was the case in these two fronts in Burma, there was no hope of the isolated troops living off the land. But the Japanese failed to take account of one recent development which had transformed this situation. The British had learned how to supply their troops from the air, dropping the necessary food and supplies by parachute from cargo carrying planes into areas in the jungle that had been cleared of trees and were protected by our troops. When once this method of supplying our troops had been perfected the critical importance of holding the road by which supplies normally came evaporated. So when the Japanese surrounded the forward British division in the Arakan and managed to cut the road from Chittagong along which the food lorries had hitherto rumbled they found that, instead of starving our forward troops and forcing them to withdraw, they had merely created a sharp thorn in their own flesh. Their own forward troops now sitting across the road from Chittagong had to be supplied by porters and mules moving along many miles of jungle paths which were liable to be attacked by fighting groups sent out from the surrounded British division.

In the same way at Imphal when the Japanese bypassed the Imphal plain and cut the road from Kohima so that supplies could no longer reach the garrison that way, all that happened was that the British divisions in the Imphal Plain were kept fed and supplied by flight after flight of Dakotas flying in from near Calcutta. Eventually the Japanese themselves had to withdraw on the Arakan front and the road from Chittagong was once again opened, and likewise the road from Kohima to Imphal was eventually cleared, though not without fierce fighting on the part of our troops driving southwards from Kohima and northwards from Imphal.

Such in short was the history of events on the Burma front that took place before I arrived there a few weeks ahead of the 11th East African Division. I was sent first to Chittagong and thence down to the Arakan front where I was attached to a unit of the 81st West African Division. It was intended that I should get some experience of conditions in this front and also learn something of the methods adopted by our troops fighting there for obtaining intelligence and information about the enemy troops facing us. During the two weeks or so that I spent with the West Africans it poured with rain continuously and my recollections of the period are of the cheerful African soldiers and their stoic disregard of the discomforts this involved. I spent most of that short period with a battalion that was in close contact with the enemy on the Maungdaw-Buthidaung track, but though patrols went out into the surrounding scrub covered hills and there were occasional reports of skirmishes with Jap troops I saw little of excitement. The unending rain limited what could be done by either side and much of my time was spent in the confines of a muddy dug out. When not trying to keep dry I and the other officers played poker dice, a game ideally suited to whiling away the hours in jungle warfare because it could be played by the light of a single hurricane lamp and did not need cards which quickly became soggy and useless.

From my short stay on the Arakan front I was transferred to Imphal where, until the East Africans arrived I was attached to the 23rd Indian Division. The journey from the Arakan was an experience I will not forget. First I had to get back to Chittagong which involved a journey in the back of an army truck along the road of which I have already spoken by which the front was supplied. This road was unusual in that in order to make the original primitive dirt road suitable for the heavy traffic that was involved the engineers had put down a surface of bricks. This had proved of little use as many of the bricks had disintegrated with the result that the surface of the road was the worst I have ever known. A series of large pot holes, some very deep, were interspersed with short bits of road with an appalling surface. I remember feeling very ill in the lorry as we bounced and crashed our way back to Chittagong. From Chittagong there was, as I recall, a two day journey on a train. It was hot, damp and uncomfortable. Thereafter the way was by road to the great Brahmaputra river where everything had to be ferried across on barges. The river, by which much of the melting snow on the lower slopes of the Himalayas travels to the sea, is about a quarter of a mile wide at the point where we crossed and running fast, so it was an exciting trip. Once across, the last lap along the road through the mountains to Imphal began. The first stage of this took one up and up until the highest point near Kohima was reached. This small mountain hill station had been desolated by the recent fighting and was a sad place as we drove through in heavy rain. From Kohima to Imphal the engineers had carved a road out of the red rock of the steep slopes of the mountains that curled and twisted like a ribbon around the flanks of green hills and across the valleys until at last it descended into the great emerald plain around Imphal. I was driven along this road at breakneck speed by an Indian driver in an old army truck. As the driver plainly did not, or would not, understand English and as I had no idea of how to communicate with him in whatever Indian language was his native tongue, I was quite unable to control our progress. Gesticulating merely encouraged him to go faster. The road was barely wide enough for two lorries to pass and, being cut out of steep hillsides, it was bounded on one side by a precipice (the Indians called it a khud). There was nothing to prevent a vehicle falling over the edge if the driver misjudged the space when passing something coming in the opposite direction. And the precipices were steep and fell away for great distances. It was one of the most hair-raising experiences of the war for me. But God was kind and by some miracle we eventually arrived. I went straight to the 23rd Indian Division that was guarding the road that ran from Palel in the south east corner of the plain over the hills to Tamu in the Kabaw valley. Here again I was attached to a unit that had considerable experience of warfare against the Japanese and learned a great deal. The 23rd Division had fought long and hard in the defence of Imphal and the troops that made it up were some of the best it was my lot to meet during the war. Though forming part of what we all called the 'forgotten army' and having had to undertake a large share of the unrewarding work involved in holding off the Japanese while waiting for reinforcements to arrive and enable the advance back into Burma to begin, they all seemed to be in wonderfully high spirits. The troops that made up the division came from all parts of India, from Nepal — the Ghurkhas, and from Britain, so it was a polyglot organisation. But they all got on very well together.

I had never before seen Ghurkha troops and I remember the first experience I had of them. It was very early one morning and I was with a battalion of Indians who were dug in on the side of a hill looking out across a valley to a further ridge. As dawn broke we stood to, as was the practice every day, and while we waited in the silence a company of Ghurkas who had been out all night on a patrol the other side of the valley came back through our lines. It had been raining and they had had a short encounter with some Japs. They were soaked and bedraggled, tired and wet. But a more cheerful bunch of little men it was impossible to imagine. They came striding along at the brisk pace they always adopted, their green hats perched saucily over one eye and held on by the chin strap which ran almost parallel to the lines of their broad grinning mouths. Their twinkling slit eyes seemed like happy headlights as they emerged through the early morning mist.

I enjoyed my stay with these engaging troops and learned for the first time that wonderful comradeship that comes to officers and men alike when they have been through a campaign together and that binds them into the best of fighting units. But again my stay with the 23rd Division was not destined to be a long one. The 11th East African Division arrived and I went back where I belonged.

Soon after I rejoined the East Africans we were visited by Lord Louis Mountbatten, the Supreme Allied Commander in South East Asia, who made it a practice to visit in person each division before it was launched into active operations. He drove round all the troops in the Division and addressed the men of each unit from the back of a jeep. He told us all what the task that he had allotted to us was. We were to advance through the 23rd Division along the road from Palel to Tamu and then from there to reach the Chindwin at Kalewa and make a bridge across the river. As I shall relate, this was remembered by the askaris throughout the subsequent campaign. Lord Louis was a personality of great charm and even the black tribesmen from the hinterland of East Africa, simple as they were, and not understanding what he said, were greatly attracted by him. He had a habit of wearing his admiral's cap at an angle which gave him a jaunty and dapper look which appealed to the Africans who always like eccentricities of dress. But perhaps what impressed these soldiers from the colonies most was that he looked so like King George VI. As the admiral's jeep drew up and we were able to see Lord Louis clearly I remember the face of one askari light up as he exclaimed in Swahili "ndugu ya mfalme" — "he is the brother of the King". So striking was the facial resemblance between the members of the Royal Family that even a simple soldier from Central Africa was impressed by it.

The other incident connected with this visit of the Supreme Commander is I think worthy of record because it shows the remarkable capacity that some members of the Royal Family acquire for remembering later the face and name of a person they met fleetingly in some earlier occasion. After he had addressed all the troops the officers were drawn up and he came down their ranks and shook each one by the hand and had a word with most of them. I was standing next to a young staff captain, Ivor Brown, who earlier in the war had been evacuated from Dunkirk on the destroyer Kelly of which Mountbatten had been in command. As he shook Ivor's hand they had a short conversation in which this came up. He then passed on to me. When, some six months later the East Africa Division was withdrawn from the front line for a rest, our task having been completed, he visited us again and went through a similar routine. This time Ivor Brown was not present — I think he had been transferred to another unit — but as the Commander in Chief shook me by the hand he paused, looked at me closely and said "are you not the man who was standing next to Ivor Brown when I last inspected the division?"!

When we started our advance from Palel the monsoon had not begun, but it was known the rains would not hold off for long. Our task was to be achieved by the time the dry weather came again, by which time it was hoped that the XIV Army could have been greatly reinforced and would pass over the river by our bridge and commence the advance into the plains of Burma retaking Mandalay and eventually Rangoon. When some years later the war had ended and Winston Churchill was to write his record of the events in which he played so vital a part, he had this to say about the advance upon which we then embarked.

"The XXXIII Corps, after taking Tamu, sent an East Africa brigade eastwards. It established a valuable bridgehead across the river Chindwin at Sittaung. The rest of the 11th East African Division went south along the Kabaw valley towards Kalewa, which they entered hand in hand with the 5th Indian Division on November 14. This was a remarkable march against great physical difficulties through an area notorious for malaria and scrub typhus. The good hygiene discipline now practised by all our units in Burma, the use of the new drug, mepacrine, the constant spraying with DDT insecticide, kept the sick rate admirably low. But the Japanese were not versed in these precautions and died in hundreds. From Kalemyo the East Africans pushed on to Kalewa and crossed the Chindwin. Here the engineers built a bridge nearly four hundred yards long in twenty eight working hours, not the least of their many achievements throughout the campaign. Thus on the central front in early December General Slim's Fourteenth Army, with two bridgeheads across the Chindwin, was poised for his main advance on to the central plain of Burma."   [*The Second World War*, vol VI, p147]

CHAPTER FOURTEEN

Monsoon Victory

The first objective in our advance was to capture Tamu, a small Burmese township which the Japs had used as a base from which they had supplied their troops operating in the mountainous country that lay between the Kabaw Valley and the Imphal plain. When the East African troops started to move forward the Japanese began to withdraw without offering much resistance. As we moved along on either side of the road from Palel it quickly became apparent that they were in very bad shape. Sickness and lack of food had taken their toll. Many had died and those that remained were often emaciated and spiritless. It was during this early part of our advance that I saw for the first time a dead man. My batman and I were walking through long grass, some three feet high, by the edge of a small stream when I stumbled over what at first I thought was a log, but turned out to be a dead Japanese soldier sprawled out in the mud. He had obviously been dead for some days as his body was black and swollen. Maggots had begun their macabre task. I remember feeling sick and nauseated and then wondering how he had died. Had he just dropped from starvation, or had he perhaps been killed by a stray shot from our infantry. I wondered, too, where he had come from and whether his family would ever know where his short life had been brought to an end. Somewhere in Japan, doubtless, his father and mother were waiting for his return. Perhaps a wife and child as well. I think it was this experience that first brought home to me in a personal sense the horribleness of war. There was nothing to be done so we walked on to the unit we were to visit. That night I spent in the open almost at the top of Sita, a mountain that was the highest point between Palel and Tamu, where we had a battalion and a gunners' observation post. It was bitterly cold and my one blanket was wet from the rain so I could not sleep, but lay awake shivering and thinking of that Japanese soldier. As our advance continued we became hardened to the sight of death as we found more and more corpses of retreating Japs; but when, after meeting very little resistance, our troops took Tamu the spectacle of that small town was enough to turn the stomach of the staunchest. The local inhabitants had all disappeared into the jungle and the Japanese had left it deserted. Broken down vehicles were scattered around – some left by the Japs and some that had belonged to the British and had been left during the retreat. Some of the latter, rusted and stripped of their tyres and wheels contained skeletons, probably of remnants of the British forces who had crawled into them too exhausted to continue the march over the hills to Palel and into India. The stink of decay and death greeted us wherever we went. The

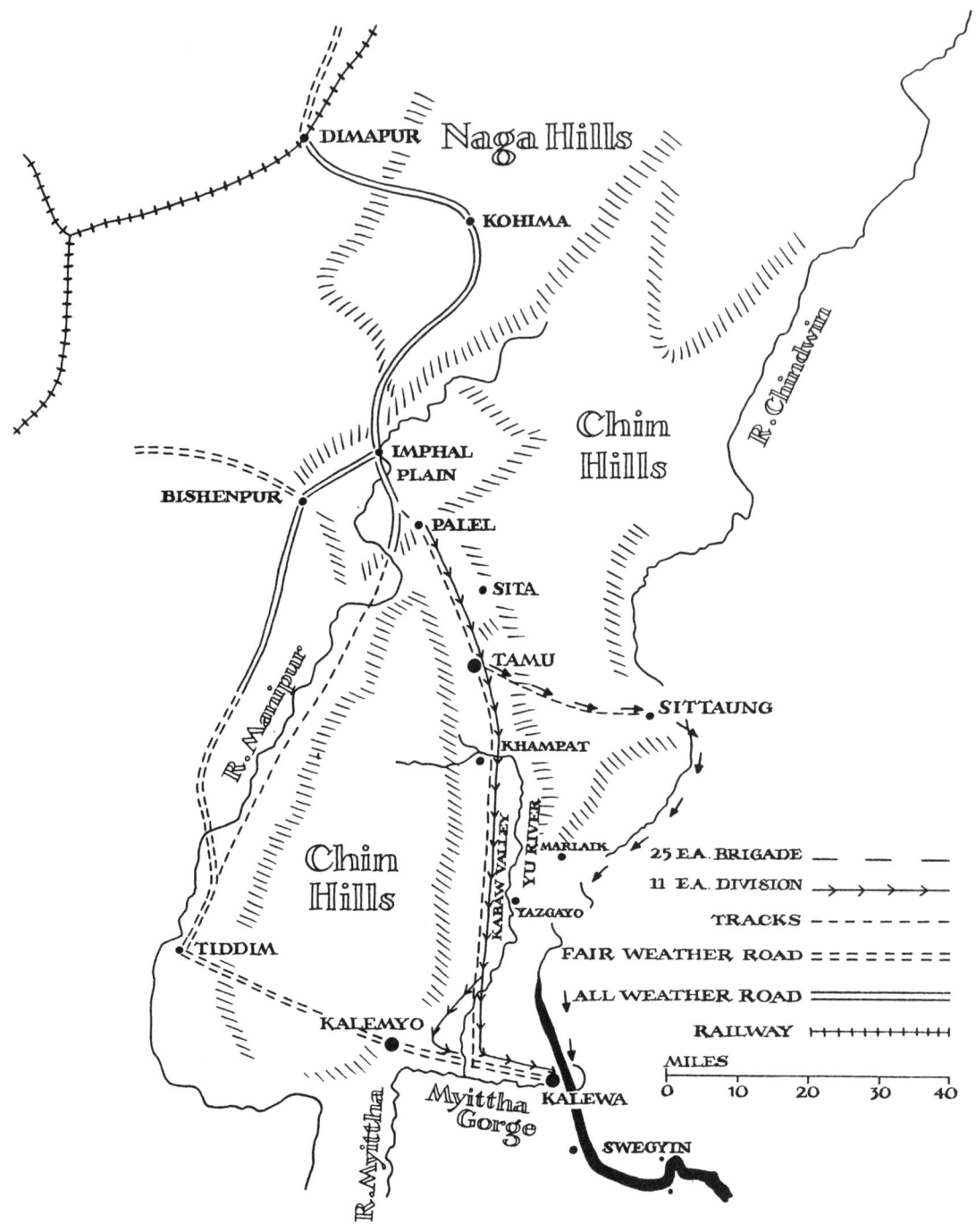

Sketch map of North West Burma.

General decided that the Divisional headquarters should be well away from this depressing and probably unhealthy spot and that we should move on as fast as possible.

The Kabaw Valley, into which we had moved after crossing the hills from Palel, runs south from Tamu and more or less parallel to the Chindwin until it reaches Kalemyo where the Yu and the Myittha Rivers join and the valley turns sharply eastward reaching the Chindwin at Kalewa. Between the Kabaw and Chindwin valleys is a range of hills covered largely with thick bamboo jungle. The flat land bordering the river at the bottom of the valley is canopied in teak forest.

It had been expected that the monsoon would start before we got into the valley but that year the onset of the heavy rains was delayed and that, combined with the fact that our advance had been unexpectedly swift, meant that we were able to move some distance down the valley before the worst of the rains came. Soon after we reached Tamu the General asked me to reconnoitre a position for an advanced Divisional headquarters as far down the valley as was practicable so that we should be close behind the advancing troops. At this time the main divisional headquarters was at Moreh near Tamu. The General said that as soon as I had found a suitable spot for the advanced headquarters he would join me with a small skeleton staff. So I set off with my orderly. A rough track ran down the valley, the maps called it a dry weather road, and, providing the sun shone, it was a pleasant route. The tall trees of the forest made a high canopy of leaf through which at intervals shafts of sunlight shone dappling the brighter greens of the undergrowth. From time to time the track crossed dried up beds of streams, or 'chaungs' as they were called locally, by means of bridges or culverts made of teak trunks laid side by side on top of and across two tall tree trunks that spanned the dip. The construction of these bridges was the work of elephants specially trained by the forestry service. During the Japs' occupation most of the elephants had escaped into the forest and reverted to the wild. A few had been marched out of the valley with the retreating British under the leadership of a most remarkable man, Major (later Lt. Colonel) J.H. Williams, who had been in the Burma Forestry Service and had a unique knowledge and understanding of elephants. He was known to everyone in Burma as 'Elephant Bill'. As I set out from Tamu to find a new headquarters for the Division I quickly realised what important work these elephants were doing, following close behind our leading infantry troops and rebuilding the bridges that had been swept away by the previous monsoon. One evening I found myself in the camp where Elephant Bill and his helpers had made their headquarters. Here they were collecting the elephants that had run wild in the forest. Each day they went out to track down any of which they had been told the whereabouts by the villagers, and usually came back in the evening with one or two more to add to the ones that had already been recaptured. That evening I sat with Bill Williams in his tiny tent as we drank rum and lime. He regaled me with the story of his march out of Burma with the elephants during the retreat. (A fascinating tale which he later told in *Elephant Bill* {Rupert Hart-Davis 1950}) He told me, too, something of what life had been like before the war working in the remote jungles of Burma as part of the Forestry Service. Rarely have I been so entertained. When I left him early the next morning he asked me to do him a favour. He said that they had no wireless in his camp and as I would shortly be with a unit that had wireless communication to the headquarters behind us would I send a message urgently to Army Headquarters. What, I asked, was the message. "Tell them" he said, "to send up as quickly as possible as much opium as could be obtained rolled into two ounce balls". He needed it, he told me, to help catch and tame again the wilder elephants that were still loose in the forest. Apparently a 2 ounce ball of opium is swallowed with relish and has the effect of making them much more amenable to the discipline of their oozies or drivers. Needless to say when, a day or so later, I was able to get the message back it caused consternation in the Quartermaster's department at 14th Army. They clearly thought that the forward troops were falling prey to the decadent habits of the local Burmese who are great smokers of opium, and they were not easily persuaded that the supplies were for a genuine wartime purpose. However ultimately the opium arrived and Elephant Bill made good use of it, eventually recovering some 60 elephants and using them to do invaluable work as the advance proceeded.

The day after I left the elephant camp I reached a point in the valley close behind our forward troops and near to the junction of the Yu River with a stream — the Khampat river. It seemed a good place for divisional headquarters so I sent a message back to the divisional commander and told him of my decision. Immediately the reply came back that he was setting out from Tamu with a small number of signallers to join me. The rest of the headquarters would follow later. The last part of that message was to prove more true than we expected, for that day the monsoon broke with a vengeance. The rains poured heavier than usual for three weeks, an average of five inches per day. The track down which I had come from Tamu rapidly became impassable. The Chaungs, hitherto nearly dried up, suddenly became deep and wide rivers sweeping away all the bridges, so carefully rebuilt by the elephants. It was six weeks before divisional headquarters was able to catch up with us. But Fluffy Fowkes[1], the divisional commander, had set out in a jeep as soon as he had received my message and managed to get about half way before the rain came. He was forced to abandon his jeep, but two days later he arrived at Khampat bedraggled but determined. Fortunately he had brought with him two signallers with a wireless and we were able to set up a forward divisional headquarters. It consisted of him and me, two signallers and a sergeant from one of the brigades and three African askaris and my orderly, Gabriel. It was from this miserable headquarters that the division was controlled for the next six weeks as it moved down the valley towards Kalewa.

As all road communications behind us were cut by the rains making the tracks impassable and the swollen rivers washing away the bridges, it was necessary to supply us entirely by air. For about two months every bit of food we and the forward troops ate and every type of supply we needed came by air and was dropped by parachute. We quickly got used to the system and once we realised how well it worked we all felt more secure than we ever would have done operating at the end of a long and vulnerable line of communication. The drill we adopted was simple. When a unit moved to a new position it formed a 'box' in the jungle. A 'box' was a defended area which was surrounded by our troops, dug in and concealed in fox holes. In the centre of the box an area of the jungle would be cleared as a dropping zone into which the Dakotas, having flown over the mountains from India, would drop by parachute the food and ammunition needed for the next step forward. At night we all settled down into our fox holes and the golden rule was to keep absolutely quiet. Jap patrols would move about in the forest and could do no

---

[1] Major General C. C. Fowkes.

damage provided we did not give away our position by firing at them or shewing a light. It did not worry us if they cut the track behind us as we knew the aeroplanes would drop more food to us at our next position. This system depended of course for its success on the total dependability of the air force. But the men supplying us were marvellous. Only about twice did a plane fail to arrive and when one remembers that every flight had to be made over mountains 10,000 feet high and often shrouded in cloud and mist, one realises what a great feat it was. Once over the mountains the pilots had to find the small clearing, in the miles and miles of jungle stretching in all directions, into which the supplies had to be dropped. So it was that we were fed and supplied as we moved down the valley.

Elephant Bill in his book (*Elephant Bill* p.289) describes vividly our progress and the work that went on behind us to try and keep the track open for the main body of troops that were to follow us.

> "The monsoons were by no mean over in the Kabaw Valley, but nothing was to stop the East African Division going down it. The rains were so violent that log bridges built one day were often washed away the next, only to be replaced the day after. Japanese lorries were bogged down all along that valley of mud. The East Africans cut millions of saplings and threw them across the road to keep it open. They (the saplings) gave out a stench as they rotted which almost matched that of the Japanese, who had dropped out all along the line, and died of disease, starvation and exhaustion.
>
> The streams were in such spate that it was next to impossible to keep long cribs in place for any length of time. We therefore used elephants to haul discarded Japanese lorries into the beds of the streams, and built our log cribs on top of them. Had it not been for the exceptionally heavy late rains in September and early October, 1944, the Japanese retreating along the Tiddim Road would have run into the spearhead of the East Africa Division, coming down the Kabaw Valley."

Elephant Bill, in that quotation, refers to the Japanese retreat down the Tiddim Road. As can be seen from the map the south end of the Imphal Plain has leading from it two roads, the one down which we had moved leaving the south east corner of the plain and going over the hills to Tamu, the other striking over the hills south west of Imphal to Tiddim. From there a track continues over the hills to join the Kabaw Valley road at Kalemyo. At the same time as the East African Division began to move forward out of the plain other British troops began to advance down the Tiddim Road. The Jap forces on this road withdrew putting up a stiff resistance and as soon as we heard of this we had a further reason for advancing as fast as was humanly possible to Kalemyo because if we could arrive there before the retreating Japanese from Tiddim they would be in a perilous state. Their only possible supply route would be cut and they would be trapped in the inhospitable Chin hills and surrounded by hostile tribesmen. Unfortunately our advance was not quite fast enough and the Japs from Tiddim streamed through Kalemyo towards the Chindwin a few days before our forward troops got into the little town. One of the reasons for our advance being slowed up as we approached Kalemyo was the nature of the country. Once I was in one of the small planes that the gunners used for observing where gunfire from their batteries was landing and for directing their guns on to the target. On that occasion the difficulties of the terrain became very clear to me. We were flying along the Kabaw Valley in the direction in which our troops were moving and all that one could see was a series of more or less parallel ridges at right angles to the line of the river. The sides of these ridges facing our advance were precipitous cliffs. The Japanese side of the ridges were more gentle slopes. It looked as if we were flying over a series of breaking waves and our troops were advancing into the breakers. The result was that as the forward troops approached each ridge they were faced with a steep cliff. On the top of the ridge would be the Jap positions, concealed beneath the all embracing jungle. The Japanese soldier became an expert at making what we called 'fox holes'. These were bunkers dug out on the forward edge of the cliff top and roofed with felled tree trunks to protect them from gunfire or bombs. All that was visible when finally one got close to them was a slit through which their machine guns could command the approaches. The formation of the country and the thick jungle cover enabled them with only a few men to hold up the advance of a whole division for several days by manning two or three of these bunker positions. Unless one was very lucky and achieved a direct hit with a shell or bomb these fox holes were impervious to artillery or infantry fire and were very difficult to find in the thick greenery. Eventually the East African askari learned that the way to deal with these obstructions was to climb up the precipitous slope under cover of darkness and then creep silently along the ridge until the fox hole was found and lob a hand grenade in through the entrance. Very often we learned that only half a dozen or so Jap soldiers had been holding the position.

It was when the division had been held up by one such Jap position on the forward edge of a ridge in front of us that I came nearer to being a casualty than I was at any other stage of the war. It had been decided to ask the R.A.F. to bomb with dive bombers the area where the bunkers were known to be. The object was to strip the foliage from the trees and undergrowth under which the bunkers were concealed, so that we could see where they were and bring down artillery and mortar fire on them. My orderly and I were standing in a slit trench on a slope about half a mile away from which we could see the target area and we were looking forward to a grandstand view of the air strike. When we heard the aeroplanes coming from behind us we stood up and looked across the valley — when we were suddenly surprised by machine gun fire and bombs. The pilots had evidently misread their maps and seeing our position on the hill had mistaken it for the Japs. Gabriel had a pack on his back and a bullet went through it — but did no damage to him or me. Gabriel smiled with his single tooth shining. "Shauri ya mungu" was all he said. "It is God's will!"

It was not long after this incident that I had an experience that taught me something of the nature of the Japanese soldier normally so enigmatic and incomprehensible. On the rare occasions when one of them was captured alive one could not understand them. They refused to speak and seemed totally dispirited. Their attitude was dictated by their philosophy which taught them that to be captured was the greatest disgrace that could befall them. It seemed impossible that they could be possessed of an artistic soul, but that was a mistaken view. Once as we were approaching Kalemyo when our forward troops had driven the Japs back from their positions on one of the ridges I have described I happened to go into one of their deserted bunkers. It was obvious that its occupants had left in a hurry and the place was full of bits of equipment and kit that had been jettisoned for their hasty departure. But what was so surprising was the amount of paper lying about. Our troops were always being told how important it was not to leave anything documentary when one left a position for fear that it might be of value to the enemy's

Intelligence. The Japs took no such care. As I was searching through all the mess to see if I could find anything that might be of value to our Intelligence I came across a small sketch book about 12 inches by 8 inches. Its owner, presumably an ordinary Jap infantryman, had evidently been an accomplished artist and on each of the twenty or so pages that the book contained there was sketched in the delicate style so typical of the Japanese a place through which he had passed on his long journey from Japan to Central Burma. Scenes in China, Indo China, Singapore, the Malay Peninsula and Burma were all represented in delightful sketches. I determined to keep the book so that when I got home after the war I could have all the pictures framed and use them to decorate my room and remind me of this phase of my life. Unfortunately however on the last page of the book was a map of Moulmein which was, as we knew, an important staging point on the Japanese route to Burma. It appeared to have barracks and headquarters marked on it so I felt bound to send the book back to Corps Headquarters for the Intelligence boys to study. I sent with it a message to Ronnie Hamilton who was in charge of Intelligence at Corps Headquarters and asked him to let me have it back after it had been studied and I duly got a reply to the effect that it would be returned to me. A day or two later we heard that Moulmein had been bombed heavily so perhaps it served its purpose — but I never got the book back and my post-war homes have not been decorated as I would have wished. Ronnie Hamilton was a cultured man and on his return to England became a housemaster at Winchester. I sometimes wonder if he had the same idea!

When we reached Kalemyo we learned that the Japs retreating from the Imphal Plain by way of the Tiddim road had passed through shortly before our leading troops had arrived. The track from Kalemyo to Kalewa followed the valley of the Mytha River from the point where it suddenly turns sharply westward. The valley is narrow and five miles east of Kalemyo becomes a steep gorge. The hills on either side are covered with thick jungle. The last line the Japanese held on the west of the Chindwin was across the entrance to this gorge where they occupied a commanding defensive position which was only overcome when a battalion of KAR had carried out a wide encircling march and placed a road block on the track behind it. Eventually the Japs were dislodged and the track to Kalewa was clear. We entered Kalewa on 2 December. The small town was in ruins having been heavily bombed by the RAF before our arrival. When eventually the road through the gorge reaches the Chindwin the valley widens somewhat and at the junction of the two rivers there is a wide sandy bay and a fair amount of open space between the edge of the trees and the river. I well remember the day on which I first saw the Chindwin. It was a perfect sunny day, a few small fluffy clouds were moving gently across an otherwise clear blue sky. Our leading troops had taken up positions on either side of the Mytha river but had not yet crossed the Chindwin. The sandy open space by the junction was occupied by a few soldiers exploring the huts and sheds that bordered the main river where there was a simple landing stage. The river, at this point about a quarter of a mile wide, was flowing fast in a muddy green torrent. On the far side trees came down to the rivers edge and the jungle extended as far as one could see. A distant line of blue hills, less mountainous than those from which we had recently emerged, formed the background. We did not know where the Japs were on the other side and it was obviously vital to get troops across the river quickly to form a bridgehead and to join up with a brigade that had crossed the Chindwin further north and was making its way down the east bank. The sappers would then be protected as they built a bridge which would enable the advance to continue towards Mandalay.

The battalion that was ordered to cross and form the bridgehead was the 4th (Uganda) Battalion of the KAR who had fought their way from Tamu with great distinction under their Commanding Officer Lt Col Duncan Geddes. Duncan, who had lost an arm earlier in the war and was a regular officer in one of the Scottish infantry regiments, was a marvellous soldier who inspired great confidence in his men. I was surprised, therefore, when he told me that his troops had refused to cross the river and he was afraid he had a mutiny on his hands. It transpired that the reason for this sudden decision by the askaris in the battalion to refuse to obey orders arose from an attractive quality in their nature. The Ugandan soldier, who was a very simple man drawn for the most part from remote villages in the countryside of Uganda, had a touching faith in the reliability of their English officers. At Palel before they had set out on their march to Kalewa Lord Louis Mountbatten, the Supreme Commander, had, as I have recounted earlier, visited the division and told us all that our task was to reach Kalewa on the Chindwin and that when we had done that another division would pass through us and carry on with the advance into the plains of Burma. When the Ugandans reached Kalewa they said, simply "We were told by the Bwana Mkubwa (the Big Chief) that we were to get to the Chindwin and then we would be relieved — now you are asking us to do more than that and to cross the river". It took a lot of Duncan's best Scots advocacy in Swahili to persuade them that we would not go back on our word but the crossing had to be made secure. Eventually they relented and it was not long before a brigade was over the river maintaining a safe bridgehead on the other side. But there were a few nasty moments.

Within a few days the bridgehead had been pushed forward so that the crossing point was out of range of enemy guns and the sappers were able to build a bridge undisturbed except by the occasional air raid. On 10th December the bridge was completed. It was 1,154 feet long and was the longest Bailey Bridge that had ever been built. When one realises that every bit of the bridge had been transported for over 150 miles from the railhead at Dimapur on rapidly improvised roads, one realises what a splendid feat of organisation and engineering it was.

With the establishment of the bridgehead over the Chindwin the task that had been allotted to the 11th East Africa Division was completed and other troops passed through to start the major advance into central Burma and on to Rangoon. We were pulled out and the Division was sent back to India to rest and refit. Christmas Day that year I spent in an army jeep driving back through Imphal and into the hills on the way to Kohima. General Slim, the Commander of XIV Army, had sworn that all his troops should have a proper Christmas dinner that year. Many of them had been on uninspiring and monotonous rations for a long time and this gesture did a lot for our morale. My little party found itself, soon after midday looking for a site in which to pitch our tents and spend the night and enjoy the turkey which, by some miracle of the military supply system, had been issued to us. We found a sheltered piece of flat ground on the side of a steep hill facing south. From it we could see the whole Imphal plain spread out beneath us and the blue mountains round it on all sides. We made a huge fire and as the sun went down we ate our turkey and then sat round the fire and talked late into the night. I remember we wondered whether the next Christmas would see us in Rangoon or still stuck somewhere on the

Irrawaddy Valley — little did we guess that by the next Christmas the war would be over, both in Europe and the Far East. The next day we drove on and eventually reached Jorhat in Northern Assam which it had been decreed was to be the division's resting area. It was an area of deep jungle and remote from any of the local towns or centres of population. The British NCOs were somewhat fed up with this assignment having expected, or hoped for, an opportunity to sample the bright lights and see some pretty girls. The reason for our isolation was, I believe, that the authorities feared that if the African soldiers were stationed too near a centre of Indian population the Indian girls might be in some danger. I dare say the authorities were right.

In the Assam hill country round Jorhat much Assam tea is grown and the tea planters were kind and sometimes invited young officers out to dinner. On one occasion, when I was returning late at night with a friend from such an evening, we were driving through the jungle and suddenly in the headlights of the jeep we saw, some ten yards ahead of us, a magnificent tiger. It stood across the track, his head turned towards us. Two things struck me when we were suddenly faced with this apparition. First, amazement at its huge size — much larger than I had ever imagined a tiger to be, and, second, the beauty of its skin as the muscles of its back legs rippled with every slight movement. Having looked at us for a second or two it moved gracefully and silently into the jungle.

A few days later I heard that I had been granted two weeks leave which I decided to take visiting Uncle Henry who was then in New Delhi. Alec Barnard came with me. It took us four days to reach Delhi — first two days by truck and train from Jorhat to Calcutta and then two days in a train from Calcutta across the plain of India to New Delhi. The train journey from Calcutta to Delhi was memorable. Even though we had been at war for some four years the train still retained the atmosphere of Victorian times. Being officers we had a First Class carriage to ourselves which was reasonably comfortable even though the leather covered seats showed signs of their age and the brass knobbed luggage racks no longer shone with the glitter of daily polishing. An Indian bearer was available to bring us water and a fan rotating, somewhat erratically, in the roof kept us moderately cool. At meal times the train stopped at a way side station and we all left the train and went into the station restaurant where excellent meals, curries and fruit were served. Second and Third Class passengers had no such luxuries. They travelled in dreadfully crowded and dirty unsprung coaches and made themselves as comfortable as they could on wooden seats. We had a pleasant ten days in Delhi. Uncle Henry, who had been Sir Edwin Lutyens' assistant when he had been building New Delhi, had remained on after Lutyens left and had done various other buildings. When we arrived he was living in a bungalow in the grounds of the Vice Regal Palace. He had a great love of India where he had been for some 12 years and knew a great deal of its history and architecture. He shewed us all the sights round about, the old city of Delhi and many temples, the Red Fort, the Roman Catholic and Anglican cathedrals for both of which he had himself been the architect. When visiting these places he drove us around in his old Sunbeam Talbot, an aged car of which he was very proud and which he drove at a furious speed and with alarming panache. He arranged for us to be invited to dinner with the Viceroy — Lord Wavell — who from time to time entertained young officers who happened to be on leave in the city. I was very impressed by the magnificent long dining room and by the red uniformed and turbaned soldiers one of whom stood behind each guest. There cannot have been very many more such occasions as less than three years later the British had left India and the great buildings were handed over to the Indians. At the time it was often said by the cynical that Lutyens' Delhi buildings would become the greatest ruins of all the ruined cities of Delhi. Happily that has not been proved to be true so far.

Our leave over we returned to Jorhat where I remained for a short period. I then learned that I had been lucky in a draw for home leave. I was to be allowed to fly back to England and have a month's holiday.

CHAPTER FIFTEEN

War's End and Marriage

The journey home took an unconscionable time, due, I think, to the fact that the cargo aircraft on which troops returning on leave were carried had temporarily been diverted to some other theatre of the war where needs were greater. The result was that three of us who had all been given leave together were stuck at Karachi for nearly three weeks. Fortunately, Karachi was a town in which it was pleasant to be stranded. It had, at that time of the year, an agreeable climate, and there was an officers' club that had access to a quiet and not overcrowded beach where we were able to bathe, lie in the sun and read. By the end of this period of protracted leisure, I became for the only time in my life, truly tanned. Eventually, we were told that we had places on a Dakota, a twin engined cargo plane that was returning to England 'in ballast'. We were the ballast. It was an uncomfortable journey and not without incident. The plane had no seats and no appreciable heating arrangements, so we had to make ourselves as comfortable as we could sitting on our kit bags. It was very noisy and very cold. We flew first to Aden where we came down to refuel and then set out across the Red Sea and along the coast line of North Africa. We were flying south of and parallel to the north coast of Africa and it was a perfect clear moonlit night. I could not sleep on account of the noise of the aircraft and the cold. So I was gazing out of the windows, across the wing of the plane on which was mounted the starboard engine.

Suddenly the propeller stopped revolving and came to rest with its blades vertical. I could not believe my eyes. But it was true and I soon realised that we were losing height slowly. I woke up my neighbour and pointed out to him the stationary propeller. He woke up the person beyond him and in a few seconds we were all awake. At that moment one of the crew came through from the pilot's cabin. He was a young Canadian who seemed no older than 18. In a calm and matter of fact voice he told us that one engine had failed and that we were going to have to make a forced landing in the desert. I confess to having been very alarmed — but there was nothing to be done except wait and hope for the best. Eventually the pilot brought us down and made a perfect landing on a bit of level and not too soft sand. We were eight miles from the coast near Mersa Matruh. Earlier the name of Mersa Matruh was well known as in the ebb and flow of the desert campaigns in North Africa the fighting troops passed and repassed it. But at this time after the Germans had been driven out of Libya and Tunisia it was garrisoned by native pioneer troops. Before we had waited very long a lorry appeared from across the desert and we were taken to the camp. There we had to wait for nearly a week until a new part for the engine of our plane was flown out from England. We were then able to continue our journey and on 17 April, 1945, we landed at Lyneham in Wiltshire on a perfect English day. It was over three years since I had left and I will never forget the smell of the newly mown grass on the airfield that greeted us when the door of the plane was opened. The spring was at its most seductive and I realised that no country could ever compete with England.

I am writing these notes over fifty years after that day of hope and happiness. So much has happened that I find it very difficult to recall accurately my feelings. But my main memory is of an overwhelming desire to get back to Chertsey to see my mother and father and sisters, to see again the familiar old home and garden and to hear the church bells ringing the traditional curfew. Whilst abroad, I had written to Pookie Powell and asked her to marry me and this she had agreed to do. The letter in which she accepted was dropped with the mail in a clearing of the jungle when we were camped near Yazagyo at the bottom of the Kabaw Valley. I was very keen to see her. When I got to Chertsey and walked up to the front door of Curfew House I wondered who would open the door, would it be mother or someone else. I knocked and almost at once the door was opened and standing on the threshold was Betty. "Hallo Bets" I said. "I'm not Betty I am Jo" replied the girl at the door. When I had left home nearly 4 years before Betty had been about 15 and Jo had been 10. Now Jo was 15 and looked exactly as I had remembered Betty! Once this gaffe was behind me I met everyone else again and little change there had been. Mother and Father were the same as ever, though they must have had a miserable time in those years, struggling to carry on as usual with no breaks or holidays and with the worries of air raids and from time to time learning of the death of some cousin or relation. Both Peter and Dick, the sons of Uncle Alan and Aunt Adèle, were killed. Peter was shot down when flying with the Fleet Air Arm over Taranto and taken to a POW camp in North Italy. Towards the end of the war he had escaped and walked the length of the country and rejoined the British where they had landed near Anzio. On his return to England he was sent to Scotland to train pilots and very shortly before the Armistice he flew into a mountain side, shrouded in mist, and died. Dick had become an engineer and died in a road accident. Andrew, the elder son of Uncle Godfrey, who had by the start of the war just qualified as a solicitor, was killed fighting in North Africa. Michael his brother had been taken prisoner by the Japs in the Far East. Eventually he was released and returned to England. I met him once immediately after the war, but he soon returned to India. I did not see him again for something over forty-five years when I met him at the eightieth birthday party of Andrew's widow, Joy. He is now Sir Michael Parsons, having recently retired from being the Vice-Chairman of Inchcapes.

Pookie and I were married in London on 3 May, 1945, at St Georges, Hanover Square. The ceremony was performed by my Uncle Godfrey who was then the Bishop of Hereford, having recently been transferred from Southwark where he had been throughout the blitz. Pookie had chosen the church as it had two statues of dogs outside the doors and she liked dogs. I was impressed as the names of the churchwardens which were written on the panelling included those of several famous statesmen including William Pitt the Younger. After the reception, we hurried to Paddington and took a train to the middle of Wales where we had a week's honeymoon at Lake Vyrnwy. The war in Europe ended a few days after we got there and a huge bonfire was lit on top of the hill behind the hotel and we climbed up to it and saw similar beacons burning on the hills in all directions.

I could not help being reminded of A E Houseman's poem:—

> From Cree to heaven the beacon burns,
> The shires have seen it plain,
> From north and south the sign returns
> And beacons burn again".

And the later, sad, verse:

> "It dawns in Asia, tombstones show,
> And Shropshire names are read;
> And the Nile spills her overflow
> Beside the Severn's dead".

My month's leave from Burma should have ended in the middle of May, but a day or two before I was due to return, I went down with mumps and I had no sooner recovered from that than I was smitten with malaria, though, fortunately, the attack of the latter was very mild. On my way out from Burma, I had passed through Calcutta where the HQ of South East Asia Command was situated. My uncle, Treffry Thompson, who had been in the Indian Army as a doctor was at that time the Director of Medical Services to the Command and he kindly asked me to lunch at the Generals' mess there. It was for me a memorable lunch and I remember being cross-examined by the Chief of Staff and other senior officers about my experiences. Uncle Treffry as medical adviser to Mountbatten had been responsible for insisting that every soldier stationed in the malarial areas of Burma took Mepacrin, a relatively new drug which protected one from the effects of the vicious mosquito that carried the disease. There can, I think, be little doubt that this insistence had done much to save us from massive casualties, as the Kabaw Valley was a notorious malarial area. When I was saying goodbye to Uncle Treffry after my lunch, I asked him what I should do to ensure that I did not get malaria when I stopped taking the nasty yellow pills which I had conscientiously taken for some three years. He said, "When you leave the area take twice the normal dose for three weeks and you can then stop taking it". This I did and the three weeks were up more or less at the same time as my honeymoon. It was then that I got malaria! I suppose I had got the infection in my blood and it had been suppressed by the pills but the final double dosage had not quite succeeded in knocking it right out. Happily, I have never since been troubled with a recurrence of it.

These two bouts of minor illnesses resulted in me not returning to the East African Division until the beginning of July when I flew back. It had been suggested to me that as I had done over 3 years overseas I could properly ask to be transferred to the home service for the rest of my time in the Army. Had I realised that the war against Japan would end with the dropping of the atom bomb a little more than a month later I would probably have fallen in with the suggestion. To have done so would have enabled me to get on with qualifying for life as a barrister and so, hopefully, enabling me to look after a wife rather better than I could on an army officer's pay. However, I decided not to take this course as it seemed to me that to do so would be a rather cowardly way of ending my service. We all thought that the war against Japan was bound to continue for some considerable time, though, once the British and American troops who had defeated Hitler could be released from Europe and transferred to the Far Eastern theatre, there could be no doubt about the ultimate outcome. So it was that I duly returned to the Division which was busy preparing for its next task. Though, as far as I can remember, we were never explicitly told what that task was to be, we were pretty certain that we were to form part of a force that when once Rangoon and Central Burma had been cleared of the Japs, would cross the Salwene River in the east of the country and would then advance into Siam. When I reached the Division it was busy training in the jungles near Ranchi in Bihar. Almost as soon as I returned I was promoted to the rank of major and given the job of GSO2(I) (General Staff Officer responsible for Intelligence) as my friend Martin Suter who had previously held the post was sent to Corps Headquarters. This was an interesting job which involved, primarily, assimilating the vast amount of intelligence information that came to us from many different sources about the Jap Army that remained east of the Salween. This period did not however last long because on 6 August the first atomic bomb was dropped on Hiroshima and a few days later a second was dropped on Nagasaki.

In any man's life there are usually a number of occasions when he hears news of some unexpected and sudden occurrence which changes his life or has a profound effect on him and others. The circumstances in which he hears this news are often engraved in his memory for ever after. Many people remember clearly where they were and what they were doing when they heard the news that President Kennedy had been assassinated. For me the receipt of the news that the first atomic bomb had been dropped was such an event. Shortly before I had returned to the Division a new divisional commander had been appointed to it, replacing 'Fluffy' Fowkes. He was Maj. Gen. Dimoline who had formerly commanded one of the Brigades in the Division. He was a genial plump man who had proved himself a good Brigade Commander and was also an excellent administrator. He had instituted a daily meeting, we called it 'Morning Prayers', which took place early every morning and was attended by the senior staff officer of each of the various elements of the Division and each officer in turn was required to tell all those present what, if anything, had happened of general interest in the previous 24 hours in his area of responsibility. In this way, it was hoped that we would never be open to the criticism frequently levelled against large organisations that the left hand does not know what the right hand is doing. On this particular day morning prayers took place in a clearing in the jungle where we were camped and the various officers were standing in a circle and I had just said my piece when a young officer called Birkenshaw whose job it was to listen to the news given out on the wireless came running into the circle, obviously very excited. He said that he had just heard on the news that an enormous bomb had been dropped on a city in Japan and it was thought that the entire city had been destroyed and razed to the ground. There was a long silence. Then we all started talking and speculating what the effect of this would have on the future conduct of the war. We quickly realised that it might mean that it would not be necessary to conduct a long campaign such as we were all expecting in order to drive the Japs out of Siam and Malaysia and Indo-China and China itself. And so indeed it proved to be. Within a few days the Japanese surrendered.

I have very little recollection of the next few months. There being no longer a war to be fought, everyone's mind was concentrated on getting back home and returning to civilian life. This applied as much to the African soldiers in the Division as to the British officers and NCOs serving with them.

My job changed from that of assimilating information about the Japanese to that of keeping an eye on the morale of the Africans who quickly began to get restive when they realised that they could not be shipped back to their native villages at once.

During this period of waiting, the officers in charge of the Africans did what they could to help them to prepare for life when they returned to their villages. Many of them had, before they joined the Army, been engaged in very primitive forms of agriculture and courses were organised for them by officers who had some knowledge of African agriculture designed to enable them to become more efficient farmers. Various other efforts were made to educate them for different trades and to help them understand how to run a business. While this was going on we gradually became aware that fundamental changes were taking place in the way that the Africans viewed the future. This change was largely brought about by two things. First, before the war, an African who was employed was likely to be paid about ten shillings per month. Even though there would often be included with this, his accommodation and his keep, it was very much less than he received as an askari who might well be paid many times that amount as well as being provided with his keep and clothing. Furthermore, while he was serving as a soldier there was, for much of his time, nothing on which these increased wages could be spent. The result was that many of the Africans had saved amounts which seemed to them to be very large indeed.

Secondly, their experience in the Army had brought them in contact for the first time, with many different races. They had met British officers and NCOs, had seen the French in Madagascar and a few who had fought in Abyssinia had seen Italians as well as Indians, Sinhalese and Ghurkhas and Burmese in the Far East. These experiences had made them realise that there was more to life than the mud huts and the bare subsistence farming that they had known before they joined the Army. They wanted somehow to improve their lot when they returned once again to their tribal areas. Many of the tribes organised societies which they intended should be used to start businesses financed by the savings of the soldiers. Some of the societies got into the hands of men who wished to use them as political parties dedicated to gaining independence from British rule.

When I began to learn about these tribal societies, I realised that many of them were innocent enough. The society organised, for example, by the Chagga tribe whose homelands are in the foothills of Mount Kilimanjaro, planned to set up a co-operative society which would cultivate coffee and sell it for the benefit of all its members. This they eventually did and I believe it has proved very successful. But some of the societies started by other tribes had more political objectives. It was at this time that my friends the Allens who had been so hospitable to me when I was in Kenya offered to let me have land on which to farm. By this time I was married and had responsibilities and what I had learned about these tribal societies led me to think that there might in the future be troubles in the African colonies. I did not like the idea of making a home and being responsible for a wife and possibly a family in a country where one was not a welcome resident. I thought, and still think, that the life of a farmer is one of the most satisfying of occupations, but these considerations made me refuse this most generous offer. Alas, that was the last I heard of the Allen family. In view of what happened in Kenya later when the Mau Mau carried out its campaign of terror against British settlers, perhaps I was wise.

I eventually left for home in December and arrived back in England just in time for Christmas. Pookie was living in the game-keeper's cottage at Bedstone in Shropshire, the tenancy of which we had taken over from her father. When, finally, I got home she was at the small station at Bucknell with a pony and trap waiting to meet me. I was entitled to a month's leave and it was spent happily at the cottage.

CHAPTER SIXTEEN

New Life Begins

The war having ended the time had come for me to plan my future. I was still determined if possible to be called to the Bar and to practice as a barrister, but it was five years since I had done any law and that had only been a very small part of the Law Tripos at Cambridge. However, the authorities which control these things had been very generous to servicemen whose academic careers had been cut short by war service. I discovered that even though I had only done four of the nine terms usually required to complete the course, I had been granted a law degree and that that was enough to excuse me from a considerable part of the Bar exams. The Council of Legal Education which was responsible for administering the arrangements and examinations for qualification for the Bar, was in those days, a very small organisation under the chairmanship of a delightful, elderly and very learned chancery lawyer, Cleveland Stevens QC. I went to see him in his chambers in Lincoln's Inn and he told me that what I had already done was sufficient to exempt me from many of the papers in the Bar exams. He thought that if I took the papers in tort and contract and equity and passed in them that would be sufficient and I would be called to the Bar. As tort and contract and equity were subjects I had studied at Cambridge, even though in the intervening years I had forgotten much that I had then learned, I thought that I could probably get them up again by study in my spare time without having to go to a law tutor or return to the University. I decided therefore to stay in the Army for a little longer and to work at the law in the evenings. This would enable me to have an income while I was studying.

The plan worked well. I was in due course posted to Eastbourne where I was stationed in the Grand Hotel which was to become a school to teach people who were to be recruited into what came to be known as the Control Commission for Germany. It did not seem to me that I was in any way qualified for this as I spoke no German and knew nothing about the country and certainly nothing about how it was, or ought to be, governed or how the legal system in Germany worked. But the authorities did not seem to consider that this was any handicap. When I got to Eastbourne, I found that the proposed school had not yet got any pupils so there was not a lot to do. I had plenty of time to study. I was fortunate too, in that when I got there I found two other young officers who had had the same idea. One was Arthur Bagnall, later to become a High Court judge in the Chancery Division and the other was Ian Fife, who acquired a large practice on the Oxford Circuit and became a respected County Court judge. We three shared a small office and, in the intervals between carrying out the limited military duties that were assigned to us, we all worked away at our legal studies.

It was while I was at Eastbourne that Pookie and I learned that she was to have a baby. This was a great excitement and we set about trying to decide on a name for it. We were easily able to decide on a boy's name. My father's name Edward appealed to us both, but we could not decide on a name for a girl. The problem was solved one Sunday in the summer when I took Pookie into the Sussex Downs where we had a lovely walk ending with tea at a teashop called 'Druscillas'. As soon as we saw this name, we were agreed that here was the name for our child if it proved to be a girl. We both liked the name and felt that it would always remind us of the happy summer's day we had spent walking on the chalk downs of Sussex. Later, when the child was born and turned out to be a girl, I wrote to Uncle Godfrey, my Bishop uncle, and told him that we were going to call her Druscilla. I got a sharp reply to the effect that at least we ought to spell her name right. "See Acts 24, v.24", he said. When I read the passage I realised that Drusilla was not spelt with a 'c'. I did not reply, as perhaps I should have done, why then is Priscilla spelt thus (See Acts 18, v.2). Shortly after this, the school for teaching people how to govern Germany, which still had no pupils, was moved to Bletchley Hall in Buckinghamshire. Bletchley Hall had been the place where, during the war, the branch of Intelligence which managed to break the German ciphers had been stationed. During the short time that I was at Bletchley, I was given the job of supervising the stores and one incident I remember well. There were a number of girls from the Forces stationed there who had come to help with secretarial tasks and the like. Of these girls one, Pauline, was particularly attractive. One day she came to me and asked if I could issue her with a pair of silk stockings, an item which was in very short supply and which was greatly coveted by the girls who normally had to put up with very much less alluring types of stockings. I asked her why she wanted them and she blushed slightly and said that she had been asked out to dinner that night and thought she might receive a proposal. She was therefore anxious to look her best. So what could I do but issue her with a pair? The next morning, Ian Fife, one of the other two hopeful barristers, came and told me that he had become engaged the evening before — to Pauline. They were in due course married and I remember driving Ian from Bletchley to Clun in the borders of Wales for the wedding. We were very nearly late but just made it. Ian and Pauline were happy ever after. We occasionally visited them in their house by the river in Putney.

My time at Bletchley came to an end in the autumn of 1946 when I finally left the Army and settled down to a few weeks of study before the Bar exams. With the good fortune that has been my lot throughout my life, I managed to pass and was called to the Bar on 7 January 1947.

The ceremony of Call to the Bar on that occasion was not the splendid ceremony that it normally is. That was because during the war, one of Hitler's bombs had landed on the end of the great Middle Temple Hall which still lay in ruins. So there was no reception for parents and friends as had formerly been the practice and as, happily, happens nowadays. Instead we were lined up in one of the Benchers' rooms and the Treasurer of the Inn, Mr Justice Cassells, shook each of us by the hand and then invited us to sign the roll of barristers called to the Bar by Middle Temple. He then addressed us and all I can remember of his speech was that he said that now we were called to the Bar we could address any Court in England or in the many countries of the Commonwealth. It seemed odd that we were apparently precluded from speaking in the Court of Scotland. There followed a cup of tea and a bit of plum cake and then we went home. Mr Justice Cassells, always known as Jimmy Cassells, was an amusing man, though a bit inclined to play to the gallery when in Court. I was always grateful to him as in later years when our paths crossed he always recognised me and reminded me that he had called me and asked how I was getting on.

Having been called to the Bar, the next requirement was to find a set of chambers where an experienced practitioner could be persuaded to take me on as a pupil. It was a requirement that one should serve as a pupil for twelve months. My father had known before the war a young and promising junior who had said he would take me as a pupil, but that was all interrupted by the war and in the meantime, the promising junior had become a QC so he could no longer take pupils. Having no other introduction to anyone practising I decided, however, to go and see him. He was Melford Stevenson QC later to become a somewhat controversial High Court judge. When I was ushered in to see him in his chambers at 3 Hare Court, I remember thinking how young he looked. He had pale sandy coloured hair which for years and years never lost its youthful shine. As I had lost the hearing in my left ear during my time in Madagascar, I started by asking him if he thought I ought to abandon the attempt to make a career at the Bar on that account. He did not reply for quite a few seconds and then said, "The only person who sits on your deaf side is your opponent — you never want to listen to him, so carry on". As I later found out there are occasions when failure to hear what your opponent has said is no serious disadvantage. If one heard one would have, perhaps, thought he had a better case than he actually had. So, fortified by this cheering reply, I asked if there was any chance of becoming a pupil in his chambers. He then told me that he had only recently left the Army himself and was setting up chambers afresh as his previous set had been bombed and had, for one reason or another, lost all its former tenants. He told me that he had recruited two young men who had good academic records and who he thought would probably do quite well, though he was not sure. They were, he said, in the next room and I could go and take my pick. Well, I went into the next room and there they were. One was Leslie Scarman, later to become Lord Scarman, a Lord of Appeal and the other was Alan Orr, later Lord Justice Orr. Both of them were destined to have brilliant careers. I chose Alan Orr and started as his pupil a few days later. Alan was a Scot and had been to Edinburgh University, where he had got a first, before going to Balliol, Oxford, where once again he got a first class degree. He was very quiet and very shy and was not, as so many barristers are, a witty conversationalist, but when on rare occasions he did say something, it was profound and wise and, not infrequently, hilariously funny. He was a wonderful pupil master and I have always been grateful to him for introducing me in the kindliest manner to the ways of a barrister with a brief. He was too kind to tell me that I was a fool and had got something hopelessly wrong. I would spend a lot of time reading his papers and preparing draft opinions or draft pleadings for him and I would put them on his desk before he left in the evening, when he would take them home with him. The following morning he would come in and in his usual charming way would thank me very much for my effort and would say it had helped him greatly. He would then let me see the opinion or pleading that he was sending out. When I read what he had written, as often as not, it bore no relation whatever to my draft, and, indeed it was obvious that much that I had written was hopelessly wrong. But by reading his version I quickly learned. This method of teaching had one fortunate result from my point of view. In order to read what he had written it was, of course, necessary for me to be able to read his writing and his writing was the worst and most illegible that I have ever come across. Worse, by far, than any doctor's. But necessity made me master it and eventually I could interpret it well. At the end of my year's pupillage the question arose whether I should be kept on as a tenant. There were several other pupils who had arrived after me and had far better academic qualifications and I knew Melford Stevenson was determined to build up his chambers by taking in as tenants only those who not only showed promise as advocates but who were also of first class academic ability. I felt therefore that my chances of being taken on were slim. But then, once again, good fortune came to my rescue. When the members of chambers met to consider who should be taken in, the senior clerk, Ernest Gill, told Melford that the typists were finding it impossible to type Alan Orr's drafts without assistance and that the only person who seemed able to interpret them reasonably accurately was young Medd. So, I believe, it was for this reason alone that I was allowed to join the set of chambers which, before long, developed into one of the very best in the Temple. That was the best bit of good fortune that came my way all my life. From then on I was to work surrounded by many brilliant men. Raymond Phillips and Peter Webster, both later High Court judges, Conrad Dehn and Bill Forbes, enormously successful silks, the latter until his tragic death a distinguished member of the Law Commission, Wilfrid Bourne, later Permanent Secretary to the Lord Chancellor, Tom Bingham, now Master of the Rolls[1] and probably the most brilliant of them all, Denis Henry, Henry Brooke and Mark Potter, all of whom later became High Court judges, and many others. To have worked for a considerable part of one's life amongst such people is a rare privilege and a wonderful experience. Perhaps what was the most noticeable quality of this talented group of men was the fact that though their political opinions, which they were never afraid of expressing, ranged across the whole spectrum from far left to extreme right, nevertheless conversation was totally uninhibited and we all got on as friends and expressed our different views without ever a cross word passing between us. I felt then, as I have felt ever since, much as Osbert Sitwell must have felt when he wrote in 'Laughter in the Next Room'

> "What a feeling of relief it afforded to find people in whose presence any idea, whether original or conventional, whether accepted or rejected by the world, whether condemned and derided or praised, could be discussed on its own merits without anger. This though an atmosphere entirely new to me, after my upbringing, in the environment I had so far known, was one, withal in which I felt immediately at home."

St Augustine expressed the same idea, when in his Confessions, he said

> "It was the talk, the laughter, the courteous mutual deference, the common study of the masters of eloquence, the comradeship now grave, now gay, the differences that left no sting, as of a man differing with himself, the spice of disagreement which seasoned the monotony of consent.... Such tokens springing from the hearts of mutual friends ... supply the heat which welds souls together and makes one of many."

Surely this quality when found in a section of society or in the members of a set of chambers betokens an important element of a liberal civilisation.

Thus it was that my name was added to those already on the board outside 3 Hare Court indicating that I too was holding myself out as a barrister ready to accept instructions from any solicitor on behalf of any client brave enough to trust me.

---

[1] Appointed Lord Chief Justice in 1996.

With Jane and Rosie at Esklets, Cleveland. The wall on the right is all that remains of the farmhouse occupied by Thomas Medd in the late seventeenth cenury and by his descendants for many years after.

Drusilla and Jane in doorway of Westerdale Church in North Yorkshire where many generations of Medds were buried.

Louisa Medd, my grandmother, wife of Canon P. G. Medd.

Canon P. G. Medd, Fellow of University College, Oxford, later vicar of Barnes and North Cerney. My grandfather.

Louisa Medd in later life. She was the only one of my grandparents alive when I was born.

E. N. Medd, my father.

A. E. G. Medd, my mother. Daughter of
William and Bertha Parsons.

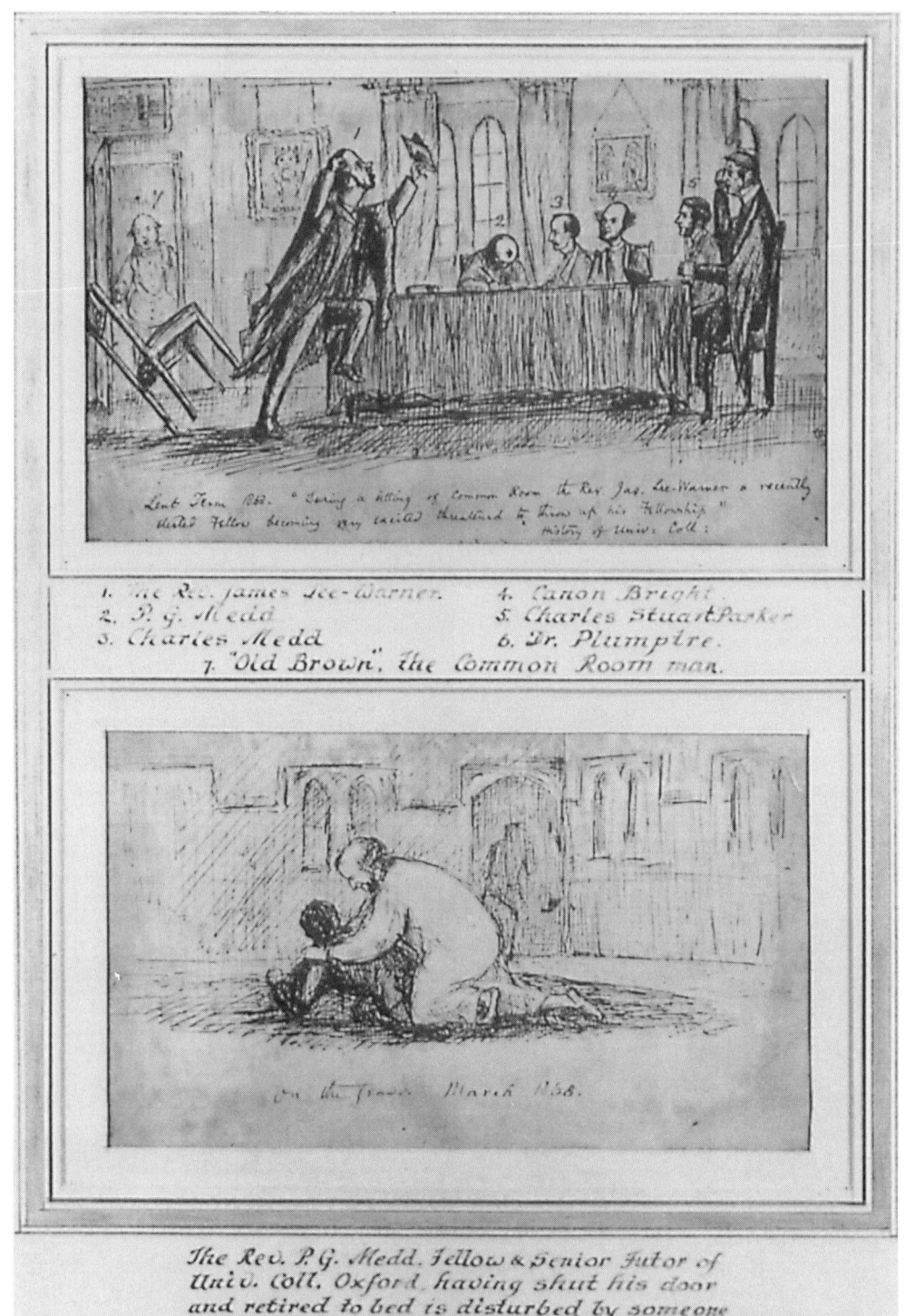

Above: Drawing of argument in University College, V.C.R., Lent term 1868. Below: Drawing of Rev. P. G. Medd chastising undergraduate who had tried to screw up his oak.

Rt Rev R. G. Parsons, Bishop of Southwark and Hereford, my uncle.

William Parsons, my grandfather.

Bertha Parsons (neé Best), my grandmother.

Emily Best, (neé de Horne) mother of Bertha Parsons.

My grandfather, Canon P. G. Medd.

With my father and Marjorie c.1923.

My mother and father, North Wales c.1930.

Father and Mother at Chertsey, c.1960.

Procession at Chertsey on coronation of George VI. The procession is passing Curfew House (on left of picture). I am standing to right of gate, my mother is behind me.

Grand Tour of Europe in 1939. Frank Tindal and myself on the dunes outside Calais. We returned to England next day.

Our car being lifted onto the ferry back to England, September 1939.

Somali syces with ponies at Larkhill, Kenya, 1942.

K.A.R. marching. Burma 1944.

At East African Artillery training camp at Larkhill, Kijube, Kenya 1942, Riding 'Georgina' at the camp by Indian mountain regiment when it was sent to the Middle East.

Kalewa on the Chindwin. The Longest Bailey Bridge ever built at that time.

At a gymnkhana at Ranchi and Assam where the division was rested after taking Kalewa.

Gunner captain, Burma 1944.

Ladies from Swindon Conservative Association at the wendy house in the garden of Deepwell Cottage.

Deepwell Cottage, Oakley, my first home, 1949, it cost £2,000.

At the end of the garden with Dru.

A family group at Chertsey 1962. Back row: Henry Medd, Father, Terence Dean, Robin Medd. Front Row: Mrs Henry Medd, Sarah Louisa Medd, Jeananne (Pookie) Medd, Mother, unknown, Mrs Terence Dean (Betty).

Sailing 'Ellsea' with George on Thames at Burcot, 1979.

CHAPTER SEVENTEEN

Early Struggles

When I first joined Chambers, I was allotted a room which I shared with Wilfrid Bourne. It was a very small room, originally intended to be occupied by a junior clerk or a typist and there, Wilfrid and I waited for briefs to come. They did not come fast. In fact, for a considerable period, they hardly came at all and we had to occupy our time with such activities as we could devise. Wilfrid was very clever and a bit temperamental. He had been to Eton and New College, Oxford and read, I think, classics. He used to come into our room and open 'The Times' at the page which had the crossword puzzle on it, he would then take a stop watch out of his pocket and put it on the table and commence doing the puzzle. If he could not complete it in ten minutes he became very cross and might not speak again for an hour or two. If he did it in five minutes he was in delightful good humour all day. At other intervals of unemployment, we played halma, a game which, as I quickly learned, required skill and forethought.

But these diversions did not improve my knowledge of the law or my skill as an advocate. Nor did they produce an income with which to support my wife and baby daughter. In order to overcome these shortcomings, I decided that the best way to learn about advocacy was to watch the best advocates at work in the courts and the best way to improve my knowledge of the law was to undertake to teach it to others. In this way, I would force myself to study deeply the subjects I undertook to teach so as to be able to lecture on them with a modicum of authority. To this end, for several years, I used to lecture two or three times a week in the evenings to accountant students and budding business men at the City of London College and the Institute of Chartered Accountants on subjects such as contract law, company law and bankruptcy.

For these lectures, I was paid £1.50 per hour and by working three evenings a week earned approximately £10 per week. This helped. I also used to go once a week to Acton where I gave free legal advice at the Citizens Advice Bureau. This was not altogether an altruistic exercise. It was good experience to be presented with a problem that was worrying some poor person and to have to try and give sensible advice that would help resolve it. The problems that affected the poor in those days were largely the same as the problems that beset them in all ages. Problems relating to housing, to divorce and to cruel and drunken husbands. These activities I found very useful though not remunerative.

The great advocate in our chambers was Melford Stevenson. He was at the height of his career and was engaged in many of the big and sensational cases of the times. It was a time when there were many bitter and contested divorces among the upper and moneyed classes. They usually got a lot of publicity in the gutter press as did claims for breach of promise of marriage which were still not uncommon. From time to time, there were sensational libel actions as well as more mundane civil cases. Melford appeared in many of these cases usually against one of the leading advocates of the day, such as Gerald Gardiner, Sir Milner Holland, Sir Valentine Holmes, Scott Henderson, Sir Andrew Clark, Gilbert Paul or Gilbert Beyfus. I learned a lot from watching these men. They were all fine advocates but their styles differed greatly.

The ways of the sensational jury advocates like Marshall Hall or Patrick Hastings were being replaced by more sober techniques. This was, I think, because fewer cases were tried with a jury and the juries in cases in which they were used were better educated and less receptive to the purple oratory practised earlier. They, like a judge sitting alone, were more likely to be persuaded by simple appeals to reason and logic. This trend has continued during all my time in the law. But when I followed Melford round the courts in those early days, there were still some who were not ashamed to use the ruses of an actor. Sir Andrew Clark was one such. He set great store on the initial impression he created. He would not arrive in court until a moment before the judge was due to enter. A little before he himself entered, his clerk, dressed in a black tail coat, would come in carrying his books and papers. These he would set out neatly on the bench where Sir Andrew was to sit. He would then unfold a small portable podium on which Sir Andrew would lean when he addressed the court, and place it on the bench with his master's notebook on it open at the appropriate page. He would then withdraw. All the motley collection of parties and witnesses and lawyers in court would be left wondering what would happen next. Then, a minute before the case was due to start, Sir Andrew and his clerk would enter in stately procession. Sir Andrew, who had a neatly clipped moustache was a tall man who had the upright bearing of the army officer that he had in his youth once been. It was a most impressive entry and he would have just taken his place when the judge would come in. Somehow the entry of the judge seemed something of an anticlimax. Sir Andrew always tried, and was often able, to dominate the proceedings by his impressive presence. Milner Holland, perhaps the best advocate of that period was very different. Quiet, and possessing a lovely voice, he was always the soul of courtesy and always had a perfectly prepared case and an impeccable understanding of the relevant law. He was the persuasive lawyer par excellence. They were all different but each in his own way was effective. Gerald Gardiner, later to be Lord Chancellor, struck me as having the qualities of a great surgeon. In his cross-examinations he seemed to be using a steely sharp scalpel to make the neat and perfect incisions in a witness who was perhaps being economical with the truth. Scott Henderson impressed with a rich and sonorous Scots accent while Gilbert Paul, who had once been a school master, achieved his ends in the manner of a terrier who yaps and worries a rat until eventually it is destroyed.

But the man who was most consistently opposed to Melford was Gilbert Beyfus, a Jew who had come to the Bar after the first world war in which he had managed to escape from a prison camp in Germany and, having reached the coast, crossed the Baltic in a small rowing boat single-handed. He had one odd physical characteristic. The lid of one of his eyes had a twitch which repeated itself every twenty seconds or so. He was a devastating cross-examiner of a very different stamp to Melford. While Melford seemed like the nimble gladiator armed with a rapier who went straight to the weak point of the witness' evidence and with a few deadly questions inflicted a deep and often mortal wound, Gilbert Beyfus on the other hand, who was much the bigger man, gave the impression of a solid giant bludgeoning his victim with a heavy club. Every minute point in the witness' evidence was examined in detail as question followed question and the twitching eyelids appeared somehow to add terror to the already frightening experience.

At the time I was trying to learn by watching men such as these, Leslie Scarman was still a junior, but his practice was growing rapidly tending to be concerned with commercial cases and Alan Orr, my former pupil master, was likewise steadily increasing in stature and in favour both with solicitors and clients. Both these men had a heavy load of paper work to be disposed of and I was fortunate in being able to do a good deal of devilling work for each of them. My first two years after joining the chambers were spent very largely in this way trying to prepare myself for the day which I hoped would not be too long delayed when I acquired a practice of my own. In those days, there was no Legal Aid and all litigants had to pay to be represented. The only exception to this was in the criminal courts where a prisoner was always entitled, for a small sum, to choose to represent him, any barrister who happened to be in court when his case was called on. The prisoner would be asked if he had with him £2. 4s. 6d. If he said "Yes", he was invited to choose any one of the barristers sitting in front of him in counsel's row. As he was in the dock behind the barristers, he was only able to see the backs of their wigs, so the choice was not normally made because of any sort of merit. The experienced criminal would usually choose the barrister whose wig, viewed from the back, seemed the oldest and dirtiest and therefore probably adorned the most experienced member of the Bar present. The advocate of his choice would go and see him in the cells and, after being given the fee (2/6d of which had to be paid to his clerk, who had played no part in the business and was not even present in court), would take instructions from the client and in due course conduct the case. A brief obtained in this way was known as a dock brief. A slightly more generous payment was made if the judge thought that the prisoner should be represented in which case he might grant a certificate for a poor prisoner's defence. This was normally, if my memory serves me right, worth £3. 4s. 6d. One did not get rich on such work but it was experience.

Once, when Pookie and I were at our cottage in Shropshire, I met a solicitor from Shrewsbury who told me that there was a shortage of good barristers in that part of the world and that if I joined the Oxford Circuit (the members of which were alone entitled to appear there), he would make sure work came my way. This seemed too good to be true so I promptly joined that circuit. I never heard from him again. But I never regretted joining that circuit. It was at the time much the smallest circuit having only something of the order of 200 members, so that one soon got to know one's colleagues well. They were a splendid lot of men, many of whom became lifelong friends. The other nice thing about the Oxford Circuit was that it served a part of England that was basically rural and to which I have always been attached. Such pleasant counties as Herefordshire, Worcestershire, Gloucestershire, Monmouth (in those days considered to be part of England though now served by the Welsh Circuit), Shropshire, Staffordshire, Oxfordshire and Berkshire were the places where the work was done. I attended the Assizes and Quarter Sessions in all these counties from time to time in my early years in search of dock briefs and I was often out of pocket because any fee earned rarely covered the cost of travelling to the court and the hotel bill if, as was usually the case, it was necessary to stay overnight.

I suppose every lawyer remembers the first case in which he appeared in his own right. The details of it are fixed in his memory in a way that later cases seldom are. I certainly remember my first case at Assizes. It was at Reading before Mr Justice Singleton. I was handed a brief by Michael Talbot a somewhat senior junior whom I later got to know well. He found himself engaged in two courts at once and it was clear he had to divest himself of one of his two briefs. I was required to defend a man charged with indecent assault of two small girls from Queen Anne's School, Caversham. They had been returning to school on a bus which crossed the Thames at Caversham Bridge and it was alleged that in the short time that the bus took to cross the bridge, each of them had been indecently assaulted by the defendant. The case did not come on until the early afternoon and I spent the morning sitting in court and watching the judge. I had been told that if you did not know the judge and his idiosyncrasies, it was a good idea to watch him trying a case before yours came on in order to get some idea of his characteristics. In the earlier case a very senior member of the circuit was appearing for the defendant and the judge, who had a sharpish tongue, was giving him a rough time. I quaked. If an experienced advocate was treated in that way what on earth would happen to me, inexperienced as I was? Happily, I had decided that it would be a great error to cross-examine the little girls on the basis that they were wrong in suggesting that what they described had not happened at all. Instead, I decided that my client's only hope was that it was a case of mistaken identity. They had only seen their molester for a very short period as the bus crossed the bridge and they might have been mistaken in saying that he was my client. They both agreed that that might have been the case. The judge could not have been more kind to the young and inexperienced barrister before him and the jury duly returned a verdict of 'Not Guilty'. After the verdict had been given, the foreman of the jury stood up and asked the judge if they might add a rider. The judge asked what it was. The foreman replied that they would like to have returned a verdict of 'Not Proven'. He was told by the judge that such a verdict was not possible in England though it was in Scotland. It was then that I began to realise that in many ways, the Scots arrange these things better than we do.

By 1949 I had begun to get a small practice and was being briefed from time to time to appear on circuit in criminal cases and found myself appearing in planning inquiries which had suddenly become something of a growth industry after the passing of the Town and Country Planning Act, 1947. But despite these welcome developments, I was still underemployed and it was then that an event occurred which opened up for me, interesting new horizons.

CHAPTER EIGHTEEN

I.C.C.U.S.

Before the war I had been interested in politics and had supported the Labour party who seemed to me to be the party that was most likely to be guided by the sort of liberal views that appealed to me. By 1949, however, we had had over 3 years of Socialist government and disastrous years they had been. In the terrible winter of 1947 there had been a fuel crisis which nearly brought the country to a standstill. Much of the legislation being passed through Parliament appeared to me to be doctrinaire and divisive. For these reasons I had, by 1949, become disillusioned with Labour for whom I had earlier hoped that I might one day stand as a candidate for Parliament. I would have liked to support the Liberals who had, in the days of Asquith and Grey, represented the sort of approach to politics that appealed to me. But the Liberals in 1949 did not look like a party that would ever regain power. It was when I was in this uncertain frame of mind that a meeting took place in the Temple presided over by Sir David Maxwell Fyfe, who had been Solicitor General in Churchill's interim government at the end of the war, and who was later to become Home Secretary and Lord Chancellor. The purpose of the meeting was to form a new society composed of members of the Bar who supported the Conservative party. In his speech, he explained that Conservative members of Parliament were busy both opposing the Government's measures for further nationalisation and also trying to develop a new approach to their own policy so that when another election came, they would be able to present to the country an inspiring manifesto which would show the way forward in the changed world that was emerging after the War. He said that the party needed lawyers sympathetic to the Conservative cause to help the parliamentary party in both these tasks. I remember his peroration which convinced me that the Tories of the future aimed to govern on principles which, it was hoped, would produce a single classless nation and which would do away with the two nations described by Disraeli. Here, I thought, was a politician seeking to put forward constructive proposals and asking for help from us. I decided to join this new society and to offer to help in any way I could. The society was to be called the Inns of Court Conservative and Unionist Society, ICCUS for short. Its first chairman was a man of whom until then I had never heard, Selwyn Lloyd, later to become Foreign Secretary, Chancellor of the Exchequer and Speaker of the House of Commons. Not long after I had joined this new society I learned that it wanted a secretary. I was invited to an interview with the Executive Committee, presided over by Selwyn Lloyd. There were three other interested candidates: Geoffrey Rippon, later to have a distinguished parliamentary career ending in his elevation to the House of Lords, Graeme Finlay who also entered Parliament and became Sir Graeme Finlay and finally my friend Wilfrid Bourne in my own Chambers, whose father had been a Deputy Speaker in the House of Commons and would in all probability have become Speaker had he not died prematurely. To my great surprise, I was chosen for the job. I soon found myself becoming more and more interested and immersed in politics.

It was not long before the society began to flourish. Most Conservative MPs who were barrsters joined, as did many barristers who were not members of the House of Commons but who were willing to give assistance. As a result it was usually possible to find someone who was an expert in any legal problem that arose upon which MPs required help. Selwyn Lloyd was to remain chairman of the society until the general election of 1951 when he became a member of the Government as Minister of State at the Foreign Office. During his term of office the society established itself as a body whose views on issues where law and politics overlapped were worthy of consideration. I remember early in its life I felt I should make contact with the Conservative Research Department which, under the protective eye of R A Butler, was engaged in research and study, the results of which would, it was hoped, help to enable a clear policy on all the major issues of the day to emerge in time for the election when it came. Its offices were in a fine house in Queen Anne's Gate and on my first visit there I was ushered into a small room in which three men were sitting. These were the researchers. They were Iaian Macleod, Reginald Maudling and Enoch Powell. At that time none of them were in Parliament, though I think that they were all hoping to be adopted for winnable Conservative seats in time for the next election. Each of them was a man of great intellectual ability and they did much under the guidance of R A Butler to lead the post-war Conservative party out of the doldrums in which it found itself after its defeat in 1945. They helped to persuade it to adopt policies suited to the conditions of the nineteen fifties. During this period ICCUS played a useful part but it was after the general election of 1951 that it really came into its own. This was largely due to the work and energy of the new chairman, J E S Simon QC. Jack Simon had just been elected for Middlesborough having defeated a sitting Labour member. He practised largely at the divorce bar but his interests covered every part of the law and his capacity for work was prodigious. The first issue to which he directed his energy was one that a committee of the society had for some time been studying, but had so far not come up with any clear or useful views. The problem was an old one, namely, how could the ordinary citizen be protected from wrong or arbitrary decisions by civil servants which adversely affected him, his property rights or his ability to earn a living. The problem had been worrying lawyers for some time and had, it was thought, worsened considerably with the introduction of the mass of legislation by which the Labour Government implemented its policies of social improvement and nationalisation. It came to a head in a case that concerned land at Crichel Down in Dorset, which had, shortly before the war, been compulsorily acquired by the Air Ministry in order to make a bombing range. After the war, when it was no longer required for that purpose the land was transferred to the Ministry of Agriculture and was managed by the Agricultural Land Commission which decided that the land should be operated as a state owned farm. In 1952 Commander Marten whose forebears had owned the land before it was taken by the government applied to have the land resold to him. The Commission advised the

Minister of Agriculture that the land should continue to be operated as a state owned farm and not returned to Commander Marten. The minister accepted this advice and there the matter would have rested had Commander Marten not been a man of remarkable determination. Eventually through sustained agitation he managed to secure an independent public inquiry. This inquiry was presided over by Sir Andrew Clarke and Melford appeared for Commander Marten. Its conclusions were dramatic and resulted in the resignation from the government of the Minister of Agriculture.

This is not the place to go into the law as it was then thought to be. Suffice to say that as a result of the Crichel Down inquiry it was made abundantly clear that where decisions which affected a citizen's rights to property depended on a ministerial decision which he was authorised by statute to take and to exercise his discretion as to how he decided it, it was not normally possible for the courts to go behind the decision to ensure that the minister had not, for example, based his decision on inaccurate information. In the Crichel Down case the findings of the inquiry made it clear that the minister had in that case based his decision on inaccurate information and that he had not taken into consideration in reaching his decision, facts which he should have considered. Had not Commander Marten succeeded in getting the matter ventilated in full before the public inquiry neither he nor anyone else would ever have known of the background facts which vitiated the decision. In other words the case showed that the law was often unable to protect the citizen from decisions by civil servants which affected his rights and which were arbitrary or based on wrong foundations.

A similar problem which had also been worrying lawyers for some time arose out of a development that had taken place over the years on the way that differences between a citizen and a public authority were settled. It was a development which had begun in the last century and gathered momentum with the advent of the Labour Government in 1945. The rapid emergence of the welfare state resulted in a vastly increased interference by the government in the affairs of the citizen. Disputes often arose between a citizen and a public body responsible for administering a particular aspect of policy. The resolution of these disputes was delegated by legislation to statutory tribunals. These tribunals were often composed of members appointed by the relevant minister himself, sometimes from civil servants in the ministry. Furthermore, there was, generally speaking, no requirement that the tribunals should give reasons for their decisions. It is not surprising that many people who came before these tribunals in these circumstances felt when the case went against them that they had not received justice. This feeling would be aggravated when they learned, as was usually the case, that there was no appeal against the tribunal's decision and no prospect of having the matter reviewed by the courts. It was the grievances revealed by these two methods of obtaining, from public authorities, decisions on a citizen's rights that were the subject matter of the committee of ICCUS. The chairman of the committee was Sir Patrick Spens, a former Chief Justice in India, but the moving spirit was Jack Simon. I was the secretary. Its membership included no less than eight MPs who were also barristers.

The result of the committee's labours was a report which was published as a pamphlet 'The Rule of Law' in which the nature of the problems was examined in some detail and the way they were dealt with in other countries, in particular France and the USA, where the citizens' rights were better protected was reviewed. It made a number of recommendations including a suggestion that there should be set up a new Division of the High Court to be called the Administrative Division.

Before the pamphlet was finally published I, myself, had an opportunity of airing the problems with which it was grappling. I had in 1953 been adopted as the Conservative candidate for the Swindon constituency. I attended the party conference at Blackpool in the autumn of 1954 and proposed a motion that had been set down by the constituency and which raised all these issues which were very much in the public eye at the time. It was an alarming experience addressing the audience of some 3000 people in the vast conference hall, but I remember well the thrill of realising that what I was saying was getting a sympathetic response. Lord Kilmuir the Lord Chancellor, formerly Sir David Maxwell Fyfe, responded on behalf of the Government and though he made no promises he made it clear that he at least understood the problems and the Government would look into them.

When finally it was published the pamphlet was well received by the press and obtained a number of good reviews. More important, notice was taken of it in 'high places' because, not long after its publication and partly, I think, as a result of its publication, a committee was set up under the chairmanship of Sir Oliver Franks (as he then was) to consider one of these questions. Jack Simon, Charles Fletcher-Cooke and I gave evidence to the committee and received a courteous hearing and were asked penetrating questions by the chairman and by Sir Hubert Parker, a judge who had earlier been the Treasury Devil, and was later to become Lord Chief Justice.

The Franks Committee when it reported made a number of important recommendations which led in due course to the passing of the Tribunal and Inquiries Act, 1971, and to the setting up of the Council of Tribunals. The effect of these two changes has been to ensure that the procedure adopted by the multifarious tribunals that now exist is fair and accords with the rules of natural justice, and to ensure that tribunals give adequate reasons for their decisions. Furthermore appeals on questions of law can normally now be brought to the High Court from the decisions of the various tribunals.

The other problem that was discussed in *The Rule of Law,* the control of decisions of administrators which affected a citizen's rights in cases where resort to a tribunal was not available, was not tackled by the Franks Committee as it was not asked in its terms of reference to consider it. It had to wait until the courts themselves managed in the next quarter of a century to develop the procedure of judicial review and the Office of the Ombudsman was established. Had our suggestion of an administrative division of the High Court been accepted it might not have been necessary to wait so long before these valuable reforms came about.

In the mid fifties public opinion was very divided on another important issue — whether or not capital punishment for murder should be abolished. Those in favour of its abolition regarded the opposition as determined to maintain a barbaric institution which achieves nothing. Those in favour of death as the mandatory penalty for murder were confident that it was a deterrent and that if it was abolished murders would become more frequent and professional criminals would go about their business armed so that, if caught, they could kill the witnesses who might well be policemen. Opinion polls showed that the country was split down the middle on this question. We, in ICCUS, felt that this too was an issue upon which the opinion of lawyers might help. Many of us had been briefed in murder trials and had some experience which we considered might be of value. Again we assembled a committee of barristers several of whom were MPs. We were, perhaps surprisingly, in view of the division in the country as a whole, absolutely unanimous in our views. First our experience told us that the vast majority of all murders committed in England were not carefully pre-planned. Far and away the majority of murders that came before the courts arose as a result of domestic tension reaching for one reason or another a point where one party could stand it no longer and gave way to violent emotion and killed. We felt that that type of murderer was unlikely to be deterred by the fact that the penalty was death. It seemed to us that the Scots, as is so often the case, had managed to develop their law more satisfactorily than we had south of the border. In Scotland a person who had killed someone would not be guilty of murder but only of manslaughter if he could satisfy the jury that at the time of the killing he was suffering from a mental condition described as diminished responsibility. This defence recognised the fact that because of their mental condition some people find it more difficult, if not impossible, to resist doing a wrongful act, even if they know that what they are doing is wrong, than do other more normal people. It seemed to us that many of the domestic murders of which we had had experience had probably been committed by people who had suffered from this sort of mental condition. We therefore recommended that the defence of diminished responsibility should become a part of the law of England as it already was of the law of Scotland.

However, this did not deal with the question of whether the death penalty should be abolished. On this question too, the committee was unanimous. We felt that the death penalty should be abolished for the majority of offences of murder, but that it should be retained for the worst types of case. We put into this category of the worst types of murders those committed by people using firearms, murders of policemen in the execution of their duty or murders of prison warders. We did not include in this category, as perhaps we should have done, murders by poisoning. These recommendations we incorporated in a pamphlet entitled 'Murder' which was provided with a garish red cover. Before the pamphlet had been written it had become clear that there would be a debate in the House of Commons on the issue and that it would be a free vote. It was, therefore, a matter of some urgency that the pamphlet should be produced quickly if it was to have any effect on MPs before they voted. The task of writing the pamphlet was given to me and I spent all of one Christmas vacation writing it. The weather during that vacation was perfect but because of the urgent need to have the report published I was not able to enjoy those glorious days. The debate in the House of Commons took place very shortly after we had published the pamphlet and I went along and listened to it. Imagine my surprise when looking down from the gallery onto the House, which was very full, I saw that nearly every member on both sides of the House had a copy of our bright red pamphlet. It was a good debate and, the Whips not being out, the division of opinions cut across normal party lines. The result showed that the House of Commons was almost equally divided on the issue. The outcome was that in 1957 the Homicide Act was passed which abolished capital punishment for all cases except for a very limited category which were known as capital murders being those that were regarded as particularly bad, such as murders of policemen, prison warders and murders committed by shooting or poisoning.

This limited application of the death penalty did not remain in force for very long and it was finally abolished some eight years later by the Murder (Abolition of Death Penalty) Act, 1965. The Homicide Act proved to be unsatisfactory in a number of ways. It raised difficult legal problems and a number of cases arose where two or more offenders had been acting together and the victim was undoubtedly shot but when it came to the trial each of the accused said that he had not fired the shot and put the blame on the other accused. It was often impossible for the jury to decide which was guilty of capital murder even though there was no doubt that one or other of the accused was.

Apart from the introduction of two categories of murder the Act introduced the defence of diminished responsibility and also introduced a reform of the law relating to provocation that was long overdue. Up to then a defendant who could establish that he had been provoked by an act of the person he had killed might be found not guilty of murder but guilty only of manslaughter which did not carry the death penalty. But it had been held that the defence was not available to a defendant who claimed to have been provoked by words alone. This could be manifestly unjust as there are cases where what a person says can be more provocative than any act. The Homicide Act corrected this and the defence of provocation can now be relied on in cases where the provocation is something said as well as where the provocation is some act.

So once again it was I think true to say that our efforts had been of some effect and had helped those in Parliament make up their minds on a difficult issue in a logical way. I remember some years later when the provisions of the Act which created the offence of capital murder had been repealed partly as a result of the public criticism of the working of the Act, I was talking to Derek Walker Smith and suggested that we had made a mistake in recommending as we did. He pooh-poohed the suggestion saying that he thought the Act had been in the best Tory tradition of pragmatic legislation. It had provided a reasonable solution which lasted while public opinion had gradually developed to the point where it was clear that a majority of the House of Commons favoured the total abolition of the death sentence for murder.

In 1958 ICCUS published another pamphlet, this time on the legal position of trade unions that was in the view of many people the cause of much of the difficulties that were afflicting the country at the time. We called it 'A Giant's Strength' which was an expression Shakespeare had put into the mouth of Isabella in 'Measure for Measure' when she said:

> "O it is excellent
> To have a giant's strength; but it is tyrannous
> to use it as a giant."

The title succinctly described the excessive power that trade unions had acquired over the previous fifty years and the way in which they had come to use it. The country had for several years been subjected to a succession of crippling strikes in many of its major industries and services. The ordinary citizen was at regular intervals put to great inconvenience by strikes in the nationalised industries such as the railways or the buses or other public services and industry was continually being impeded by strikes of workmen. The great muscle possessed by the unions enabled them to exert extreme pressure on employers and on the Government which often resulted in the Government or the employers giving in to excessive and inflationary wage demands. Furthermore the fact that there was little that could be done to control the way that the unions dealt with their members gave rise to numerous cases where individual workmen suffered grievous injustice as a result, for example, of the union operating a closed shop policy. A closed shop policy was one which insisted that all workmen in a particular trade or calling must belong to a particular union. The result of this was that if a workman did not wish to join the union and refused to do so or the union refused to accept him as a member he could not work in the trade concerned and that might well mean that he was unable to obtain work if that was the only trade he knew. The power that had been acquired by the unions had come about as a result of their historical development. At the end of the nineteenth and in the early years of the twentieth century their activities were severely restricted by a series of court decisions ending in the famous decision of the House of Lords in 1901 in the Taff Vale case. This led to a strong reaction and the passing of the Trades Disputes Act, 1906, by which the pendulum was made to swing to the opposite extreme. The effect of the Act was to put the unions in a privileged position under the law in that the courts were no longer entitled to entertain any action against a union or its members or officials in respect of any wrong alleged to have been committed by or on behalf of the union. This immunity extended to all wrongs whether or not they were committed in contemplation or furtherance of a trade dispute. There were other developments which had by the nineteen fifties produced the result that trade unions had in effect been placed in a position where they were above the law which applied to other citizens.

The committee of ICCUS that studied these problems and which finally produced 'A Giant's Strength' was not hostile to the unions. It realised only too well that the ordinary worker, unless able to combine with his fellow workers, was in an inferior bargaining position to his employer. It followed that in order to produce a fair balance as between employer and employee workers should be allowed to form trade unions to represent and protect their interests. What was needed, however, was a legal structure which enabled the unions to carry out their essential task in a way that was fair both to their members and to the public. It was also necessary to ensure that the members of a union were protected against high handed action by union officials.

It was in an effort to achieve this balance that we made a number of recommendations relating to the right to strike, the registration of unions, model rules for unions, the settlement of inter-union disputes and the operation of restrictive practices by workers.

The pamphlet was eventually published in June 1958, and once again I spent a large part of my vacations writing the pamphlet and trying to put into words the product of the committee's cogitations. We had hoped that, as had happened with our earlier pamphlets, it would be published by the Conservative Political Centre but Iaian Macleod who was at the time Minister of Labour in the Conservative Government vetoed this suggestion. He thought, I suspect, that it would be too explosive at a time when the Conservative Government was wooing the unions in the hope that they could be made to co-operate with the Government. Fortunately, Christopher Johnson, who was MP for Carlisle, undertook the job and it was published under the umbrella of his publishing company. It was well received, but the Government at that stage took no steps to reform trade union law and the unsatisfactory position continued until 1974 when the first of the various Acts of Parliament was passed which now regulate the position in a way that largely accords with the views we then expressed. When, earlier, Barbara Castle was Minister of Labour in the Labour Government, she tried to introduce a Bill on similar lines but found it impossible to convince the more extreme members of her party of the need for such reform.

All these excursions into law reform took place many years ago and long before anything was actually done to put right the defects to which we tried to draw attention, but an incident which occurred in the nineteen seventies brought home to me the simple fact that no worthwhile reform can be achieved overnight and that it often takes many years for the great British public, through its representatives in the House of Commons, to accept the need for it.

It so happened that some sixteen years after 'A Giant's Strength' had been published I was appearing in a case in the House of Lords in which Jack Simon, who had by then become one of the Law Lords as Lord Simon of Glaisdale, was one of the judges. It was the day on which the trade union and Labour Relations Act, 1974, had been given a second reading in the House of Commons. I had finished my final speech and was leaving the court room when a flunkey in a tailcoat and white tie came up to me and handed me a note. I thought, "Oh heavens, I am going to be asked to go back and explain some point I have not made plain to their Lordships". When I read the note it was from Lord Simon and was concise. It was in these terms:

Question What is the definition of a Tory reactionary?

Answer A person who suggests a much needed reform nearly twenty years before it becomes law.

CHAPTER NINETEEN

Hopeful Politician

My experience as secretary of ICCUS brought me into contact with many Conservative politicians of the period shortly after the war. Jack Simon was undoubtedly the one who made the greatest impression on me, but there were many others, Derek Walker-Smith, Charles Fletcher-Cooke, Harry Hylton-Foster, Lionel Heald, who made me realise that there were, at that time, many men in the House of Commons who were not just party hacks but were men with ideals who were doing a worthwhile job in Parliament. The work I was doing for ICCUS which I have tried to describe, I found fascinating and I reckoned that there was a future for someone who wanted to try in a small way, to reform some of the aspects of English law and practice which gave rise to injustice or which were in some other way, unsatisfactory in the changing world into which we were moving after the end of the war. I therefore decided to try and get into the House of Commons. I determined to model myself on Edward Grey, the great Liberal Foreign Secretary and lieutenant of Asquith. He seemed to me to be the model statesman, devoid of personal ambition and motivated solely by his high sense of duty

So it was that I asked to be included in the list of potential candidates that was kept at the Conservative Central Office for the information of any local constituency party that might need to select a new candidate to fight an election. After an interview with the vice chairman of the party, I found myself on the list of approved candidates and waited for something to happen. I did not have to wait for long as I soon learned that the Swindon constituency were looking for a candidate. Swindon was then a borough constituency which at the general election in 1951 had returned a popular Labour member with a majority of some 6,000. With a majority of that size, it was obviously a seat which it would be difficult for a Conservative to win unless there were a wholly unexpected and massive swing in favour of the Conservative Government that was then in power. I did not think that that was likely to occur, but as I had had no experience of electioneering and as a general election would be likely to be held within a year or two, I decided to let my name go forward so that, if I did happen to be chosen, I would gain valuable experience and then be better equipped to be considered for a winnable seat after the general election. It turned out that there were only two other people interested in fighting Swindon and the three of us in due course, appeared before the local selection committee and, greatly to my surprise, I was chosen. Shortly afterwards, on 24 July 1953, I was adopted by a full meeting of the whole constituency party.

Since the middle of the nineteenth century when Isambard Brunel had built the Great Western Railway, Swindon was the centre at which the steam locomotives used on that line were built and repaired. The men who worked in the loco sheds lived, for the most part, in the streets of small terraced houses surrounding the works. They were old fashioned workers, very proud of the GWR rolling stock. Very often when I called on them canvassing, they would take me into their living room and proudly show me a model which they had themselves made, of one of the locomotives that had been built at Swindon, the 'King George V' and the 'Caerphilly Castle' were two of the favourites. The models were usually displayed on the mantelpiece and were often masterpieces of accurate reproduction. Before the Second World War, there had for many years been a strong Liberal vote in the town, but by the time I got to know it, the railwaymen and their families tended to vote Labour. There was, nevertheless, a substantial minority that supported the Tories. The other main employers in the town at that time were Vickers who produced parts for the aeroplane industry, Plesseys, electrical engineers and Garrards who manufactured parts for gramophones. These industries were relative newcomers to the town and many of their employees lived in the huge new housing estates that were being built on the fringes of the old town as part of the Government's policy of expanding a number of towns away from London which would, it was hoped, encourage industry to migrate from the metropolis to the country.

In order to get myself known as quickly as possible, I decided to spend most of the long vacation visiting the local branches of the Conservative party and calling at the homes of as many voters as possible. I set myself the task of calling at every house in the constituency before the general election which was likely to be in 1955 or 1956. This was an ambitious target which in the event, I did not quite achieve. I did, however, visit the homes of some 75% of the electorate and by the time the election came in May 1955, I had made myself reasonably well known. It was an experience that I have never regretted. I found that, at the vast majority of houses, I was courteously received and usually the occupants were prepared to discuss politics and the problems that were then exercising them. Occasionally, I was told that the whole household voted Labour and had always done and so there was no point in me wasting my time on them. Once or twice, as soon as I had said who I was, I had the door slammed in my face, but this was rare. I did not always come away feeling that I knew which way they would vote when the time came. But I did come away feeling that I knew with what it was that they were preoccupied in their daily lives. It was a good education for me.

Visiting was not, of course, my only activity. Looking through my diary for those years, I find that hardly a week passed in which I did not attend some function in the town. Often I was required to make a speech and sometimes what I had said was reported in the local press. The result of all this activity was that when, in May 1955, the general election was announced, I felt that I had at least made my mark in the constituency. The sitting Labour member had sometime before, indicated that he intended to retire and would not stand again and Francis Noel-Baker was chosen to succeed him. Francis was not a typical Labour candidate. He was the son of Philip Noel-Baker, a clever and high minded man who had been Secretary of State for Commonwealth Relations and Minister of Fuel and Power in Attlee's government. Francis was well off and it was said that he owned a Greek island in the Aegean which he visited from time to time and ruled with the firmness of a benevolent aristocrat. I got on well with him and he was a fair and generous opponent so we never, as sometimes happens, sank into crude personal attacks on each other. When the election was announced, he was not all that well known in the constituency and I felt that with reasonable luck, I should be able to reduce considerably the Labour majority and might, just possibly be able to win the seat.

The date chosen for the election was Thursday 26 May, which happened to be my birthday. That seemed to me to augur well for my success. So we plunged into the campaign with enthusiasm and vigour. At that time, the television had not become the powerful influence in the battle for votes that in subsequent elections it was to be. People still came to meetings and listened to the speakers and we were fortunate at Swindon that meetings were usually well attended and often lively. Meetings were arranged for most of the weekdays in the three weeks before the election, sometimes two or even three meetings an evening. In addition, I held open air meetings at strategic points such as at the gates of the various factories as the workers were arriving or leaving.

I was anxious that the visiting speakers should be good and I applied to Conservative Headquarters for one or two cabinet ministers to come but I was told that, as Swindon was not considered to be a marginal seat, that is one in which the Tory candidate has a good chance of displacing a sitting Labour member, it was not possible to spare a minister to speak there. I therefore decided to ask some of the friends I had made during my time as secretary of ICCUS and was fortunate in that they responded splendidly with the result that, at almost every meeting, I was supported by a first class and experienced speaker. Three of them, I particularly remember. Airey Neave had made a name for himself by escaping from Colditz, the notorious German prison camp, during the war. He had written a best-seller about his experiences and was regarded as a war hero. In 1953 he had won a by-election and become MP for Abingdon. He made quite a stirring speech which went down very well with the Swindonians. Another person who had recently become a member was a young lady who had impressed me both by her charm and her vigorous good sense. She was called Margaret Thatcher. At that time, she had not got into Parliament and it would not be true if I said that I saw in her a future Prime Minister, but I felt sure that she could make a good fighting speech. In this, I was proved right. She came to Swindon and spoke to a meeting of ladies in the Town Hall. She was terrific and I well remember the enthusiasm with which she was applauded by that gathering of housewives.

The third speaker who came to help me out was Melford Stevenson, the head of my chambers. He was not without political experience having fought the Malden constituency in the 1945 election where he had been beaten by Tom Driberg, a very left wing Socialist. It was traditional in Swindon that, on the last Saturday before the day of the election, there should be a big meeting in the Regal Cinema, a large cinema just opposite the entrance to the railway workshops. I had been told that it was often a very rowdy meeting and I thought Melford would be a good person to have on such an occasion. When we arrived, we found that the theatre was packed and a considerable number of people were standing at the back. I remember as he came onto the platform looking at the sea of faces in the auditorium and in the gallery at the far end of the cinema. In the middle of the front row of the gallery was the secretary of the local Communist party, a gentleman I had met several times before. He was plainly the leader of a team of hecklers.

As soon as Melford started to speak, the heckling began and insults came thick and fast from the gallery and other parts of the theatre. But they did not know their man. Melford had a wonderful gift of repartee and there was nothing he enjoyed more than dealing with interrupters. His strong line was a devastating form of sarcasm. After a few minutes when two or three of the hecklers had been dealt with effectively to the amusement of the bulk of the audience, absolute calm was established and when my turn to speak came, I was listened to with what appeared to be respectful attention.

During the campaign, Pookie and I stayed with the chairman of the association, Sir Geoffrey Tritton, at his fine house at Stanton Fitzwarren a village a few miles out of Swindon. He and his wife were wonderful hosts and could not have been more kind. When we got back exhausted after a long day of canvassing and meetings, he would pour me a large whisky and soda and we would discuss the day's events and plan our tactics for the morrow. He had himself stood as the Tory candidate at the previous election in 1951 and he knew the constituency well and its idiosyncrasies, so his wise advice and cheerful encouragement often saved me from making stupid mistakes and kept my spirits high.

The last few days before polling day were spoiled by fairly continuous rain. There can be few activities that are more depressing or more likely to lower one's morale than canvassing in the pouring rain. I remember on one such day when I was returning in the evening to the campaign headquarters, I came into the square in front of the Town Hall. It was deserted except for two people, one of whom was talking into a loud speaker while the other held an umbrella over him. Not a soul was listening to the orator who was none other than my opponent, Francis Noel-Baker. He looked as miserable as I felt and I thought perhaps we would both feel better if we went into the local pub and had a drink together. But we could not do things like that while an election was on.

Eventually, polling day arrived and there was nothing more we could do but wait and see how the voters would speak. After a good dinner with the Trittons, we went to the Town Hall where the counting of the votes had begun. There is something peculiarly exciting in the atmosphere while this is taking place and one watches the voting papers being counted, those for each candidate being grouped together and wrapped in bundles of 100. Each bundle is then put with the other bundles for that candidate on a long table. So each candidate has a line of bundles, and at any moment, it is easy to see which candidate has, up to that moment, collected the most counted votes. When we arrived at the count, the bundles for 'Medd' made a line longer than that for 'Noel-Baker' and I was suitably cheered until I realised that the bundles that had, up to that moment been counted, had come from the part of the town which was predominantly Tory and that the votes from the more distant parts, which were likely to be mostly Labour, had not yet reached the Town Hall. As the evening wore on, my line of bundles was gradually overtaken by those of Noel-Baker and shortly after midnight, the count was completed and showed that Noel-Baker had won by some 3,000 votes.

When once the result was declared, the candidates were required to go onto the small balcony of the Town Hall which overlooked the square so that the people in the square could hear the results. Francis Noel-Baker led the way onto the balcony which was very narrow and as I came onto it behind him, I was surprised, as it was raining hard, to see that the square was full of people whose upturned faces were lit up by the street lights. As I stepped out, there was a crashing noise and we were both suddenly soaked in water. It was as if a bucket of water had been thrown over us. The upturned faces burst into laughter. At first, I thought there had been a practical joke, but soon it became clear that the heavy rain had proved too much for the guttering on the roof and a piece of it had given way and released the deluge onto our heads. I wondered if, perhaps, it was the Almighty's way of showing what he thought of parliamentary candidates.

The election over, I returned to my practice in London and continued with my normal life.

CHAPTER TWENTY

County Council and Failed Politician

In 1562, the lawyers of the Middle Temple decided to build a new hall in which they could lunch and dine and hold the moots and readings by which the students acquired a knowledge of the law and were introduced to the art of advocacy. The new hall took the place of an old building, on the site of what is now Pump Court, which had originally belonged to the Military Knights Templar. This old building had been the centre of the communal life of the Inn. The Treasurer of the Inn when the new building was commenced was Edmund Plowden, a member of an old Catholic family that lived, and indeed still lives, at Plowden Hall under the west slopes of the Long Mynd in that part of Shropshire where I had been stationed early in the war. Because of his religious beliefs, he received no preferment despite his acknowledged excellence as a lawyer. Equally because of the universally high regard in which he was held, he never suffered the persecution often meted out to Catholics during the reign of the first Queen Elizabeth. For these reasons, he was able to manage and supervise the building of the hall and his period as Treasurer of the Inn was extended from the usual one year to six years. The hall was completed in 1572. With its magnificent double hammerbeam roof and oak panelled walls, it is one of the finest buildings of the period. The walls are now adorned with the coats of arms of the Inn's Readers and Treasurers. At the west end of the hall, behind the High Table, are a number of portraits of members of the Royal Family who were Benchers of the Inn. Of these, the portrait of Charles I by Van Dyck in the centre of the wall is the most impressive.

When I was working in London and not engaged in a case outside London, I usually lunched in this great building where one could get a light lunch cheaply and quickly. I always sat at the same table at the south western end of the hall where many of my friends lunched regularly. On my return from Swindon after the election, I was cross-examined vigorously by my companions about the campaign and how I had tackled it. Several of them were planning, if possible, to make a career in politics and hoping soon to find a constituency which they could fight. Now that nearly forty years have passed since that election, it is not, perhaps, without interest to note who some of those enthusiastic young men were. First there was Geoffrey Howe, later to become successively Solicitor General, Chancellor of the Exchequer, Foreign Secretary and deputy Prime Minister in successive Conservative administrations. At that time, he was busily engaged with his friends from Cambridge days in developing the Bow Group and its periodical *Crossbow* which discussed and proposed a wide variety of progressive ideas designed to appeal to the younger generation of Tories then making their presence felt. Then there was Patrick Jenkins who was to become Local Government Minister in Margaret Thatcher's government and Patrick Mayhew who, having held the posts of Solicitor General and Attorney General, became Secretary of State for Northern Ireland in John Major's government. Not all my friends, however, were Tories. Dick Taverne was then a Labour candidate who later became an MP and ultimately changed to the Liberal Democrats. There have been a number of staunch Liberals who lunched at that table. Among them was Arthur Mildon, later a Circuit judge, who, like me, never succeeded in being chosen to fight a winnable seat. Another was Stephen Tumim[1] who also became a Circuit judge before being appointed Chief Commissioner for Prisons in which position he has succeeded in bringing to the public's attention conditions that prevailed in many of our older prisons. As a result of his numerous reports on conditions in particular prisons, he has initiated improvements that should make them institutions that are less of a disgrace to a civilised country.

During the years that followed the 1955 general election I, along with many of my friends in ICCUS and those who lunched at my table, tried to get ourselves adopted for safe seats. Most of them succeeded but Arthur Mildon and I failed. I was once told that before he was eventually adopted for a winnable Conservative seat, Enoch Powell had been rejected by 27 other constituencies and that it was thought that that was a record. Well, if it was, it was a record which I managed to beat. By the time that I gave up trying I had been considered and rejected by some 29 constituencies. Faced with such a disastrous record, I cannot help but ask myself the question, why did this happen? Although there were a number of occasions when I think it can fairly be said that I had bad luck, nevertheless, the basic reason for my failure was the fact that for some reason I am constitutionally incapable of selling myself to an audience. If I am given the task of putting a case for someone else, or if I am required to explain a political idea or make a political speech, I can usually hold my audience's attention and keep them interested but somehow when I tried to persuade a selection committee that I was just the man to represent them in Parliament, I failed dismally. Though I must accept that this was the main reason for my failure, there were, I think, two other factors operating at that time which tended to reduce my chances. First there was a noticeable tendency amongst the activists on the local selection committees to prefer, or even to demand, a local candidate. There was a widespread feeling that there were too many 'carpet baggers' in Parliament. The second factor which was also making itself felt at that time was a feeling that there were too many lawyers in Parliament. Lawyers in the eyes of many constituency members were insincere and would be quite as ready to argue a case in which they did not believe if it suited their interests to do so. I do not believe that this is a fair view of lawyers. But it was a view that certainly existed then and continues to be the opinion held by many laymen even now. It is a view which fails to take account of the fact that when a barrister is exercising his profession, his first duty is to his client and that, therefore, if his client's interest required that a case be put on his behalf then it is his duty to put that case, even though it may be a case that the barrister himself does not find attractive. When, however, a barrister who is a Member of Parliament speaks in that capacity, the position is different.

---

[1] Subsequently appointed Principal of St Edmund Hall and also knighted (1996).

He must put his own genuine views. In my experience, lawyer politicians are every bit as sincere in the opinion they express as are non lawyers — sometimes more so.

When the Conservatives won the 1951 election and Churchill formed his post war government, Walter Monckton, who had recently been elected for the Bristol West Constituency, became Minister of Labour. Later, in December 1955, when Anthony Eden had become Prime Minister, he was made Minister of Defence which resulted in him being in that position during the run up to the Suez crisis in 1956. For a short period, he was Paymaster General and shortly thereafter, he became chairman of the Midland Bank and left politics. This meant that a new candidate had to be found for the Bristol West constituency. It was a safe Conservative seat and had many attractions. The great Edmund Burke had sat for Bristol and before Walter Monckton, its member had been Oliver Stanley who had, sadly, died suddenly just as he appeared about to be offered one or other of the senior cabinet posts in the new government. I was fortunate and after a preliminary interview with a small selection committee, was put on a short list of three who were to appear before the full executive council. Of the two other competitors, one was an elderly man who had been in local government in Bristol and who I discovered had, during the war in Italy, been in the same regiment of gunners as my dear friend Raymond Phillips. The other was a good looking unmarried young man who was the son of a Bristol surgeon. He had, I think, been an active Young Conservative in the constituency. I was fortunate, I discovered later, in that Walter Monckton, who I had met once or twice when our paths crossed at the Bar, had very kindly written a letter to the chairman of the association strongly commending me. When I entered the room in which the committee, which as far as I can remember consisted of about twenty five people, were sitting, I noticed that in the front row were five or six pretty young girls and a few young men, all of whom were obviously members of the Young Conservatives. I was never to see another selection committee at which there was such a high proportion of Young Conservatives. My speech went well, but it was clear to me as I spoke, that I was cutting no ice with the young people in the front row. Eventually, the chairman told us that the handsome young man had been chosen. In due course, he was elected to Parliament where he sat for several years for Bristol West and finally retired after receiving a knighthood and having made little mark in the House. He was, however, a wonderful gardener and presided over one of the most beautiful gardens in the west of England.

In 1958 another opportunity arose when a candidate had to be found for the Isle of Wight constituency. Before the vacancy occurred, there had been a certain amount of comment in the press and elsewhere that local constituency associations were not following the procedure recommended by the Central Office for choosing candidates and as a result, were sometimes adopting people who were wholly unsuitable. The Isle of Wight constituency made it clear that it would follow the recommended procedure and in due course, I was invited to appear before the selection committee in Newport on a Saturday in November. When the day arrived, it was pouring with rain and blowing hard. I drove to Portsmouth and boarded the ferry to the island. There was only one other passenger on the boat and as we set off on the short but rough crossing, we had a cup of tea together. He too was going to Newport to appear before the committee. He turned out to be William Rees-Mogg, then, I believe, the editor of the Financial Times and later a distinguished editor of The Times and the holder of a number of important public appointments. He is now Lord Rees-Mogg. When we arrived we were put in a small waiting room and the agent told us that there was one other person on the short list. Rees-Mogg and I were duly called in and asked to address the meeting. As I made my carefully prepared speech, it rapidly became clear to me that the audience were not in the least interested in me or in what I was saying. I wondered what I had done to induce such an atmosphere of boredom in the committee. After we had both been before the committee, we were told that we could go home and then in due course, we would be told of the result. This was in itself unusual. The normal practice was for the final contenders to be kept until the committee had voted and decided who had won. The winner was then called to meet the members of the association. But what seemed even more odd was that there was no sign of the third person who was on the short list. So Rees-Mogg and I made our way back to the ferry where, once again, we sat drinking cups of tea on that depressing, rain swept journey. Rees-Mogg told me that he too had felt that the committee were not interested in him. We both came to the conclusion that the association had made up its mind before we arrived who it was going to choose and that we had only been invited down in order that it might appear that they had adopted the correct procedure. They had no intention of really considering either of us as possible candidates. We were both pretty fed up at having had to waste the whole of a Saturday at some expense on what was inevitably to be a fruitless expedition. A day or so later, I received a letter in which I was told that the successful contender had been a Mr Woodnut who was a boat builder in Bembridge.

Of course, if a party wants to choose a local person as their representative, they should do so, but in fairness, the 'carpet baggers' should not be put through what is necessarily the somewhat stressful experience of appearing before a selection committee when the decision has in effect, already been taken.

Such were my experiences with two of the many selection committees before whom I appeared in those years in my attempt to get adopted for a winnable seat. I have described them in some detail as I think they show the sort of hazards that a person ambitious to get into the House of Commons may face in his efforts. In the other constituencies for which I was considered, I have no doubt that my failure to impress the committee was largely due to that personal inability to sell myself to which I have referred. There were a number of constituencies in which, from what I was told afterwards, I came very near to being chosen. Southport, where my friend at the Bar, Ian Percival, later the Solicitor General, was chosen, Hemel Hempstead, SE Leicester, Tavistock and Basingstoke (the constituency where I then lived and where, doubtless they knew me too well) were all such. I sometimes wonder how different my life would have been had I succeeded in what was then my ambition.

These events all took place more than thirty years ago and things have changed a lot since then not least the nature of the life of an MP. In those days, it was possible to be an effective and useful MP and also practise at the Bar. The careers of many of the friends I made when I was helping to run ICCUS, such as Jack Simon, Charles Fletcher-Cooke, Derek Walker Smith, David Renton and Airey Neave among many others, are proof enough of this. But nowadays it is much more difficult to combine the two occupations. The work of MPs has become much more demanding of their time, while solicitors and barristers' clerks view with less enthusiasm than was once the case, men whose heart they feel is divided between two mistresses. One result of this is, as has often been said, that the legal calibre of barristers who are in Parliament is lower than it was in the past with the result that it is difficult for a government to find law officers of the very high standard that once prevailed in the days when men like Sir John Simon and other doyens of the bar were available to do the job.

The changes have, furthermore, meant that the life of the modern MP has become much less attractive than it was in those years, thirty to forty years ago, when I was so keen to become one. The old fashioned back bencher who was not ambitious for office and who was entirely independent has almost disappeared. Amongst all parties, politics has become a whole time occupation for most MPs, the ultimate objective of whom is to be appointed to office when his or her party is in power. This has a very limiting effect on the likelihood of a member being prepared to take a line that is not popular with the party whips. It also means that there are many fewer members who can bring to Parliament the experience they have gained from a life spent in part in some other occupation, such as farming, the city, a trade union, business or industry or one of the professions.

I finally gave up my efforts to get into Parliament in the early sixties by which time I had acquired a considerable and interesting practice at the Bar which absorbed all my energies. But in the years after 1955, I had continued my efforts. One odd result of these efforts was that in 1959, I got elected to the Hampshire County Council by mistake. It happened in this way. The Basingstoke constituency at that time consisted of the town of Basingstoke itself and a considerable number of villages in the surrounding countryside extending as far as Andover. I was then living in Weston Patrick, a village in the constituency some six or seven miles from the town. The town of Basingstoke had two local government wards: Basingstoke West and Basingstoke East and each ward had a branch of the local Conservative association. The West ward had always returned a Conservative to the County Council while the East ward had, for as long as anyone could remember, always returned a supporter of the Labour party. One evening I was rung up by the sitting member of Parliament, Sir Patrick Donner, who told me that members of the two ward branches in Basingstoke were quarrelling amongst themselves and he asked me to go, as an independent outsider, and try to bring peace. I was made chairman of the committee of the two branches. Fortunately, it was possible to restore peace, but in 1959, a meeting of the joint committee was held for the purpose of deciding who should be chosen to stand as the Tory candidate in each of the two wards during the forthcoming county council elections. The meeting was held at 8 o'clock in the evening and I came down from London after a tiring day in court and plunged into the meeting before I had had any dinner. We started by considering the safe Basingstoke West ward. There were several people who were anxious to be chosen and there was much debate and discussion as to who would be most suitable. The discussion dragged on and on. No sooner had agreement seemed within reach than another proposal was floated and the debate started again. But, eventually, agreement was achieved by which time it was nearly 10.30 and I was very tired and hungry. We then turned to consider the East ward where it was considered that a Tory had no hope at all. No names were put forward and no helpful suggestions were forthcoming so in desperation, I said that I would stand provided that the association did not expect too much of me, as I knew that in the period before the election I was due to take part in a long case which would preclude me from doing a great deal of canvassing and speaking during the evenings. The members of the committee, as anxious as I was to get home, agreed to the suggestion and the meeting closed. I went home to dinner and bed. I need not recite what I did during that campaign, suffice to say that when polling day came, there was, across the country, a large and wholly unexpected swing to the Tories with the result that when eventually the votes came to be counted, I had won by a majority of 3!

I greatly enjoyed my three years on the Hampshire County Council. At that time, the council was not divided on party political lines in the way that most local authority councils now are. The great majority of its members were independent and only the towns of Basingstoke and Southampton returned members who had stood as representing the Labour or Conservative parties. I and the two or three other Conservative members considered ourselves as independent and acted accordingly.

After I had attended a number of meetings of the full council, I decided that the time had come for me to take the plunge and make a maiden speech. But the question was, on what subject should I speak? When I received the agenda for the next meeting, I noticed that there was to be put before the council, a proposal that the riparian owners adjoining the great Hampshire Chalk streams the Test and Itchen should be given the power under new bye laws to license suitable people to shoot swans on the rivers. The reason given for the need for this new power was that the number of swans had greatly increased in recent years and that they ate large numbers of the small trout fry and so seriously reduced the stock of fish in the stream. It seemed to me that the probability was that the 'suitable people' who would be issued with the licences would be the river keepers employed by the owners of the fishing rights and it might well be that they would shoot all or most of the swans. I did not think that the people authorised to shoot swans should be people who had, or whose employers had, an interest in destroying all or most of the swans. So, I decided to propose that the council should refer the proposal back to committee for reconsideration. In due course, I made my submission and was able to pull the leg of the relevant committee for not having considered who in fact owned the swans — might it not be the Queen who certainly had rights in relation to swans on the Thames? To my amazement, my proposal was carried almost unanimously. From then onwards, I was considered to be the council's authority on birds and was put on a subcommittee charged with the task of trying to find ways of controlling the damage done by bullfinches in orchards. Such was one of the unexpected results of joining the County Council. Other less unexpected but equally interesting tasks came my way. I was put on the Education Committee and the Subcommittee on Special Schools. This I found fascinating. Unless one actually goes and sees the schools specially provided for handicapped children, deaf, spastic etc, it is very difficult to appreciate the difficulties teachers in these schools manage to cope with and the appalling problems with which they are faced.

Until 1972 when the Lord Chancellor's Department took over the building of new courts, the provision of courts was the responsibility of the local authorities and as a general rule, the Assizes and County Quarter Sessions were held in a large court which usually formed part of the County Hall. In Hampshire, the large court was held in an ancient building on Castle Hill. It had hanging on one of its walls what looked like a huge dartboard but which was said to be the top of King Arthur's round table. By 1960, this building had become hopelessly inadequate as a court and the council decided to put up a new building which would contain sufficient court rooms and other accommodation to cater for the greatly increased needs that then existed. Not many courts had been built in the years preceding this and the requirements of a modern court had changed since the nineteenth century when the majority of county halls were put up. Shortly after I arrived on the council, the plans and a description of the proposed building came before it. There was one other barrister on the council, Ewart James and he and I looked at the plans and though we thought that the appearance and the general idea of the court complex was excellent and the final building would be a handsome feature of Castle Hill, there were a number of practical points which needed to be considered in some detail and which suggested that alterations should be made if the building was to prove as efficient as it undoubtedly was handsome. So a small committee was formed on which Ewart and I served, which studied the proposed plans from the point of view of the users of the building. We were able to make a number of suggestions for improving the eventual layout most of which were accepted. So far as I know, the finished building has proved a success. In the years since then, there has been a great deal of court building carried out under the direction of the Lord Chancellor's Department and gradually, as experience has been gained they have improved, so that the most recently built complexes have for the most part proved excellent. It is probable that several of the earlier ones would have benefited from more consideration of the plans by the people who were destined to use the finished buildings.

My time on the County Council came to an abrupt end after the next county elections after three years, when the earlier swing to the Tories was reversed and Basingstoke East reverted to its traditional loyalty with the Labour party.

One other bit of good luck came my way during these years which I should record. Mac Murison came to live in our village and he and his delightful family soon became great friends. He was a merchant banker who worked for Schroder Wagg. He was also a non-executive director of the Equitable Life Assurance Company, the oldest life assurance company still in business in England; which in 1962 was celebrating its 200th anniversary. After the celebrations, several of its older directors retired and through Mac's good offices, I was invited to join the Board. It was thought that the society might benefit by having one of its directors a practising barrister. The society had been formed in 1762 at a time when many other similar companies started to operate by taking annual payments from individuals in return for a promise to provide an annuity to them or their dependants at some future date, or in the event of the individual's death. In the case of life insurance this was obviously a risky business because whether the total of the annual payments would be sufficient to pay for an annuity which fell due several years later depended on whether the individual lived long enough and also depended on how long the person to whom the annuity was to be paid survived. The reason the Equitable survived while all its early competitors went under was because it had the good fortune to have amongst its directors at a critical time, two remarkable men, Sir Charles Gould, its president and Richard Price. Both these men understood the nature of the danger that faced societies of this sort. The danger was that the total of the premiums paid together with any interest obtained on their investment, would not be enough to pay the annuities as they became payable. Richard Price, the son of a nonconformist minister, was an able mathematician who himself became a minister. He was interested in trying to solve the problem of calculating the amount of premium that it was necessary to charge in order to be sure that there would be funds available to pay the annuities when they became due. He prepared the first reasonably accurate life tables from the records of mortality available in the towns of Norwich, Northampton and Chester. From these tables it was possible to calculate what premiums should be charged for the various types of annuities required by the society's members. Gould and Price were both cautious and honourable men and erred on the side of caution by charging premiums slightly higher than the life tables suggested and in this way ensured that the society was built on a sound financial base.

I remained a director of the Equitable Life for nearly twenty years until 1981 when I was appointed a judge. It was an experience that I found immensely valuable. The other members of the Board were able men, for the most part, distinguished in their own particular occupations. They included stockbrokers, merchant bankers, a publisher, the chairman of the P&O steamship company, a future chairman of the governors of the Bank of England, farmers and landowners and a solicitor, as well as an author, the son of a former Prime Minister and a professor of business studies (later to become chairman of several important public companies). With such a wide cross section of experience, the Board was well placed to take wise decisions. In my time with the Equitable, I learned a great deal about the way the City works and of course, about the business of a life insurance society all of which was of great value to me. I also made a number of friends. Lord Baldwin of Bewdley, the son of Stanley Baldwin, pre-war Prime Minister, was a governor at Abberley Hall, my old prep school and lived in Worcestershire and I stayed with him on a number of occasions when doing cases on circuit in that area. He was a most modest man, but full of common sense. He and his wife were generous and kind hosts and in the years before he died, we became good friends. I hope that my contribution to the working of the society was of comparable value. The experience convinced me that for a lawyer whose practice includes commercial work to serve on the Board of a company provides a background which helps him greatly in giving sensible and common sense advice to clients engaged in business transactions. Likewise, a lawyer on the Board can be of real use. I never ceased to admire the vision of the directors of the Equitable when they were considering problems of investments or other normal business matters but when, as happened occasionally, a situation arose when litigation or serious legal problems might result, they sometimes needed to be restrained from taking rash decisions and be persuaded to act with greater caution.

CHAPTER TWENTY-ONE

Odd Cases and Coal Miners

By the early nineteen sixties, I was over forty years old and it was time to abandon any hope of a political career and concentrate on my work at the Bar. By then, I had a respectable and varied practice consisting mainly of work on circuit, both criminal and civil, as well as a certain amount of planning and rating work. In these years there was a great upsurge in planning appeals following the introduction of the far ranging legislation introduced by the Labour government in the Town and Country Planning Act, 1947. Anyone wishing to change the use to which land or a building was put, had, as a general rule, to obtain permission from the local planning authority which was usually the local county or county borough council. If the application was refused, the applicant had a right of appeal which took the form of a public inquiry before an inspector appointed by the minister. It was at these inquiries that barristers were often employed, sometimes to put the case for the planning authority, but, more often for the applicant whose application had been refused. Very often, feelings ran high in the locality where it was intended that the proposed development should take place. When, for instance, a developer wanted to build a new housing estate on the edge of some attractive village, the residents would often rise in wrath and voice their objections at the inquiry in no uncertain way. I often found when I was appearing for the developer, that the fury of the locals was vented on me, even though if I had been putting forward my own personal views, I would often have agreed with them. But, of course, I was not putting forward my own views, I was doing my best to put forward the arguments that my client, the developer, wished to put before the inspector.

However the English being tolerant and understanding people, this fury rarely went beyond, as Hartley Shawcross once put it, 'letting off steam'. There was, however, one occasion when I was assaulted by an objector who hit me over the head with a rolled up map! There is a very attractive stretch of the Thames near Marlow which is overlooked by a local beauty spot, Winter Hill. Under the meadows on either side of the river, there are vast deposits of excellent gravel. At that time there was a great demand for gravel for building purposes particularly for the building of motorways which was then in full swing. Before the appeal with which I was concerned, there had been an application by a local firm of gravel extractors to dig gravel in this area which had been turned down by the Minister on appeal. The case for the extractors had been that there was a huge demand for gravel in this part of the country and that this site was one of the most accessible. In his decision, the Minister had said that he accepted that there was a great demand, but nevertheless, he would refuse the application on the ground that the gravel workings would spoil the lovely view from Winter Hill and be detrimental to the local environment. My client, a year or two later, made a similar application to be allowed to extract gravel but he had found a field that was entirely surrounded by high trees and woodland and his case was that to extract gravel from it would not affect the beauty of the valley as the workings would be invisible because of the surrounding trees. When this appeal came to be heard, the gravel extractors who had been the appellants in the earlier appeal, opposed the application on the grounds that there was no shortage of gravel in the area and the demand did not exist. I had been supplied with a copy of the Minister's written decision in the earlier appeal and so after a director of the objecting firm of gravel extractors had given his evidence to the effect that there was no demand for the gravel, I was able to point out, by showing him the Minister's earlier decision, that what he had said in evidence was inconsistent with what he had said at the earlier inquiry. He could not deny this and became very cross. A few minutes later when the inquiry adjourned for lunch he came up from behind me and hit me on the head with a rolled up map. I was caught by surprise but was not hurt!

Barristers can be very boring if they recite the details of the cases in which they have been involved and I must not fall into that trap. I find, however, looking back over the years that the details of the vast majority of the cases in which I have appeared have faded from my mind. It is only when the facts are exceptional or when something amusing or particularly memorable occurs that the case is fixed in my memory. One such was when I was briefed as a junior to appear in the High Court in Dar-es-Salaam in what was then Tanganyika, shortly to become Tanzania. My leader was Leslie Scarman, who by then had become one of the leading QCs at the common law Bar. Our client was a wealthy South African, Guy Hulett, who controlled a number of companies that ran sugar plantations in various parts of South Africa. At that time, Tanganyika imported all the sugar it needed and the British government thought that if instead of importing it, sugar could be grown in the country, the economy would be eased. Guy Hulett was asked to carry out a survey of the country to see if there was anywhere sugar could be grown on a large scale. Sugar plantations can only be successfully established on certain sorts of soil and in places where the climatic conditions, rainfall, temperature etc are suitable. He went all over the country and came to the conclusion that there was only one area that met all the requirements. This was a valley in the hinterland which was some two hundred miles from railhead and which did not have a road by which it could be reached. Hulett reported that the area would, he thought, grow sugar, but it could only be a commercially viable proposition if an all-weather road or a railway was built to enable the sugar to be brought out. When the report was received he was asked by the Minister of Agriculture if he would carry out a pilot scheme for a season to make sure that the plan was likely to succeed. He agreed to do this at his company's expense provided the necessary rail or road link was provided. It was his case that he obtained an assurance that it would be provided and so he proceeded with his pilot scheme. During the next year, his company spent a very large sum of money clearing the bush and cultivating the land and planting and harvesting sugar, but he then learned that the government was in an economic crisis and that no money was available to build the road or railway. The result was that all the money and effort expended by his company was wasted. He was very angry and even though he was advised that his prospects of suing the government successfully were minimal, he determined to bring an action to try and recover damages for the loss his company had suffered. He was convinced that the reason for the government's failure to build the railway and or road was not economic problems but the fact that very shortly the country was going to become independent and that Julius Nyerere, who would head the Tanzanian government, had refused to have a South African company operating in the newly independent country.

Leslie and I set off and went, first to Durban, where we stayed for a week taking instructions from our clients and learning all there is to know about the management of sugar plantations. One fact which I learnt and which surprised me was that in Africa, the tall sugar in plantations is a favourite haunt for a particularly unpleasant, poisonous snake and when the sugar is harvested, often quite large numbers of these creatures are found in the crop. In order to get rid of them, the harvested sugar plants are placed in a large metal dish-like machine which is then rotated at high speed so that the centrifugal force has the effect of throwing all the snakes to the edge of the dish where they can be removed. There were quite a few snakes in the load we watched being treated in this way.

From Durban, we flew to Dar-es-Salaam via Portuguese East Africa where we spent the night on the island of Mozambique. During the war when I had been with East African troops, I had learned a little Swahili and when we landed at Mozambique I found myself talking Swahili to a porter at the airport. I very nearly had my brief withdrawn from me. Guy Hulett was furious. He was a typical South African and regarded it as quite improper to talk to a native African in his own language! The island of Mozambique was, at the time, divided into two parts. One half was the town of attractive Portuguese houses built round a square lined with acacia trees. The other half was a prison. We were told that there was very little crime in the country as the criminal law was so severe. One's property was quite safe, we were informed, because anyone found guilty of theft had his hand cut off. Even so, there seemed to be plenty of prisoners in the prison.

On reaching Dar-es-Salaam, we were put up in the English club, a comfortable building on the shore of the bay round which, when the country had been a German colony, some fine houses had been built. Here we met our opponent who had arrived from England the evening before. He was Brian McKenna QC who was made a High Court judge soon after his return home. He was very annoyed because, after he had retired to bed the night before, a thief had climbed up a drain pipe and entered his bedroom by the window and stolen almost all his clothes. When we met him he had just been to the market where he had gone, dressed in his pyjamas, in order to buy himself a new outfit of more suitable clothes in which to appear in court.

The case was heard before the Chief Justice, a Dane who remained absolutely silent throughout the several days that the case lasted. The hearing itself was not of particular interest but I particularly remember Leslie Scarman's cross examination of Trotman, the Minister of Agriculture. It was the most masterly cross examination I can ever remember. We had a bundle of correspondence relating to the negotiations which had taken place between Hulett and the government. It ran to just over one thousand pages and Leslie's total mastery of every page of this enabled him to question Trotman in such a way that he was, eventually, forced to agree that he had led Hulett to believe that a road or railway would be provided, an admission that he had resolutely denied up till that point. But despite that, we lost the case as the law was against us. So we set out for home. It was the very end of July and the long vacation was due to begin as soon as we were due in London. The reason the case really sticks in my mind is that I realised at the last moment that the plane came down in Rome, I had never seen the Eternal City and on the spur of the moment, I decided to spend a few days there. This I did and have never regretted it even though it was almost unbearably hot. My few days there made me realise something of the wonders to be seen there and it made me determine to visit Rome again for a longer visit at a more congenial time of year. This I was able to do with Pookie, a couple of years later. During the years that followed my visit to Tanganyika, I was briefed twice more to appear in East Africa. This involved me in visiting Kenya and Tanganyika during the interesting period, shortly after they had become independent.

One further case in which I was briefed at this time was that which the tabloid press christened 'the Red Mini Murder'. I mention it both because its facts were unusual and also because it brought me into contact with the well known novelist C P Snow, who sat in court throughout the trial in order to obtain material for a novel, 'The Sleep of Reason' which he subsequently published. In it, he described a court scene in which the legal characters portrayed with considerable insight in the book, bore an uncanny likeness to those who took part in the actual trial at Oxford Assizes. I was led in this case by William Howard QC and our client was Valerie Newell, a very attractive girl of twenty three who, having been born and brought up on a farm in North Wales, had come to live in a flat in Reading. There, she met a married man called Cook, who lived in Swallowfield, a village near Reading, with his wife, who had inherited a certain amount of money, and his children. He fell in love with our client and a passionate relationship ensued. The Thames near Pangbourne flows beneath hills covered with beech woods; along one ridge of these hills, there is a narrow lane which runs from a public house, the Highwayman, towards Peppard. Late one Saturday evening in March, 1967, a Mr Franklin, who was a fireman, was returning home along this lane when he came upon what looked like a the result of a road accident. A red Mini appeared to have run off the road and smashed into a tree. Beside the car, a woman was lying on the ground with serious injuries to her head. In the front of the car was a man, who turned out to be Mr Cook. He was slumped over the front seats and Mr Franklin thought he might have been drunk. Another man was bending over the injured woman. This man told Franklin that he was going to get some towels for her head and he went along the road to a blue Ford Escort car that was parked some 80 yards further up the road. Mr Franklin heard the boot lid of that car slammed down and then it drove off and the man disappeared. An ambulance was called and the injured woman, who turned out to be Mrs Cook, was taken to hospital where, shortly after midnight, she died. She was found to have a fractured skull. Early next morning, a police constable who had heard about the accident visited the point in the wood where the Mini had been found against the tree. He noticed that some distance from the tree, there was a large pool of blood. He realised that if the injury to Mrs Cook had occurred as a result of the Mini hitting the tree, the blood would have been near the tree. As it was, the pool of blood seemed to suggest that she had been injured some distance from the tree. When suspicions were aroused, a number of other facts emerged which seemed to point to Mrs Cook not having died as a result of an accident but from some other cause. A post mortem revealed that she had suffered none of the sort of injuries that one would have expected if the car had run into the tree with her in it. She had no injuries to her chest or of the sort usually found in such accidents. It was also clear that Mr Cook had suffered no injuries, although he had been in the passenger seat of a car that had collided violently with a tree, one would have expected him to have at least been bruised. So the police began to make inquiries. The first question was, who was the man that Mr Franklin saw by Mrs Cook's body who drove off in the Ford Escort? Announcements on the radio and television asking him to come forward, or for anyone who could give information about the car, produced no results. After some weeks, during which the police had no success, all policemen anywhere in England were asked to examine any blue Ford Escort that they came across and to interview their owners. For some time this produced no result, until one day, a police constable stationed near Portmadoc in North Wales came across a blue Ford Escort owned by a man called Jones whom he knew and who ran a timber merchants business near a quarry in the area. He asked to examine the vehicle and on looking into the boot, found signs of blood. He asked the owner if he had the car jack and was told that he had not. The quarry had a quite substantial pond in it and the police decided to search under the water. They found a car jack of the sort that has two parallel bars and was issued to Ford Escorts. When the jack was examined, it was found to have traces of blood on it and the two bars were the same distance apart as two parallel fractures that had been found in Mrs Cook's skull. When this evidence had been found, it did not take the police long to charge the timber merchant, Jones, Cook and Miss Newell with murder. The allegation was that Mrs Cook had died from injuries received when she had been hit over the head with the car jack from Mr Jones' car. At first it seemed that there was no evidence against Miss Newell. There was no suggestion that she was present at the scene of the murder and there was little evidence that she had known what was being planned. However, after the trial had been going for a day, Jones changed his plea of not guilty to one of guilty and he agreed to give evidence for the prosecution. That evidence was fatal to Valerie Newell, because what he said was that she had known him when she lived in Wales and that she had arranged for him to come to the Reading area and murder Mrs Cook in return for a payment of £10,000.

By the time the trial ended, it had become clear that there had been a prearranged plan made by the three of them, that Mr Cook would take his wife to dinner in Pangbourne and give her plenty to drink and then drive her up onto the hills by the lane to the Highwayman pub where Mr Jones would be waiting for them, having driven down from Wales in his Ford Escort. The murder would then be committed and the Mini driven into the tree to make it appear like an accident. Cook and Jones would then drive off in the Ford Escort. Unfortunately for them, Mr Franklin arrived before they were able to leave the scene of the fabricated accident. The jury did not take long to convict Cook and our client of murder and they were both duly sentenced to life imprisonment.

After the trial was over, James Irvine, who had appeared for the prosecution entertained all the counsel who had been engaged in the case at his home in Buckinghamshire so that we could meet C P Snow. It was obvious when I talked to Snow that he had been intrigued by the way in which the trial had been conducted and was particularly impressed by the cross examination of the pathologist who had examined the body, by Douglas Draycott, who had defended Cook. He was right to have been impressed as it was a masterly cross examination.

During my time at the Bar, I appeared in a number of murder trials, perhaps twenty or twenty five, and only two of them that I can remember, were pre-planned and pre-meditated murders of the worst sort. This was one of them. My experience confirmed the view that many with more experience than I, had expressed when I was writing the pamphlet 'Murder', of which I have already spoken. The vast majority of murders are done on the spur of the moment or at moments of great tension or exasperation.

The next eight years was a very busy time for me. My practice grew so that I was always busy and often away from home for long periods. Furthermore, during this period, I was appointed to a number of part-time posts which involved duties that had to be fitted in on top of the exigencies of my practice. In March 1964, I was required to go to Worcester after a tiring day in court in London so I drove down after court and arrived in my hotel at about 7.00pm. As I was very tired, I went to bed at once and decided to do such work as was necessary for my case at Worcester, in the early hours of the next morning. I had hardly gone to sleep when the phone by my bed rang. It was the Lord Chancellor's Private Secretary saying that the Lord Chancellor was minded to appoint me as Recorder of Abingdon and would I accept. In a very sleepy voice I accepted and was soon sleeping soundly again. Thus it was that I mounted the bottom rung of the judicial ladder.

The office of recorder was an ancient one and in the case of Abingdon was created by a charter of 1609 granted by James I. This charter having recited that Abingdon was a "very populous Borough and chief town in our County of Berks" went on to provide that "we are therefore willing that the Borough from henceforth and for ever be and remain a Borough of the Peace to be under a recorder, William Dayrell, Esquire, learned in the laws of England". Unfortunately, although the charter provided that the borough should "for ever" be under a recorder, the office of the Recorder of Abingdon came to an end in 1971. This was as a result of the passing of the Courts Act, 1971, which put into effect, the recommendations of a Royal Commission presided over by Lord Beeching. The Act abolished all the courts of Quarter Sessions (which included courts presided over by recorders) and in their place, created the Crown Court in which criminal cases were to be heard. Thereafter, when a person was appointed a recorder, he was not allotted to a particular borough but was appointed recorder of the Crown Court and became, rather like a taxi driver, liable to go and sit wherever his services were needed. Though some such reform was necessary to improve the administration of justice in the big metropolitan areas where the old system was under great strain, it has always seemed to me that it was not necessary in the country areas such as were served by the Oxford Circuit. In those areas the old system worked well. The chairman of the County Quarter Sessions or the Recorder of Borough Quarter Sessions got to know well the area covered by his jurisdiction and became familiar with the foibles and characteristics of the probation officers, police, solicitors and barristers who were frequently before them. They also quickly became aware of any trends in the incidence of particular crimes in their areas and were able to take such action as was possible to rectify them. However, the new system has now been working for over twenty years and we are all familiar with it. As well as losing the local connection, there has undoubtedly been a vast increase in the number of civil servants that are deemed necessary to administer the present system and I have a strong feeling that, had the old system been allowed to continue in the county areas, the counties and boroughs responsible for administering those courts, would have managed with a much smaller administrative centre and the judges would have been, as they once were, much more in touch with the people in their area and in particular, with the sort of people who were called upon to form juries.

Abingdon had thirty-eight recorders after William Dayrell, the first appointed by James I. I was the last and when the Quarter Sessions came to an end, the council gave a splendid dinner to mark the occasion. It was held in the council chamber, a beautiful room in which are hung many fine paintings including two Gainsboroughs of George III and his Queen. One of the guests present at that dinner was Mr Justice Thesiger who was descended from Frederick Thesiger, later Lord Chelmsford, who had been MP for Abingdon, Attorney General and finally Lord Chancellor and of whom a dignified full length portrait also hangs in the room.

The court room in which the recorder sat at Abingdon was part of an old building that had formed part of the gatehouse to Abingdon Abbey, a large Benedictine abbey that was dissolved at the time of the Reformation and of which only a very few bits of the original buildings now remain. The court room on the ground floor had had, at a much later date, an upper floor built above it. This was the council chamber of which I have spoken. The court itself was small and the ceiling was supported by a very large beam which crossed the court about half way down its length. This beam, which was shewing signs of giving way in the middle, was supported at the centre of its span by a large metal pillar behind which was the dock. The result of this arrangement was that, often the prisoner being tried was hidden from the bench behind this pillar and it was necessary for the judge and the accused to engage in a form of hide and seek before sentence was delivered. At the back of the court was a gallery in which the idle and unemployed in the town would sit and watch the proceedings, which sometimes provided enjoyable entertainment. On the front edge of this gallery was a row of black leather buckets filled with sand for use in case of fire. At the end of the dinner, in honour of my retirement, I was presented with one of these buckets which now serves as a waste paper basket in my library. It has the arms of the Abingdon Corporation painted on it and the date, 1825.

Not long after I was appointed, I was called upon to try a case that was widely reported in the national press at the time. The accused was a detective constable in the Oxford police who was charged with stealing a diamond ring that had belonged to a lady who had lived with her husband until he had murdered her. The detective was sent with others, to the dead lady's home to investigate the death and after the officers had carried out their necessary duties at the house, the accused was left to guard the house and make sure that no-one interfered with anything that might be needed as evidence in the murder trial. It turned out that shortly before she died, the old lady had shewn her neighbour a diamond ring that was in her jewel case and was thought to be very valuable. She had, on that occasion, told her neighbour that she, the neighbour, could have it if she were to die. A day or two after the death, the neighbour came to the house and inquired about the ring. It was nowhere to be found. Suspicion fell upon the accused who had been almost the only person in the house between the time when the ring was shewn to the neighbour and the time when it was found to be missing. However, nothing could be proved and in all probability, nothing more would have happened had not, about a year later, a parcel addressed to the accused, arrived at the police station where he was working. It was intercepted and was found to contain the ring and a covering letter from a well-known jeweller in London saying that the ring was not as valuable as had been thought and that the jeweller would not sell it and so he was returning it. At the trial, a type-written letter was produced, which had been sent to the jeweller and appeared to have come from the accused, in which the jeweller was asked to value the ring with a view to selling it. The accused was defended by John Griffiths, who later became Attorney General in Hong Kong. The defence was simply that the ring had not been stolen by the detective and that the letter to the jeweller had not come from him but was a forgery. The letter to the jeweller had been written on a typewriter, certain letters of which, when printed, shewed unusual characteristics. Evidence was given that none of the typewriters in the police station had those characteristics and the family of the accused gave evidence that he had never had a typewriter in his home. The jury had great difficulty in deciding the case and eventually, after asking me to give them further directions on the law, acquitted him.

Another case stuck in my memory because of a remarkable coincidence. The defendant was charged with some driving offence and was also acquitted. He was a successful businessman who had, shortly before, been made chairman of a large public company, Slough Estates Ltd, I cannot remember his name but it began with 'M'. After the case was over, I drove home and on arrival, read the post that had arrived since I had left in the morning. Amongst the mail was the school magazine from Abberley Hall. On reading the news of old boys I saw two entries next to each other;

> "M........ has been appointed chairman of Slough Estates Ltd
> Patrick Medd has been appointed Recorder of Abingdon"

I had, of course, no idea that we had both been at the same prep school.

In 1967 I was appointed a deputy chairman of Shropshire Quarter Sessions, an appointment which proved to be most enjoyable. I knew Shropshire well and had a number of friends in the county. It is one of the most rural counties in England and one got the impression that the administration of the county and the magistracy had not changed its style greatly since the nineteenth century. Shortly before I went there, the three senior judges who presided at the Quarter Sessions were Lord Powys, Lord Maenan and Sir Wintringham Stable. The first two were both in their nineties while the latter, a High Court judge who had before the war been in our chambers, was eighty. They were all in full possession of their faculties and I never heard any criticism of their judicial abilities from the Bar or anyone else who appeared before them. When I joined, the two nonagenarians had just retired and the chairman was Stable, who was affectionately known as 'Owlie'. On the day before the Autumn Sessions were due to start, the chairman used to invite all the magistrates in the county to a dinner held in the judge's lodgings in Shrewsbury, a fine Georgian house in the centre of the town. These were enjoyable and valuable occasions. The legal chairmen got to know the magistrates from the various parts of the county and problems were aired and discussed. The following day, the Sessions began. We usually sat in four courts each being presided over by one of the legally qualified chairmen with whom sat a number of magistrates. The Sessions usually began on a Tuesday and we prided ourselves on the fact that, almost always, we got through all the work by the end of the week. Time was not wasted. After Owlie Stable retired, my old friend Michael Talbot became chairman. He was a Shropshire man born and bred. His father had been rector of a village on the border of Shropshire and Staffordshire and was a member of the Talbot family, one of the oldest families in the county. Michael was an able man and was an excellent judge. There were many who regarded him as the best judge on the Circuit and, indeed, better than many a High Court judge. He was genuinely devoid of ambition and was very content when he was made a Circuit judge. He once told me that he had only ever had one ambition and that one he had achieved. It was to be chairman of Shropshire Quarter Sessions. In later years, after the Quarter Sessions had, as at Abingdon, come to and end, he and I managed from time to time, to arrange that we both sat at Shrewsbury at the same time. This involved us staying at the lodgings together. These were good occasions as he was an entertaining conversationalist and many an evening we sat up after dinner and he regaled me with tales of Shropshire life when he was young. He knew most of the great landowners in the county and his descriptions of them, their eccentricities and their way of living in the years between the wars fascinated me. I often wished that I had been able to record them as they enabled my imagination to picture the very different conditions that prevailed in those days.

There were a number of other part-time legal appointments which I took on in those years. Legal Adviser to the General Optical Council and Legal Adviser to the General Medical Council were two which brought me in contact with various aspects of the medical professions. They both involved being present at hearings of disciplinary proceedings before the two councils and giving any legal advice that was necessary and making sure that the proceedings were conducted fairly and in accordance with the law.

Another post which came my way was the secretary on the National Reference Tribunal to the Coalmining Industry. This was a body that was set up after the General Strike in 1926 to provide a way of avoiding damaging strikes in the coal mines by enabling disputes to be brought before the tribunal and settled by a panel of three, consisting of a legally qualified chairman and two lay representatives, one chosen by the unions and one by the Board. When I first became secretary, the chairman was Lord Morris of Borth-y-Gest, a Lord of Appeal and one of the most courteous and kindly people it was possible to imagine. I learned a lot from him by watching how he handled the representatives of the miners' unions and those of the Coal Board. At that time, the secretary of the National Union of Mineworkers was a Scot, Laurence Daly, who put the case for the miners. He was an able advocate and very shrewd trade unionist who enjoyed a 'wee dram'. The President of the union at that time was Joe Gormley, who often acted as Daly's 'minder' driving him safely home after meetings. Shortly after I took Silk in 1973, and became a QC, I handed over the secretaryship to Michael Baker, a young member of my chambers. I thought it would be a good idea to give a farewell party to the members of the tribunal, the trade unionists and the Coal Board officials who regularly appeared at hearings, in order to say goodbye, and to enable them to meet the new secretary. The date chosen for the party, which I gave in my flat in the Temple, was in the last week before polling day in the general election of February 1974. As the issue in that election was, as has been said, who was to govern Britain? the elected government or the National Union of Mineworkers? it was, obviously, necessary that politics should not raise its head in any form at the party. I had no worries on this score as we were, of course, a totally neutral judicial body. However, I was not prepared for what occurred. The party proceeded quietly and without incident for about an hour and all our guests got on well together and then the members of the tribunal and the Coal Board representatives departed, leaving only Joe Gormley and Laurence Daly of our guests. These two, however, shewed no sign of wishing to go and appeared happy to continue to enjoy my whisky despite my efforts tactfully to suggest that they left. Eventually, my wife and I decided that the only thing to do, as we were getting hungry, was to take them both out to dinner at a small restaurant we occasionally frequented, at the lower end of Fleet St. My wife undertook to escort the two guests to the restaurant while I went to my chambers a few hundred yards away in order to collect a cheque book so that I could pay for the dinner. I said I would meet them in the restaurant. I got there first and waited in the road outside looking up Fleet St for the others. Soon, I heard a great commotion and some lusty singing of Scottish songs and then I saw that the singing was from a party of three people proceeding, arm in arm, down the middle of the street. It was my wife, being escorted by Joe Gormley and Laurence Daly towards our restaurant. By some miracle of good fortune, there were no press photographers in the street to record the scene. Had there been, the two Union men would surely have been recognised as they were frequently in the news at the time and it is not difficult to imagine the headlines in the papers a day or two before polling when it was realised that the companion with whom they were carrying on in this way was the wife of a newly appointed QC who happened to be the secretary to the tribunal. But all was well and after a rather noisy dinner, we managed to put them into a taxi and send them on their way.

It was not long after this that Arthur Scargill became president of the NUM and his militant approach resulted in the Union deciding not to use the tribunal to resolve its disputes, with the result that until the end of the Miners' strike in 1984, no further hearings took place. By 1984, however, I had been appointed a co-President of the tribunal, together with Stephen Sedley, who was later to become a High Court judge. In the years after 1984, I had to hold a number of hearings of the tribunal, but as, by now, the industry was being rapidly run down, it became a less significant activity.

By the end of 1967 my practice was such that I considered I would be justified in applying to the Lord Chancellor to be considered for appointment as a QC. In the preceding years, I had been overwhelmed with work with the result that I was able to spend less and less time with my family and indeed, looking back, this situation was, I think responsible to a great extent, for the break up of my first marriage. I decided that I would apply in 1968. It is always a risky business becoming a QC. But, nevertheless I decided to try. Before, however, the time for making applications arrived, an event occurred which altered the direction that my professional life was to take.

CHAPTER TWENTY-TWO

Taxman's Counsel

Sometime in the early summer of 1968, I was engaged in the defence in a criminal case at Reading when I got a message from Cyril, my clerk, that the Attorney General, Sir Elwyn Jones, wanted to see me in his room in the Law Courts. Cyril did not know what he wanted. I went to see him a few days later. He had a large pile of files in front of him and he opened the top one and said "Oh Medd, I am considering appointing you as Standing Counsel to the Customs and Excise at the Old Bailey". This was, to me, a most extraordinary proposal. I have never practised in the Old Bailey and I knew nothing about the Customs and Excise. I think my jaw must have dropped and shewn my surprise because before I had answered, he said "Oh I am sorry, I opened the wrong file". He then told me that he was offering me the appointment as Standing Counsel to the Inland Revenue in succession to Raymond Philips who had recently taken Silk. This was not so entirely a surprise as Alan Orr and Raymond had each held the position for five years and I had, occasionally, done the odd case for them when they were unable, for some reason, to do it themselves. But I had not considered myself in the running for it as there were several very bright young men who seemed more suitable than me. This presented me with a difficult decision as one was required to do the job for at least five years as a junior and that meant that my application for Silk would have to be put off for several years with the result that I would be somewhat older than was normal when I applied to be a QC. On the other hand, it was regarded as a step in the direction of an appointment to the High Court Bench. Many distinguished men had held the post and become distinguished judges. Indeed, only two people since the post was first instituted, had not become High Court judges. Raymond Asquith, the brilliant son of the great Liberal prime minister was the first, and he had not become a judge as he had tragically been killed in the first war. Had he survived, he surely would have been. His successor, Sir Reginald Hills, who had been a fellow officer with Raymond in the Guards, held the post for many years — from the end of the First World War until well after the end of the second. He never wanted to take Silk or to be made a judge and so he continued until he retired in the 1950s. He was followed by Alan Orr. Both Orr and Philips, who followed him and Harry Woolf who followed me, were duly promoted and proved to be excellent judges. When I was offered the job, I had been told that Alan Orr and Raymond Philips had both been led to understand that they might reasonably expect to become High Court judges in due course. In the circumstances, I thought I should take up the offer. I knew that it would involve me in very hard work but it would be very interesting and it would, I thought, improve my chances of reaching the top of the profession. I therefore told Sir Elwyn Jones that I would be happy to accept. It was a decision I was never to regret though, as it turned out, my ambition of going on the High Court Bench was never achieved.

During the period from 1968 to 1973, the great majority of the work I did was for the Inland Revenue, either in court or advising on problems relating to tax which arose with remarkable regularity. The result was that, by 1973, when I took Silk, I had become something of an expert in these matters and for the rest of my time at the Bar, until 1981, I found myself involved in many interesting and important tax cases. So, though I failed to achieve my ambition, I enjoyed the life I had chosen immensely. The work was intellectually stimulating and I often found myself immersed in the affairs of big industrial companies or of well known personalities. Frequently, when people learned what I did, their first reaction was that it must be a very dull life, not half as interesting as those exciting criminal cases about which one reads in the papers. How wrong this view is. The legal problems raised by tax cases can be very intricate and difficult. The taxpayers may be big companies or famous people and in order that the legal questions raised may be understood, it is often necessary to understand the detailed working of some trade or business. This, I often found to be fascinating. During my time, for example, I conducted cases that required me to master the facts relating to the mass manufacture of boots and shoes, of china, of how wallpapers and curtains were patterned, of the workings of a huge dry dock in Glasgow (which as it happened I had known in my early days as an apprentice), of various aspects of the motor trade or the brewing industry or the management of a chain of cinemas and so on.

One of the problems with which the Inland Revenue is regularly faced, is how to prevent tax payers from carrying out and benefiting from unacceptable schemes of tax avoidance. The years before I became the Revenue junior had been years of very high taxation with the result that people with large incomes were constantly on the lookout for ways of avoiding at least some of the burden. This gave rise to the emergence of a new category of advisers, usually accountants, who called themselves tax consultants, and who studied the tax legislation with great care in order to find provisions which, if carefully manipulated, could be used to reduce the amount of tax payable by their clients. In 1935, Lord Tomlin, giving judgement in the House of Lords, in the Duke of Westminster's case said, "Everyone is entitled, if he can, to order his affairs so that the tax attaching under the appropriate Acts is less than it otherwise would be. If he succeeds in ordering them so as to secure this result, then however unappreciative the Commissioners of Inland Revenue or his fellow tax payers may be of his ingenuity, he cannot be compelled to pay an increased tax".

This statement of the law had provided a shield by which the intricate and often very complicated schemes devised by these gentlemen had been protected from attack by the Inland Revenue. People who were liable to be taxed in the ordinary way on their income from a trade or from investments would enter into some complicated transaction which they would never have dreamed of entering into except for the fact that by doing so, they would avoid paying tax, or would be able to obtain a repayment from the Revenue of tax which they had never paid. One of the earliest schemes devised by 'tax consultants' for this purpose was what became known as dividend stripping. This was a device by which a trading company, say a farming company, which had for a given tax year, made a loss and had ceased to trade, changed the objects clause of its memorandum of association so that it could trade in shares. It then acquired the shares in a company which had a cash balance equal to or greater than its farming losses, which it could pay out as dividends on which tax had been paid. Having acquired the shares in this company, the farming company which controlled it caused it to issue dividends equal to the amount of the farming company's losses. It then sold the shares of the company that had issued the dividends. Because a dividend had been paid out, the shares were worth less than they had been when the farming company had originally bought them by the amount of the dividend and the shares were sold at a loss.

Thus, if one looked at the activity of the farming company as a dealer in shares, it had made a loss equal to the amount paid out in dividends. Because it had made a loss, it was entitled, as the law stood before 1960, to be paid by the Inland Revenue, the amount of that loss. This practice, which was described by Lord Denning in one case as "digging for wealth in the subterranean passages of the Revenue, searching for tax repayments" became, for a period, extremely popular amongst that part of the public which enjoys getting something for nothing. Many people began to arrange their affairs in this way so that, to use Lord Tomlin's words "the tax attaching under the appropriate acts was less than it otherwise would be".

To test whether this practice was legitimate, the Inland Revenue took one case, Griffiths v Harrison, to the House of Lords. Whether or not the shareholders were entitled to a repayment of tax depended on whether what the so called traders in shares did (i.e. buy the shares, cause a dividend to be issued and then resell the shares at a loss), amounted to the carrying on of a trade. When the case was heard in the House of Lords, three of the judges held that it was trading and that the practice was legitimate and two, Lords Reid and Denning held that it was not. This was a most unfortunate result. It has always seemed to me that the Revenue were very unwise to take that particular case to the highest tribunal and it would have been wiser to wait for a case in which the repayment of tax claimed by the taxpayer was very much larger than the comparatively small amount involved in Griffiths v Harrison. As the repayment of tax was being claimed by someone who knew he had not paid the original tax borne by the company whose shares had been bought, the real enormity of what was being done would then have been very apparent to the court. I feel sure the views expressed by Lords Reid and Denning would have prevailed. As it was, having lost the case, the Inland Revenue was driven to legislate in order to stop the practice. To do this involved passing legislation that was monstrously complicated. It was contained originally, in Section 28 of the Finance Act, 1960, one of the most incomprehensible provisions that ever found its way to the statute book.

During the period that I was the Inland Revenue counsel, I took part in many cases in which the various provisions of that section had to be interpreted and which wound their way laboriously up to the House of Lords. It was not for several years after the passing of the Act that most of the problems of interpretation had been resolved by the courts. When it is remembered that there are, for cases of this sort, no less than five possible steps in the appeal ladder, it is not difficult to realise how expensive for both taxpayers and the Revenue it was to get these matters decided. In addition, the lengthy delay involved, in appealing in this way meant that for several years there was uncertainty as to what was the correct interpretation of the law.

The problems to which the widespread practice of tax avoidance, in the years when levels of taxation were high, gave rise are set out in a book by Nigel Tutt *The Tax Raiders — The Rossminster Affair*. There, the activities of two accountants, Messrs Tucker and Plummer, who spent their time devising avoidance schemes which gave rise to tax savings to themselves and their wealthy clients of hundreds of millions of pounds are described, as also are the efforts by the Inland Revenue to counter them. As the amount of tax that was being lost to the Treasury was very considerable, it was clearly the duty of the Inland Revenue to endeavour to stop the loss. The problem was how best to do this. The difficulty was that there were many ways in which a person might rearrange his financial affairs and thereby subject himself to less tax than he might otherwise have had to bear, without anyone considering that he had acted wrongfully. Such cases could fairly be said to fall within the principle laid down in the Duke of Westminster's case. So the problem became: where was the line to be drawn that divided such cases from those which made Denis Healey, the Chancellor of the Exchequer from 1974 to 1979, say that it was intolerable that "a small number of wealthy corporations or individuals should escape their responsibility to society by tax dodging on a massive scale"? Such people were, after all, only rearranging their financial affairs so as to make themselves liable for less tax than they would otherwise have had to bear.

One way of dealing with the problem would have been to pass legislation which gave the Inland Revenue, if in its opinion a scheme was a purely tax avoidance scheme and had no commercial purpose whatever other than the avoidance of tax, power to declare that the scheme was ineffective in its purpose. This approach had already been adopted in New Zealand but had led to serious difficulties. Several cases had come before the courts in which innocent traders had got caught up and been penalised in circumstances which were generally considered to be unfair. Besides, such a solution was contrary to a well established principle of taxation that had first been developed as long ago as the time of the civil war, namely, that a taxpayer was only bound to pay such tax as was clearly laid down by Parliament. If the tax for which he was liable depended on the discretion of someone in the Inland Revenue, it could hardly be said to be 'clearly' laid down by Parliament. Another alternative was to legislate against a scheme so that in future, it would not enable those who indulged in it to avoid paying tax. This alternative, too, had disadvantages. The legislation needed to bring it to an end was often necessarily complex and did not always succeed in its object. Furthermore, it was often too late in reaching the statute book, because tax payers who had used the scheme had already received the benefit of it by the time the Inland Revenue had learned of the scheme, how it worked and brought forward the necessary legislation.

It was thus, very important, if it was possible, to persuade the courts that these schemes were, as the law then stood, wrong and should be countered. An opportunity to do this arose when Mr Plummer himself appealed against a decision by the Inland Revenue refusing to allow him to deduct certain sums, which he claimed were annuities, from the total of his taxable income. When this case reached the House of Lords, the judges were divided in their views. Three decided in favour of Mr Plummer and two, Lords Diplock and Dilhorne in favour of the Inland Revenue. So once again, the tax avoider won. This was a great disappointment as it had seemed to me while the case was being argued that we (I was on the Revenue's side), had persuaded at least three of their

Lordships that we were right. So for the time being, the type of avoidance that Plummer had been engaged in was held to be legal and many wealthy people paid the accountants substantial fees to explain how the scheme worked and the Inland Revenue was deprived of enormous sums of tax that it had legitimately expected to collect. Fortunately, however, there were other cases on their way up to the House of Lords where the whole question of the proper approach of the courts to complex schemes of a purely tax avoiding nature, was to be considered. They reached the House of Lords after I had left the Bar and become a judge. In these two cases[1], a new approach was developed which enabled the courts in appropriate cases, to strike down transactions which formed part of a series of transactions which, themselves, had no commercial purpose other than to avoid tax.

---

[1] Ramsey v Inland Revenue Commissioners (1981) I A K E R 865.
Furniss (HMIT) v Dawson (1984) I A K E R 530.

CHAPTER TWENTY-THREE

Queen's Counsel

In 1973, I was appointed a QC, or as is commonly said in the profession, I was granted Silk and became entitled to wear a silk gown in court. Thereafter, I did not have to do the sort of work that took up much of the time of a junior barrister. Drawing pleadings and appearing in interlocutory matters became a thing of the past and because I was normally employed only in the longer and more difficult cases, being called in to lead the junior who had drawn the pleadings and done most of the preliminary work, I was concerned in fewer but bigger cases. This was pleasant. It meant that I was able to plan my professional life better. Instead of the hectic life of the busy junior, rushing from case to case day after day and often sitting up late at night preparing the following day's work, I was able to spend several days preparing a case very thoroughly and then spend a week or two conducting it. The responsibility was, of course, greater because often the amount at stake in a civil case was very considerable or in a criminal case one's client was in danger of a long prison sentence or some huge penalty. But if one does not like taking difficult decisions or accepting heavy responsibility, one should not become a barrister. Fortunately, I was not worried unduly by this.

Taking Silk can be a disaster. There are cases where a busy junior finds that after he takes silk, few solicitors brief him, perhaps because though they were happy enough with his performance as a junior, they did not have confidence in his capacity to handle the bigger cases that come the way of a QC. Fortunately, I did not have any difficulty in this respect. The Inland Revenue were kind and sent me many of their important cases and other solicitors, who knew that I had often appeared for the Revenue, sent me briefs for their clients who were in dispute with the taxman. Perhaps they thought that one who had been a bit of a gamekeeper was likely to be able to guide a poacher through the thickets and undergrowth of revenue law. I also found myself appearing in quite a number of commercial and ordinary common law cases which was the sort of work in which those in my chambers tended to specialise. One bit of good fortune for which I was particularly grateful, came my way. I began to receive instructions from the Malaysian Government to appear in the Privy Council. This arose because a young man whom I had come across when he was working for the Inland Revenue in England went to Malaysia to be employed in their government departments. So I was fortunate and soon found myself with plenty of work of an interesting character and of the sort that I enjoyed. A large part of it involved conducting cases in the Court of Appeal, the House of Lords and the Privy Council.

Shortly before I took Silk, Pookie and I had been divorced and I had married Elizabeth Spencer whom I had known for many years. I do not think that any good comes of holding post mortems after failed marriages die, but the last years when Pookie and I had been together had not been happy. This was certainly, in part, my fault. I had concentrated too much on the effort needed to succeed in my profession with the result that I had failed to give the attention to Pookie and her problems that they deserved. As the years passed, we seemed to grow further and further apart and she suffered a series of nervous breakdowns resulting in her going into hospital for several quite lengthy periods. This put a great strain on the family. When eventually she recovered and after we had separated, she embarked on a career of her own as a probation officer and met with considerable success. I think she enjoyed that work and found happiness in it and in her friendship with a Roman Catholic priest she had known when we lived at Malshanger and who was, I think, instrumental in her conversion to the Roman Catholic Church where she found peace and comfort. She died of cancer when she was only fifty-nine and it was very sad that she was prematurely prevented from enjoying for longer, the new life that she had made for herself.

For my part, the years after I took Silk were exceptionally happy. Elizabeth and I first lived in a house, 52 East St Helen Street, which we had created out of four derelict cottages near the river in Abingdon. The work of conversion was brilliantly carried out under the supervision of Dudley Evans, an architect whom I had met during the war and who had remained a good friend ever since. It had only a tiny garden but I had originally hoped to be able to buy a neighbouring bit of waste land which led down to an old coal wharf on the river's edge where I would have been able to create a riverside garden. This plan, however, miscarried as the owners of the coveted land were given permission to build flats on it and no longer wished to sell. Deprived of the chance of exercising my creative instincts by making a garden, I turned to boats. Ever since my Glasgow days, I had wished to build a boat to my own design. I therefore, decided to take advantage of the fact that we now lived in a riverside town and designed a small cabin cruiser which we could keep on the river. When she was completed, we launched her into the Thames from a small slipway just above Abingdon Bridge. She was christened 'Ellsea' and for a number of years, she enabled us to enjoy happy days on the river. She became a familiar sight to the boating community on the upper reaches, who viewed her with, I suspect, some amusement on account of her somewhat unusual appearance and the fact that she was powered only by a small Stewart Turner engine which did not give her a great turn of speed. She made very little noise, just a quiet chug chug as she glided gently along the stream. She was not at all like the modern fibre glass pleasure craft that speed up and down the river followed by a wash that erodes the banks and disturbs the bird life. A year or two before I built her, I had become the chairman of the Cheshire Home that was built in the grounds at Burcot, the home of the former Poet Laureate, John Masefield. As the land on which this home was built ran down to the river, I moored 'Ellsea' there and the residents at the home enjoyed watching her comings and goings. Her name 'Ellsea', was meant to represent the phonetic spelling of LC, the initials of Leonard Cheshire, the great wartime RAF Officer who founded the movement which provided and ran homes for seriously disabled people.

We lived happily in Abingdon for six years. Two of the four cottages I had restored were made into a small house next door to the larger one in which we lived. Elizabeth's eldest son, Michael and his new wife, Jane, bought this off us and in due course, Muffy, their first son and Elizabeth's first grandchild was born. This arrangement, as can be imagined, was a happy one for us.

In 1976, however, we all decided to move. Michael and Jane needed a larger house as another grandchild was expected. So it was that we came to live in Clifton Hampden at Little Place, a house which we originally rented and later bought from the Gibbs estate. Little Place was built in the early years of the eighteenth century as a small two down, two up cottage and since then has been extended on a number of occasions. It stands at the bottom of a bit of rising ground facing south across the water meadows bordering the Thames and commanding a lovely view over the river to Wittenham Clumps, two small hills whose summits were once fortified by Roman camps and which dominate this part of the valley. On the rising ground behind the house, we have gradually created a garden extending to some two acres. For a short time, early this century, Lady Ottoline Morrell, the wife of a wealthy MP and patroness of the Bloomsbury set rented the house while Garsington Manor, a beautiful manor house a few miles away which was to become her country home, was got ready for occupation. While she lived at Little Place, local tradition has it that she asked her friend Gertrude Jekyll to lay out the little bit of garden that then went with the house.

I do not know what truth there is in this story but it is certain that when we took over the property, the small part of the garden nearest to the house had been terraced with three levels intersected by yew hedges. Six Irish yews, each over 20 feet high stood in pairs like giant pillars on either side of the steps leading from one terrace to the next. Over the years, they had spread out so that they met across the path and made all the area near them dark and overgrown. Our first task was to open up this part of the garden by cutting down the Irish yews and cutting back the yew hedges to manageable proportions thus allowing light onto the terraces. In doing this, we found, concealed under the overspreading hedges, paths made of old paving bricks of an attractive colour. This was an unexpected bonus and enabled us by re-using the bricks, to lay new paths around the house and past a small pond and fountain which we built. Now this part of the garden gets plenty of sun and has flourished in consequence.

The upper part of the garden had not been seriously laid out or tended for many years so we were able to start from scratch creating a kitchen garden, orchard and croquet lawn. Behind the wall that bordered the furthest side of the lawn was an area of nettles and elder bushes which had once been the village rubbish tip, but had not been used as such since the local authority started refuse collections in the village. One winter Elizabeth and I decided to try and clear it, so we set about pulling out the nettles and cutting down the elders and removing the many old iron bedsteads, bottles, batteries and other household rubbish. When we had done this, we found we were left with a large mound, riddled with rabbit warrens and consisting of blackish soil formed largely by the ash tipped by the villagers. When we had the soil of this mound analysed, we found that, unlike that in the rest of the garden which was alkaline, it was slightly acid. As a result, we were able to plant it with rhododendrons, and azaleas which have since done well. The whole area has now been made into a little wood with a variety of trees and shrubs surrounding a small pond where frogs and dragon flies are gradually appearing and a few woodland birds are starting to make their homes. The creation of this garden has been the source of great

Little Place.

View from Little Place across water meadows to Wittenham Clumps in winter.

The path through the small woodland garden.

The croquet lawn and gazebo.

Entrance to the kitchen garden.

Upper pond.

Lower pond.

Elizabeth in the Kitchen Garden, 1987.

View from the Kitchen Garden through the hawthorn arch to the croquet lawn.

pleasure to me. As one of my friends, who has watched it developing over the years, put it, "it is like watching a child growing up; each year one notices some way in which it has matured". Certain it is that it has given me great pleasure.

The little village of Clifton Hampden on the river halfway between Abingdon and Dorchester-on-Thames was, until recently, all owned by the Gibbs family. In the nineteenth century, a member of the family, Lord Aldenham, who became Governor of the Bank of England, did much to improve the village. He evidently became a friend of the famous Victorian architect, Gilbert Scott, who was employed to restore and modify the little church which stands on a rocky outcrop overlooking a curve in the river. In addition, he built the manor house, the village school and the bridge. When I told my father, shortly before he died, that we were coming to live in the village, he told me that his father, when he was a fellow of University College, had known Lord Aldenham and when he was trying to raise money for the founding of Keble College, he asked Lord Aldenham to dine with him in College in the hope of being able to ask him to help. Unfortunately in the middle of dinner, a college servant came up to my grandfather and said "Excuse me Sir, Mr Disraeli wants your guest in London at once". So, Lord Aldenham had to leave the table and go, post haste, to London. When he reached Downing St, the Prime Minister asked his advice as to how the money needed to buy the shares in the Suez Canal company could best be raised. The money was needed at very short notice as, if it could not be raised quickly, it was feared that the French would buy the shares and so control the Suez canal which was, at the time, a vital link in our route to India. As is well known, the Government eventually raised the money through Rothschilds bank. Happily, so far as Keble is concerned, this incident did not prevent Lord Aldenham, and other members of the Gibbs family from contributing most handsomely to the building of Keble College. They paid for the splendid chapel and also for the library.

Towards the end of the First World War in August 1918, my father and mother spent their honeymoon at the Barley Mow in Clifton Hampden. The inn is on the other side of the river from Little Place and the lights from its windows are the only lights we can see from our bedroom windows. I was born in May 1919 just nine months after they had been on their honeymoon. It is, therefore, perhaps not surprising that I feel as if I belong in the village now. Two of Elizabeth's children have settled down nearby so she, too, is content. We have certainly been very lucky in the way our home life has developed.

Although we regarded Little Place as our home I had during my later years at the Bar, a small second floor flat in the Temple at 2 Garden Court, where I stayed when working in London and where, from time to time, Elizabeth was able to join me. 2 Garden Court is mentioned in Charles Dickens's novel *Great Expectations* as the place where Pip met his uncle from Australia. Alas, I cannot say that the meeting took place in my flat as the modern Garden Court is a late Victorian building which replaced that with which Dickens must have been familiar. The sitting room of our flat, looked out over a double herbaceous border which ran between the magnificent sixteenth century Middle Temple hall and the lawns running down to the river. Not many people can boast of living in such delightful surroundings in the centre of London and no more that a hundred yards from their place of work. In 1969 I had the good fortune to be elected a Bencher of the Middle Temple. This made life at the flat more congenial than it might otherwise have been because when Elizabeth was not in London, I could dine in Hall and did not have to cook my own dinner (which usually consisted of fish fingers and frozen peas) and moreover, was able to enjoy the company of the other Benchers. These were senior members of the Inn, many of whom were judges, and who through various committees administered the affairs of the Inn. I was put on the Executive Committee and was appointed one of the Inn's two representatives on the Council of Legal Education, the body that was responsible for supervising and providing instruction for the final vocational stages of a barrister's education. Through work on these two committees, I quickly gained an insight into the workings of the Inn's administration and the all important education of prospective barristers. It was a period of change and there was much questioning both of the part played by the Inns of Court in the upbringing and disciplining of their members and of the way in which young, aspiring barristers were educated.

Some years later, a Royal Commission under the chairmanship of Lord Benson, an eminent accountant, was given the task of enquiring into these and other matters affecting the provision of legal services and to consider what changes were needed in the public interest. The commission reported in 1979. It made a large number of sensible recommendations, and after a very careful and extensive consideration of a vast amount of evidence, which to a large extent had been marshalled and presented by the then chairman of the Bar Council, Peter Webster, who was a silk in my own chambers, the commission concluded that the two professions of barristers and solicitors should remain separate. It also made several suggestions as to how education for the Bar might be improved and made available to all classes in society. It had, in the past, always been possible for a clever boy from any walk of life who could pass the necessary exams, to be admitted to practise at the Bar. The members of the commission were anxious that this position should continue and that the Bar should not become a profession, entry to which was limited to people whose parents could afford the very substantial cost of educating them through university and law school without assistance. In the past the clever sons of poorer parents were able to qualify for the Bar by obtaining grants from local authorities which helped them to pay for their university education, and for the final vocational training. Scholarships granted by the Inns of Court helped them support themselves during pupillage and for a year or two in the early, unremunerative period on first entering chambers. We had in Fountain Court several such people. One was the son of a steel worker in South Wales, another the son of a poor village schoolmaster in Scotland and several whose parents were so badly off that there would have been no hope of them practising unless they had managed to get assistance of this sort. Unfortunately, due to financial straits, as more and more local authorities became disinclined to award grants to young people to help them through the period of vocational training and the fact that the cost to the Inns of providing the vocational courses was steadily increasing, it became more and more difficult for people of humble background to qualify for the Bar. At the same time, another trend began to make itself felt. The number of people wishing to practise at the Bar began to rise steadily. This trend has continued throughout the twenty years that have passed since then. The result was that not only was it becoming more difficult for children of less well off families to find the funds to enable them to be educated up to the right standard, but even if they could manage to become qualified it was sometimes impossible for them to find chambers that could accept them as pupils and even if they managed to get a pupillage, they often could not find chambers from which they could practise. Quite simply, more people were wanting to practise at the Bar than could be accommodated in the sets of chambers available. This has been aggravated by the fact that in more recent years the reforms introduced into the legal system by the Government have resulted in less and less work being available for qualified young barristers to do. Solicitors, despite the recommendations of the Benson Report have now been granted greater rights of audience in the courts than formerly and more and more of them are taking advantage of the chance to do work that used to be done by young barristers and which enabled them to gain experience of relatively simple work in their early years. These manifold problems were beginning to make themselves felt in 1969 when I first became a Bencher and have increased in their intensity over the quarter of a century that has since passed.

In the autumn of 1971, Raymond Philips was appointed a judge of the High Court and I became head of my chambers. This had the effect of bringing forcefully home to me, the serious nature of these problems. Our chambers had grown from the small group of some six men who had returned from the war and started in Hare Court in 1947 to a much larger body in chambers at 2 Crown Office Row. When I took over as head, we were grossly overcrowded and there was an unremitting demand from newly qualified young people to become pupils to join the chambers. The chambers were popular because they had proved successful. Many first class men had joined and we had plenty of work. But there was no physical space to take in more. Already all the silks in the chambers had to share their room with someone else which was very inconvenient. Fortunately a year or two later, the Middle Temple obtained vacant possession of three houses on the border of the Temple in Essex St. They had been built in the seventeenth century and needed considerable renovation. We decided to ask the Inn to convert them into a single set of chambers facing into the Temple at Fountain Court. Several members of the chambers were apprehensive and were reluctant for us to move. They feared that the great increase in rent that we would have to pay would be more than they could afford. However, after a rather tense chambers meeting, there was a small majority in favour of the move which took place on a very hot Saturday in July. The move was made memorable by the fact that Mark, our youngest clerk, then about 18, managed to fall into the fountain fully dressed.

When we were established in our new quarters, we soon realised that it had been a wise move. We were able to expand and to organise ourselves more efficiently. We were able to take in a number of young people and took good care to ensure that they were not all from better off families. Several were young men of very modest parentage. Many of them have done well. It was not long before we were amongst the largest and most successful sets of chambers in the Temple. As I have said, at this time, it was becoming even more apparent that the cost of getting started at the Bar was proving prohibitive to many clever young men. It was not so bad if one's parents lived in London and one could live with them but if they lived away from London and it was necessary to share a flat or pay for digs, it was more difficult. Many parents could not afford to provide their children with the necessary finance. To help overcome this, the Inns made great efforts to increase their scholarship funds. The Middle Temple, under the vigorous treasurership of Desmond Ackner, set up the Queen Mother's Fund which soon became sufficiently large to increase substantially the number of good scholarships available. But this was not enough. Christopher Bathurst who was always very thoughtful about the interests of the poorer aspirants suggested that our chambers should finance a number of scholarships to help pupils over their first year or two. This we decided to do and were one of the first sets of chambers to start a practice which has since become commonplace. We also made it a rule that when new young tenants devilled work for elder men, they should be paid for the work they did. Previously it had simply been regarded as a good way of the young men getting experience which, of course, it was. But often the barrister for whom the work was done, received a benefit, particularly if the young man was any good.

I remained head of Fountain Court chambers from 1971 to 1981. During that period, the number of members of chambers rose steadily from 18 in 1971 to 30 in 1981. I tried to ensure that as one of the most successful and prosperous sets it played fully its part in trying to help overcome the problems that I have described. I hope we succeeded in doing our little bit.

When in 1947 Melford Stevenson had invited me to join the chambers, he told me that there was only one rule that he insisted was never broken by any member of the chambers. That rule was that there was never a cross word spoken by members of chambers to each other or to members of the staff. It was a very good rule and I always told young men when offering them a place that that rule remained the essential foundation of a happy set of chambers. The Bar as a whole is composed of people who are civilised and problems do not often arise but occasionally one hears of a set of chambers where the members have quarrelled bitterly with the result sometimes that members have left or been forced out, or the chambers have split up. Generally this does nobody any good. It only leaves a nasty taste in the mouth. It was always my objective that Fountain Court should be a happy ship and I think that it was. This was due to a very large extent to the fact that we were blessed with a wonderful staff. When I took over, Cyril Batchelor was the senior clerk. He was a most remarkable man who had played a large part in developing the chambers. He was trusted absolutely by our solicitor clients. He was immensely knowledgeable about the intricacies of the workings of the courts and was frequently consulted by solicitors as well as by barristers on these matters, an understanding of which makes all the difference to the smooth working of litigation. In several years he was Chairman of the Barristers Clerks Association and introduced a system of training for people who wished to become clerks. By so doing, he did much to destroy the traditional image of the barristers' clerk as a relatively uneducated man who spent much of his time in the bars of public houses near the Temple, chatting to solicitors' clerks with the object of obtaining briefs for his 'gentlemen'. People now seeking to become barristers' clerks are required to take exams in subjects designed to make them able to run efficiently a set of chambers, to keep simple accounts and handle helpfully, solicitors' clients and barristers. The result has been a complete change, for the better I consider, in the way barristers' clerks work. This change has not, however, in the great majority of chambers, affected the special relationship that exists between a barrister and his senior clerk, although the fact that nowadays the number of practitioners in chambers is much greater than it was means that it is more difficult for the clerk to give as much time as once he did to the affairs of any one barrister. The perfect clerk so arranges affairs that the barrister is relieved of all the tiresome chores and is left free to get on with his work. In addition, the clerk is able to advise and help in matters affecting the barrister's career. In short, he becomes a trusted friend and confidant as well as an efficient manager. So it always was in Fountain Court. I profoundly hope that it will always be so. It would be sad indeed if the modern trend to concentrate on market efficiency were to take away the human element in the relationship.

Cyril retired shortly after I became head of chambers and David Hemley took over. He, too, was an exceptional young man. Immensely efficient, imperturbable and totally loyal. He too retired after I had left and since then has run a successful business in Surrey.

CHAPTER TWENTY-FOUR

Some Odd Jobs and a Little Ambition

Of course, the duties of a head of chambers do not take up a great deal of his time. Most of that side of his life can be carried on when he is out of court or after working hours. His normal work continues. In my case in the years after I took Silk in 1973 as well as doing the ordinary court work and sitting as recorder and chairman of quarter sessions I was from time to time asked to hold a public inquiry into some incident which had caused some public anxiety. The first of these that I was asked to do arose as a result of a riot that took place in Reading gaol in which a prisoner and one or two warders were injured. At that time Reading gaol was used to house young offenders who had been sentenced to borstal training and had started their sentence in some other institution but had proved to be so disruptive or difficult to handle that they were sent to Reading which was reserved for those worst offenders under twenty one who the normal borstal institutions could not control. As can be imagined when all brought together in one place they proved to be an unruly crowd. I do not now remember precisely what caused the riot except that it occurred when the prisoners were queuing for breakfast. I remember when on the first day I arrived to hold the inquiry, I was met by the governor who took me to see the cell in which Oscar Wilde had been housed when he served his sentence in this prison many years before. It was a gloomy place and nothing in the old Victorian building had changed over the years that had intervened. The prison still stands and is visible on the south side of the railway line before going through Reading station when travelling from London to Didcot and the west. In my report submitted to the Home Office after I had held the inquiry I made certain recommendations and was thanked by the Permanent Under Secretary. Not long after that the prison ceased to be used to house the most intractable of young offenders.

Another inquiry I was asked by the Shropshire County Council to hold concerned a children's home on the outskirts of Shrewsbury. Complaints had been received by people living in houses nearby that they had heard loud screams coming from children in the home and on at least one occasion after dark had seen a child being beaten by the warden of the home in a room lit by electric light of which the curtains were not drawn. This was a bad case and it turned out that the warden was something of a sadist and some of the young girls who were employed to help at the home were only given very inadequate instructions as to how to handle difficult children and did not understand the rules that had been laid down by the County Council with regard to corporal punishment. Again after the inquiry (in which I was helped by a former chairman of the County Council) we made a number of recommendations particularly designed to ensure that the people employed in such homes should be instructed in and should understand what the law allowed them to do to children who needed disciplining.

There was one other inquiry which I held at the request of the Ministry of Health. In this I was assisted by the Matron of St Mary's Hospital, Paddington who was a most impressive lady. She was highly intelligent and of a humane and understanding disposition. She was quick to see the essence of a problem and had an enviable gift of insight into a witness's mind. She would have made an admirable judge. The events which gave rise to this inquiry were very unfortunate and somewhat unusual. They took place at a hospital in North London where an old man was a patient. There came a time when the doctors considered he should be allowed to go home, so his wife was informed that he would be returning. On the day he was released from the hospital the nurses on duty got him up in the morning and dressed him. He was then helped into a wheel chair, wheeled out of the hospital, put in an ambulance and driven to his home. On arriving, the wheelchair was taken from the ambulance and pushed to the front door of his house where his wife was waiting for him. When she came to greet him she realised that he was dead. It is not hard to imagine the shock and horror that must have overcome her. No one who had played a part in getting him home, neither the nurses nor ambulance men, had realised that at some stage he had died.

By the time we had heard the evidence it became clear that this sad event had happened as a result of the fact that the hospital had at the time been desperately understaffed and that nurses were working very long hours and wards were being manned by about half of the number of nurses that they required. The result was, of course, that nurses were not able to do everything in the ward that needed to be done and were often working when they were very tired. In these circumstances mistakes were bound to occur. What had probably happened in this case was that the patient was left unattended in his wheelchair for a short period and had quietly expired during that time. Thereafter, no-one had noticed before he arrived home.

One bit of good fortune I had during this period was to be appointed the chairman of the tribunal that had as its other members, in the words of the statute that set it up, 'two or more persons appointed by the Lord Chancellor as having special knowledge of and experience in financial or commercial matters'. This tribunal was brought into being when Parliament had, in 1960, introduced certain very complicated and draconian provisions designed to counteract tax advantages arising from the less attractive sort of tax avoidance schemes. During the time that I chaired this tribunal there were five other members and a remarkable lot they were. They were a merchant banker, three accountants and a solicitor and were all the best type of city man. Lord Chorley, later to become the President of the National Trust, was a distinguished accountant as were also Eddy Ray and Philip Couse, both of whom were to become president of the Chartered Institute of Chartered Accountants. Hugh Stevenson was a merchant banker from Warburgs while Roger Payton was a solicitor who also happened to be a director of Morlands Brewery in Abingdon. As he put it in a letter to me, we therefore had a second common interest — at least he hoped I had an interest in Morlands' products. By the time I became chairman of this tribunal the number of appeals coming before it had fallen somewhat and we did not have to sit very often. When, however, we did sit, it was always a pleasure to be assisted by such able men. Another part time appointment I held for a short time was Legal Adviser to the General Medical Council, which is the body that is responsible for hearing disciplinary cases against doctors. It was staffed largely by Scots who, besides being good doctors, are nearly all, it seemed to me, ideally qualified to be judges. They are independent, wise and fair — though I sometimes thought they were rather hard on their colleagues who had in some way fallen short of the high standards they require.

I have mentioned these activities in which I was engaged in my years as a QC to show the sorts of things that came the way of a silk in practice in those years. It was never a dull life, though it could be exhausting. At the end of a week's work, I always looked forward to the journey from Paddington on Friday evening which took me back to the peace of Little Place and the domestic pleasures of home. On summer evenings, as I looked out of the window of the train at the quiet Thames flowing in the valley below the Chilterns and the Berkshire Downs and the countryside of the Oxford plain, I realised how fortunate I was to live in such a beautiful part of England with such a lovely wife as Elizabeth.

After I had been a QC for some four or five years I was approaching sixty and I began to wonder what the future had in store for me. I had, by this time, sat as a recorder for over twelve years and had done a fair amount of work that was of a judicial nature. It was work which I found interesting and I felt that I was capable of doing it reasonably well. I therefore rather hoped that I might be invited to go on the High Court Bench. I knew that when Alan Orr had been appointed Standing Counsel to the Inland Revenue he had been given an undertaking that after he had done five years in the post and had been in practice as a silk for three or four years, he would be appointed a High Court judge. Though I never asked Raymond Philips, I think he was appointed Standing Counsel for the Inland Revenue on the same basis and both these men duly became High Court judges. Nothing of the sort was said to me when the Attorney General appointed me, but I felt that in the light of what had happened to my two predecessors, I was justified in assuming that I would, provided I did my work well, have a good chance of following them. The difficulty was that if I was not appointed a judge by the time I was sixty, I would have to retire before I could have earned a full judicial pension. Eventually, after a good deal of heart searching, as I did not want to seem importunate, I decided to ask Peter Rawlinson, whom I had known for many years and who had been the Attorney General for much of my time as the Revenue Junior, for advice. He told me that "as the pattern has now been established you can reasonably expect to be favourably considered for the post". By this, I took him to mean that as both Alan Orr and Raymond Philips had been appointed to the High Court after doing five years in the Revenue post and a few years as a silk, I could look forward to similar treatment provided that I had not disgraced myself in any way. He also told me that any member of the Bar was entitled to ask for an interview with the Lord Chancellor's Permanent Secretary in order to ask him whether or not he was in the running for a High Court judgeship or had no hope of such an appointment. After this helpful interview, I decided I would not ask for an interview with the Permanent Secretary as there was, it seemed, a chance that before long I might be considered. There was another reason too why I did not particularly wish to see the Permanent Secretary at this time. The Permanent Secretary was Wilfrid Bourne, one of my oldest friends who had shared a room with me in Hare Court many years before. I felt that going to see him might seem like asking favours of a friend and I did not want that. So I decided to soldier on in the hope that before too long, an invitation would come.

Not long after I had been to see Peter Rawlinson, however, an event occurred with altered the position. Peter Webster and Tom Bingham both of whom were younger than me and were in my chambers were appointed to the High Court. They were both brilliant men. Tom Bingham particularly, had, I think, always been recognised by everyone who knew him as one of the most exceptional men of his generation to come to the Bar. This meant that if I were to be appointed, three members of one set of chambers would have been appointed in rapid succession. I thought it was unlikely that the Lord Chancellor would want to do this and further, Wilfrid Bourne would not want to advise him that yet another of his own old chambers should be considered. So I reached the conclusion with some sadness that I no longer had any hope of achieving what had been my ambition. I decided to go and see Wilfrid Bourne as Peter Rawlinson had told me I could. So it was that I found myself talking to him in his room high up in the Victoria Tower of the House of Lords. He told me, with the greatest courtesy, that I had no hope of appointment to the High Court but said that there was a vacancy for a Circuit judge to take charge of the courts at Newcastle-upon-Tyne and would I be interested in that. He had remembered that my father's family had come from the north of Yorkshire and that I had relatives living in Northumberland. It was a kind thought but I had little hesitation in refusing the offer as it would have meant that Elizabeth and I would have had to move to the northernmost tip of England miles from all our children and most of our friends. So I returned to my practice. Not long after this, Wilfrid Bourne, who had become a Bencher of the Middle Temple, met me one day in the Inn and asked me if I would be interested in becoming the senior National Insurance Commissioner in succession to Sir Rawdon Temple who was about to retire. It was a job that had a limited amount of judicial duties but considerable administrative responsibilities. In the past, Sir Robin Micklethwaite had been appointed from the Oxford Circuit. I eventually decided not to take this post as I did not think I would enjoy the work and David Hemley, my clerk, told me he did not think it was the sort of thing I should do. Not long after all this, I decided to apply to the Lord Chancellor to be considered for appointment as a Circuit judge. I had been told that if I did this, I should ask one or two judges who knew me and who had had experience of me appearing before them, if they would allow me to use them as referees. I therefore wrote to two judges before whom I had appeared many times to ask if they would support my application. One was Lord Russell of Killowen who before being elevated to the House of Lords had presided in the Court of Appeal in many cases I had done in that court over the previous years and the other was Lord Diplock before whom I had argued many cases in the House of Lords. The two letters I received in reply were warmer than I had ever expected. Charles Russell ended his by saying "I can assure you that my experience of you will lead to the warmest recommendation" while Diplock said he would gladly be a referee and added "But if Quintin[1] asks me I shall tell him that, in my view, he would be foolish not to appoint you to the High Court Bench instead". These two letters came as something of a surprise to me and I wondered what to do. My diary entry for 19 February 1980 records the event. It said that the letter from Lord Diplock:

---

[1] Lord Hailsham of St Marylebone, Lord Chancellor

"was more generously worded than I had expected". I spoke to Peter Webster and Tom Bingham (both of whom were still in chambers having told me of their appointments which were not to take effect until April 1980) and they both thought I ought to speak to Wilfrid Bourne again and find out finally whether I have any chance of the High Court. Mark Potter then told me that Jack Simon was very keen to be of help to me so it all seemed to change. My feeling that I had failed totally to make progress receded a bit. Today, I went to see W B. He was very helpful and frank. He was certainly impressed to see K D's letter, which I shewed him. I also explained that I thought that a person who had been Revenue Junior rather fell between two stools as he practised in the chancery court and yet was not eligible for the chancery Bench. The judges who had seen him perform were therefore never asked for their opinions of him. Conversely, the judges in the QB division on the whole see little of him so he does not spring to mind as a possible when the matter is being discussed. Wilfrid said that he would ask Denys Buckley (then the senior chancery judge in the Court of Appeal) and he thought Diplock would have a word with Hailsham. He asked if I would be interested in the Family Division. I said "Yes!" For the first time for a year or so I feel that my future may take a turn for the better. But, I must not be too sanguine.

As I had walked to the Houses of Parliament to see Wilfrid that day, I had been struck by the loveliness of the sunny day and the improvements that had been brought about by the cleaning of the buildings. I said:

"The grass in Parliament Square and the newly cleaned government offices in Whitehall made the area round the Houses of Parliament seem spacious and airy. The statue of Oliver Cromwell beside Westminster Hall now stands in a new lawn. This greatly improves the side nearest the square. The Abbey, its stonework also partly cleaned, is looking superb. The new square beside the entrance to the House of Commons, underneath which is the MP's car park, has greatly improved the part inside the railings. But I cannot pass it without thinking of poor Airey Neave who was assassinated as he drove up the ramp".

I had known Airey Neave well both as a member of the Oxford Circuit and as MP for Abingdon. He had been responsible for my being chosen as Chairman of the John Masefield Cheshire Home when we first went to live in Abingdon. He was a brave man and had made a daring escape from the notorious prisoner of war camp at Colditz during the war. He came to Swindon during the general election of 1955 and spoke for me. I liked him very much.

Of such things were my thoughts as I went to visit Wilfrid Bourne. When I came out I felt a bit more confident and decided I would not apply to be a Circuit judge for another year or so in the hope that my luck might have changed. So I returned to my chambers and settled down once more to my work. As it turned out, the ensuing year proved to be full of interest and excitement so that I soon forgot about my future. The present kept me fully occupied.

CHAPTER TWENTY-FIVE

More Cases

During the last three or four years before I became a judge, I was briefed in a number of cases, mostly tax cases, which were of some importance either because the amount of money involved was very great or because there was an important point of principle at stake. Of course, as a general rule, a litigant who is an ordinary member of the public is not interested in points of principle. He is only concerned to win the case. When, however, one of the parties to an action is a government department or some sort of public body, it may be very interested in a point of principle. There will often be many other cases which turn up on the same point so that even if the amount at stake is small, the result will be serious for that litigant if the case is lost. It may find itself having to pay out considerable sums in settling other cases which raise the same issue. This situation arises quite frequently when the case is an appeal by a taxpayer against the amount for which he has been assessed to tax by the Inland Revenue. The amount of tax for which the taxpayer thinks he has been wrongly assessed may be small, but if the Inland Revenue were to lose, many thousands of other taxpayers would be affected and much revenue would be lost to the Crown. I remember well one case where this was the case. I was appearing for the Inland Revenue who were appealing against a decision of the General Commissioners who had decided in favour of a self employed carpenter who often worked away from his home and when that happened, he spent a small sum on buying sandwiches for his lunch. They had decided that for one year he was entitled to deduct £52 from his total earnings when calculating his taxable income. They estimated that that was the difference between what it cost him to buy sandwiches when he was away from home and what it would have cost to lunch at home. So the amount of tax at stake was a very small sum — namely the tax on £52. When Mr Justice Templeman, who was trying the case realised this, he said to me "Why on earth Mr Medd, are the Revenue contesting this matter" the solicitor for the Inland Revenue who was sitting behind me tugged my gown and said "tell him that if the appeal goes against the Revenue, approximately £10 million of tax would be lost to the Crown". Eventually, the Inland Revenue won the appeal, though I must admit to having some sympathy for the little carpenter[1].

---

[1] *See Caillibotte v Quinn (1975) 2 ALLER 412.*

Two other cases in which the amount of tax in dispute was small but which raised issues which the Inland Revenue considered to be of importance because they would affect many other taxpayers, were appeals by two practising barristers. The first[1] raised the question whether the books bought by a barrister for his law library and were in the nature of capital assets, were to be treated as 'plant' for the purposes of income tax. If they were properly to be regarded as 'plant', the barrister was entitled to certain capital allowances in respect of them and this had the effect of reducing the amount of tax he had to pay. This case was brought by James Munby, a successful junior, practising in Lincolns Inn who had, some years before, been a pupil in my chambers, so I knew him well. The case was first heard by Mr Justice Fox who had decided that the books were not 'plant' and so did not come within the terms of the Act which laid down when capital allowances could be claimed. In reaching this decision, he felt that he was bound by the decision some fifty years before, in 1926, by Mr Justice Rowlatt who was a very distinguished judge who was always considered to be a great authority on matters of taxation and who was, incidentally, the uncle of the under-matron at Abberley Hall whose engagement party had resulted in me being given champagne for the first time. In the case which concerned the law books of a practising solicitor, Mr Justice Rowlatt had said "I cannot bring myself to say that such books . . . . are 'plant' ". So before Mr Justice Fox, James Munby lost. But he appealed to the Court of Appeal where I was briefed by the Inland Revenue and Frank Heyworth Talbot QC, who was then in his eighties and was the doyen of the tax Bar, appeared for James Munby. The appeal came before Lord Denning, Lord Justice Pennycuick and Lord Justice Browne. The difficulty for the Crown was that in the fifty years since Mr Justice Rowlatt's decision there had been a number of cases in the Court of Appeal and in the House of Lords in which the judges had all approved and applied a statement of the law made by Lord Justice Lindley in another case in the Divisional Court where he said that the word plant meant "whatever apparatus is used by a business man in carrying on his business — not his stock in trade which he buys or makes for sale; but all goods and chattels, fixed or moveable, live or dead, which he keeps for permanent employment in his business". As the Act applied to professional men like barristers and solicitors as well as to business men, then it was clear that books came within this definition.

I scratched my head to try and find an argument that did not involve saying that Lord Justice Lindley's decision was wrong as the court would not overrule a dictum that had on numerous occasions been accepted by the House of Lords. The only argument I was able to put forward was that when one looked at all the cases, one found that they all concerned equipment or apparatus that was used by a business man or professional man in a physical way. That is, it was moved mechanically or performed its function by some physical act. Books, though they might properly be called apparatus, were not used to do anything physical. They were only read. They were like intellectual warehouses where bits of legal knowledge were stored. So I did my best to put this argument over; but the three judges did not accept it — and I think they were quite right not to have done so. So James Munby got his capital allowances for his law books and I am bound to say, I am glad as the decision applied to me and my law library as well as to all other barristers and

---

[1] *See Munby v Furlong (1977) 2 ALLER 953.*

solicitors and indeed many other professional men. I conclude my description of this case by allowing my vanity to intrude. The Master of the Rolls and Lord Justice Pennycuick complimented me in their judgements on the way I had argued the case.

The other case which concerned a practising barrister and which, again, though not involving any great amount of money, the Inland Revenue regarded as of importance was one in which I was concerned, not as a barrister but in a judicial capacity. When I had become a Bencher of the Middle Temple, I was asked to be a General Commissioner of Income Tax for the area of the Inn. This was a post which did not, in the ordinary way, involve any very great amount of work. Normally, cases coming before the commissioners related to the tax returns of barristers or solicitors who practised in the Inn and they were nearly always settled very quickly. There had not been a contested case for many years, but in 1980, Ann Mallalieu who was a barrister practising mainly in the criminal courts in and around London, appealed against a decision of the Inspector of Taxes refusing to allow her to deduct from the total of her earnings when computing her taxable income, the cost of purchasing, cleaning and laundering the clothes such as black suits, black dresses and white shirts which she was required to wear in court. Again, the amount at stake was small, only the tax on £564 but if she were to win, every lady barrister and probably every male barrister would try and jump on the bandwagon and much revenue would be lost to the Crown. John Monroe, an able chancery barrister and I were asked to try the case as General Commissioners.

I will not go into the details of the case which turned on the interpretation of a section of the Income Tax Acts, which had often given rise to difficulties. There was one report of an earlier case in the court of appeal which seemed to us to explain how one should approach the problem when it arose. That case was *Bentley Stoke and Lowless v Beeson* which had concerned a firm of solicitors who had claimed to deduct the cost of lunches given to clients. I had read the report of this case many times as I had often been called upon to advise in cases where the principles laid down in the judgement of that case were relevant. When we had heard all the evidence and arguments, I agreed to write our judgement. In doing this, I considered carefully how the facts which the evidence had established fitted into the reasoning laid down in the *Bentley Stokes and Lowless* case. Our conclusion was that Ann Mallalieu was not entitled to deduct the cost of cleaning and repairing her black clothing from her total earnings in order to compute her taxable income. John Monroe agreed with me and I was quite convinced that we had come to the right conclusion. But Ann Mallalieu appealed to the High Court. Some time after we had heard the case, I was appearing in another case in the Court of Appeal and when it had finished, Eric Moses, who was the solicitor of Inland Revenue instructing me, said to me "Mr Justice Slade is giving judgement in the Mallalieu case in the next door court, shall we go and listen to the rest of his judgement?" I readily agreed and so we slipped into the back of Mr Justice Slade's court and listened to what he had to say on the subject. He decided that John Monroe and I were wrong and he allowed the appeal. Imagine my astonishment when I heard him end his judgement by saying something to the effect that "the learned General Commissioners who heard this case have quite failed to understand the reasoning in *Bentley Stokes and Lowless v Beeson!*" If there was one case on the books, the reasoning of which I thought I completely understood, it was that one. Mr Justice Slade was a very good judge who was later promoted to the Court of Appeal. But, I thought, even Homer may nod. The Inland Revenue appealed to the Court of Appeal and I thought "well the Court of Appeal will put him right". But I was wrong. The Court of Appeal, presided over by the Master of the Rolls, Lord Donaldson, said that Mr Justice Slade was right and we were wrong. The Inland Revenue got leave to appeal to the House of Lords and so the matter came before the courts yet again. After it had been heard, I was having lunch one day in the Middle Temple when Lord Diplock, who had been one of the judges who heard the case in the Lords, came up to me and told me that their lordships had allowed the appeal and agreed with my judgement. "Isn't it odd", he said, "how many judges have misunderstood the reasoning in *Bentley Stokes and Lowless!*" In the House of Lords, there had been one dissenting voice, Lord Elwyn-Jones, who thought that the judges of the High Court and Court of Appeal had been right. I was glad that my view had been vindicated by four of the five judges in the highest court in the land. But it was a close run thing. Of all the judges who had had the case before them, six had held that the Inland Revenue had been right and five had held that Ann Mallalieu's view should have prevailed. Perhaps this shows that it is often possible for sensible men to hold opposing views as to what a few quite simple English words mean. The issue in the case was, quite simply, were the expenses incurred by Ann Mallalieu 'expenditure wholly and exclusively laid out for the purposes of her profession as a barrister'?

Not long after this case had reached a conclusion, Ann Mallalieu, who is a highly intelligent and attractive person and who has, I believe, always been a supporter of the Labour Party, was made a life peer and now sits in the House of Lords. I do not, however, think that the two things were, in any way, connected.

Another case in which I appeared for the Inland Revenue and in which the decisions both of the High Court judge and of the judges in the Court of Appeal were overturned in the House of Lords was called *Tyrer v Smart*. It concerned the well known Rentokil group of companies one of the subsidiaries of which, became a public limited company by offering its shares to the public. At the same time as shares were offered to the public, shares were offered to employees of the company who had been with the company for at least five years at a price of 20/- per share. The shares were offered to the public at what was called 'the striking price' after tenders had been received by the company. The striking price turned out to be 25/- per share. The Inland Revenue assessed Mr Tyrer, one of the company's employees who had bought 5,000 shares at 20/- per share on the sum that the Revenue considered to be the benefit he had received from the company by being able to buy the shares at 20/- each and not at 25/- each which he would have had to pay had he been a member of the public. The Inland Revenue claimed to be entitled to do this under the provisions of the Act which laid down that an employee was to be assessed to tax on the 'emoluments' from his employment. 'Emoluments' were defined in the act as including all 'perquisites and profits whatsoever' as well as salaries, fees and wages. So the question that had to be decided was whether by being able to purchase the shares at 20/- each rather than at 25/- each amounted to a 'perquisite' of his employment. The Special Commissioners before whom the appeal first came were presided over by Mr Hubert Monroe QC one of the best tax lawyers of the day and they held that Mr Tyrer had received a perquisite and that, therefore, he should pay tax on the benefit he had obtained by purchasing 5,000 shares at the lower price. Mr Tyrer appealed and I was briefed by the Inland Revenue on the appeal which came before Mr Justice Brightman. He held that the

Commissioners were wrong. It was his view that the benefit Mr Tyrer had received had resulted from his decision as a private individual and not as an employee to take the commercial risk of investing in the shares. In other words, he thought that the benefit did not come to Mr Tyrer from his employment but from his personal decision to invest. This decision seemed to me to be wrong. It was true that Mr Tyrer's decision to take advantage of the benefit resulted from his decision to invest in the shares. But that did not seem to me to mean that he had not received a benefit from his employment when he did decide to invest. So the Inland Revenue appealed to the Court of Appeal and once again, I appeared and once again, we lost the appeal. The three judges taking substantially the same view as Mr Justice Brightman. This was disappointing as I remained convinced that the decision reached by the Special Commissioners was right and that the judges who had heard the appeals were wrong. Nothing that any of them had said had changed my view. The Inland Revenue solicitor asked me whether I thought we would win if we appealed to the Lords. I said that I thought we ought to win but in a situation like this, I was always mindful of what Oliver Cromwell had once said in a letter to the General Assembly of the Church of Scotland which had stubbornly held to an opinion that most other people thought to be wrong. He had said, "I beseech you, in the bowels of Christ, think it possible that you may be mistaken." Well, the Inland Revenue, to my surprise, had sufficient faith in my view and the case eventually came to the House of Lords and, as we were the party appealing, it fell to me one Monday morning, to open the case for the Crown. Rarely have I had such a rough passage. It was clear from the start that their Lordships were inclined to take the same view as the Court of Appeal. None of my arguments seemed to be going home, but I reminded the House that they were only entitled to say that the Special Commissioners' decision should be overturned if they considered that they had gone wrong in law. If there was any evidence before the Commissioners which entitled them to reach the conclusion they did without them going wrong in law, they were bound to let the decision stand.

By the time it came to adjourn for lunch, I felt that I had made no impression and that all five of the Law Lords hearing the appeal were against me and I had come to the end of all the arguments I thought I could put. To continue would mean that I was repeating myself. So when we were about to adjourn, I told Lord Diplock who was presiding that I had no more to say, but I asked him to allow me to be free to continue after lunch if anything further occurred to me. After lunch, I rose to tell the judges that I had one more short point I wanted to put to them. No sooner had I started than it immediately became apparent that Lord Diplock had changed his mind and now accepted what I had said and soon, I realised that all five of the judges had, over lunch apparently, swung right round. So I quickly sat down and left the field open to my opponent, who was Michael Nolan (now Lord Nolan) an old friend. He found himself facing heavy fire from all quarters. He was not able to make them change their minds again.

The decision of the Lords was given on 13 December 1979 and it was a unanimous decision by all five of the Law Lords in favour of the Inland Revenue. A day or so later, I received a charming letter from Brian Davenport who was then the Inland Revenue's standing counsel but who had not been in the case. He wrote:

Dear Patrick,

 Walking past Somerset House (the HQ of the Inland Revenue) a day or so ago, I thought I saw the flag flying at the top of the topmost flagstaff. Going in to inquire whether there was a new Royal Baby or some event of equal importance, I was told by the car park attendant that the happy event was a great victory in Tyrer v Smart — unanimously the cause of virtue had prevailed........"

I also received a most generously worded letter from Eric Moses, the Solicitor of Inland Revenue, who, typically, belittled the enormous amount of work that he and his department had put into preparing the case. I will conclude my account of this small event in my life by saying that the room in Somerset House that the Solicitor of Inland Revenue occupied at that time, was a beautiful regency room with windows that looked out across the Thames. It was at the top of a unique Georgian staircase and was the room in which, I believe, the Board of Admiralty used to sit at the time of the Napoleonic wars and over which there was a flagpole. No doubt the flag did fly from there when the news of Nelson's victory at Trafalgar reached London!

One day not long before the general election in 1979, in which the Conservatives defeated the Labour party and Margaret Thatcher began her long period as Prime Minister, I was sitting in my room in Fountain Court when the phone rang and my clerk told me that Lord Elwyn-Jones, who was still the Lord Chancellor wanted to speak to me.

When he came on, he asked me if I would act for Lord Llewellyn-Davies in a tax case. It was, he said, to be treated with the utmost secrecy but it was of great importance to the Labour Government because Lady Llewellyn-Davies was the leader of the Labour peers in the House of Lords and if the case was lost, her husband would certainly be made bankrupt and she would have to resign. Lord Llewellyn-Davies was a very distinguished architect and he had been employed to design and supervise the building of a considerable number of hospitals in the Middle East and elsewhere for which he had, of course, received very substantial fees. He had received an assessment for income tax which demanded that he pay rather over one million pounds tax on these fees. Not surprisingly, if the assessment was correct and he was rightly liable for such a huge sum, he would have been in acute financial trouble and would probably have to be made bankrupt. It was, obviously, a worrying case but with some trepidation I agreed to take it on. Shortly after this conversation, Lady Llewellyn-Davies came with her solicitor to have a consultation with me in chambers. She proved to be a most intelligent and sensible woman, full of good sense and was charming as well as elegant. It turned out that her husband had been persuaded to enter into a tax avoidance scheme dreamed up by a clever accountant who was well known to the Inland Revenue. When Revenue officers realised this, they began an intensive investigation which ended up by them issuing the assessment. When I received the instructions upon which I was called to advise they turned out to be voluminous and included some two thousand pages of correspondence and many pages of complicated accounts covering many years. When I had absorbed all the information with which I had been provided and after I had had a consultation with my client's accountants, I reached the conclusion that there was a small part of the assessment to which there was no answer, but that there was a good chance of establishing that the great bulk of the sum demanded by the Revenue was wrongly claimed. I therefore, advised that the relatively small sum against which it was impossible to argue should be paid and that we should contest the balance. As, however, I did not consider that we had a cast iron case and as the amount of the assessment was such that if we were to lose, my client would probably have been made bankrupt with all the consequences that would have flowed from that, I considered that it was a case which, if possible, should be settled. It seemed to me that a fair result would be achieved if it were possible to persuade the Revenue to accept in final settlement, a much smaller sum, the payment of which would not bankrupt my client. In this way, the Revenue would get some tax, even though there was at least a doubt whether it was entitled to any and though eventually, Lord Llewellyn-Davies would pay a sum for which he might not be liable, he would be spared the worry of expensive litigation and saved from the risk of bankruptcy. I was, therefore, instructed to go to Somerset House to meet a member of the Board of the Inland Revenue to see if this could be achieved. This I duly did. I was shewn into a small room where I faced across a table, a member of the Board, the solicitor of Inland Revenue, their accountant and senior inspectors. I explained why I considered we had a good case and that they might feel that a bird in the hand was worth two in the bush. They all sat in polite but stony silence. When I had finished my plan, I was firmly told that they could not consider a settlement. So there was no option but to continue with the appeal. The question that arose in the appeal and upon which it turned was one of accountancy. It arose because the contracts under which architects are often employed (RIBA standard contracts) provide for the architect to be paid fees at intervals as the work of designing the building and supervising the construction proceeds. These fees are known as stage payments and the contract lays down the percentage of the total that is to be paid to the architect at each defined stage. In practice, of course, an architect does a great deal of work during the early stages when he designs the building and prepares specifications and the like and later when he is supervising the building work he is not so heavily engaged. For this reason, the contract provides that a high proportion of his total fee for the whole job is to be paid at an early stage. The design and construction of a large building such as a hospital may, of course, take place over a considerable period, often three or four years, and it is only fair that the architect should receive something for the work he has done as the work proceeds. The question that this case posed was whether, as the Revenue contended, the architect should be assessed to tax in the year in which a stage payment was made on the basis that the stage payment was to be regarded as contributing to his profits for that year, or whether, as Lord Llewellyn-Davies contended, he should pay tax on the whole of the fees he received for a particular contract in the year in which the final payment was made and when the full amount was known and when it was possible to compute accurately his profit on the whole contract being the fees he had received less the expenses he had incurred over the whole period.

The law was clear that the answer to this question depended on what was the accepted and proper practice of accountants. It was, therefore, necessary for the appellant to call evidence to show what the accepted and proper practice was. And it was vital that that evidence should be of the highest quality. In other words, it was crucial to our case that we should call an accountant as a witness who was regarded by the profession as the best possible authority on accountancy practice and who could put forward his expert views in a convincing manner. I thought that Eddy Ray, the senior partner of one of the large firms of accountants, Spicer and Pegler, was such a man. I knew him because he had sat with me on a tribunal of which I was chairman and felt sure that he would be a good witness. Furthermore, his firm had, for many years, been in the forefront of those who took an interest in the education of young men in the mysteries of the accountants' profession. He agreed with the view of the accountancy practice that was held by Lord Llewellyn-Davies's advisers so we decided to call him.

In due course, the case came before the Special Commissioners of Income Tax. I will not recite the details of the case which was concerned, as can be imagined, with highly technical matters of the practice of accountants when trying to arrive at a true and fair view of the profits of an architect when he was engaged in a long lasting building contract of the sort that had formed Lord Llewellyn-Davies's relationship with the bodies that employed him to design and supervise the building of hospitals. It suffices to say that Eddy Ray gave his evidence very well and was a most convincing witness with the result that when, some time later, the decision of the Special Commissioners was announced, they accepted the arguments that we had put to them and the assessment was discharged. It was a great relief to me that all had turned out satisfactorily. The Inland Revenue appealed against the decision which was heard by Mr Justice Warner after I had been appointed a judge, so the appeal was conducted by another Queen's Counsel. Mr Justice Warner upheld the decision of the Special Commissioners and the Inland Revenue accepted that decision. Lord Llewellyn-Davies was not made bankrupt and Lady Llewellyn-Davies remained leader of the Labour peers in the House of Lords. Tragically, Lord Llewellyn-Davies died very shortly after the litigation ended. The case shows however, that there are tax cases which are of immense importance to the taxpayer and where the amount of money in dispute may be great. They can be very nail biting cases for the barrister who is called upon to conduct them.

With Elizabeth on beach at Pittwater.

With Elizabeth and Dru by Sydney Opera House and in front of the harbour Bridge.

In Dru's little house in Phillip Street.

October, 1981, in my full togs on the day I was sworn in by Lord Hailsham the Lord Chancellor.

Talking to Lord Nolan at opening of combined Tax Tribunal Centre. In front Lord Mackay, Lord Chancellor, talking to Basil James, Special Comissioner of Income Tax.

With the Lord Chancellor, (Lord Mackay of Clashfern) and Paul Heim (left) at opening of courts of Combined Tax Tribunals, 44 Bedford Square.

Corner of the President's room at 44 Bedford Square. This room was once the drawing room of Lady Ottoline Morrell and later of Lord Oxford and Asquith after his retirement. Asquith had been Prime Minister during the first world war.

CHAPTER TWENTY-SIX

Last Years as a Barrister

Not long after I had finished Lord Llewellyn-Davies's case, I heard that there was a vacancy for a Circuit judge in Oxford and I decided to ask to be considered. It was an appointment that I thought would suit me perfectly. Little Place is only about seven miles from Oxford so it would mean an end to long journeys to courts far away on the circuit and an end to weeks in London. I liked, too, the idea of working in a university town where one could perhaps be of help to law teachers and keep in contact with the young and new entrants to the profession. One would have access to all that Oxford has to offer. I knew well, as old circuit friends, the two judges who were already sitting there. I would not be in strange territory. I was afraid, however, that the Lord Chancellor might think that he ought to appoint an Oxford man. Nevertheless, I decided to try my luck. In due course, I was interviewed by two men from the Lord Chancellor's office and not long afterwards received a letter telling me that the Lord Chancellor would like to appoint me and asking if I would accept. So the matter was settled. There was only one difficulty. I had been instructed in two important cases which were to be tried in Malaysia and the dates of the trials had been fixed for some two months later. I did not wish to give up these, as I had done a lot of work on them and I was not unmindful of the fact that my clerk, David, had already negotiated a very good fee. Furthermore, I was looking forward to going to Malaysia, a country I had never visited. I asked that my appointment might be postponed until I had done these two cases in the Far East and this was readily agreed.

As the summer vacation was approaching and as it had been arranged that I should take up my appointment in October, Elizabeth and I decided to combine business with pleasure and take a holiday in Asia after the cases were over. Unfortunately, Elizabeth could not accompany me to Malaysia as she was teaching Spanish during school term, so I set out alone and we arranged that we would meet in Sri Lanka and have a holiday there after I had finished the two cases, by which time her school would have broken up for the summer holidays.

I flew out to Kuala Lumpur a few days before the first of the two cases in which I was to be engaged was due to begin. In the first case, I was briefed by the State of Johore in a case which raised difficult, but uninteresting, points of law relating to the powers of the state over virgin land which by the National Land Code of Malaysia was vested in it. The State was given power by the code to alienate the land for periods and to charge rent to those to whom it was alienated. The code also provided that in the event of the due rent not being paid, the State had power to forfeit the lease. The case concerned a large area, some 20,680 acres, of virgin forest land which had been alienated to a sugar company for a period of 99 years. The sugar company had charged its interest in the land to a bank in return for a substantial loan. It had then spent some 18 million dollars in developing the land as a sugar cane plantation and in building a sugar factory on it. After some ten years it failed to pay the rent and, as the land code enabled it to do, the State forfeited the company's right to occupy the land.

The sole question that arose was whether or not the court had power to relieve the company against the forfeiture. No such power was given in the land code, but in England the courts had developed an equitable doctrine of relief against forfeiture in cases between a landlord and a tenant. Should that non-statutory development of English law be read into a written land code? The company argued that in fairness it should. The company had originally appealed to the High Court in Johore where the Chief Justice had decided in its favour and held that the court had the power to relieve against forfeiture and it was against that decision that the State of Johore, for whom I now appeared, appealed to the Federal Court of Appeal.

The few days before the case began had been taken up with preparations for the hearing. I wrote in my diary:

> "The next day the legal adviser for the State of Johore, who is instructing me arrived together with another Indian barrister, Mr Pillay, who is also to be my junior. The legal adviser Alauddin, is a pleasant little bearded Malay. Rather earnest and humourless but straight forward and anxious to help. Pillay, who arrived with his wife, a vast mountainous woman wrapped (except where her bulging midriff could not be contained) in a sari, and three children. Pillay never stopped talking in a nearly incomprehensible pidgin English. They all came up to my room where I had hoped to be able to glean information about the case. This was hardly possible with the children and mother romping around and trying the wireless and TV which were in the room. However, eventually I was able to get rid of the Pillay family and then had an interesting and helpful consultation with Alauddin."

It was not quite how consultations with QCs are conducted in England.

Later, I was able to contact some of the other counsel involved in the case. There were, in all, seven of whom one was a Malay, three were Indians (one a Sikh), one was Chinese and two were English. The company was represented by an Englishman who had been a judge in Malaysia and after retiring had returned to practise at the Bar. His junior was Chinese, a charming and very clever man called Wong Kim Fatt. During our consultation, Mr Pillay had told me that he did not trust Wong Kim Fatt and that he was convinced that Wong Kim Fatt's clients had bribed the Chief Justice before the earlier hearings in the High Court as he was about to retire and needed money. He had no shred of evidence of this outrageous suggestion but seemed somewhat put out that I refused to consider it as an argument to be put to the court. The bank which had lent money to the company was represented by an Indian, Mr Chelliah and the Sikh, Mr Gill. One evening I was asked to dinner by the Sikh who, I was told, was very rich and more concerned with commerce and business than the law. He had an interest in the hotel where I was staying and was clearly given most favoured nation treatment. The dinner was a magnificent feast. It went on and on, course after course and my glass was never empty. I think that the total number of courses was sixteen. I noted in my diary, "oddly, though I must have eaten a large amount, I felt no ill effects and indeed enjoyed it more than the sort of Chinese meal one sometimes eats at home". During this meal, I was given a detailed description of the idiosyncrasies of the judges that were to form the court. One, an Indian, Mr Justice Abdoolcadder was, I was told, very difficult. He had no interests save the law, was arrogant and thought that he alone knew it all. He was rude and interrupted continuously. The president of the court, Wan Suleman, on the other hand, was courteous and good. This intelligence proved valuable when we started the case next day. I also learned during that dinner that only once before had a QC come out from England to do a case in Malaysia, that was Sir Dingle Foot who had been out some four or five years before. There had been objections to any being allowed to come raised by the Bar Council of Malaysia, but a hearing in the High Court had decided that I should be allowed to appear.

The day before the appeal was due to be heard I visited the court buildings in order to get the feel of the place before I actually had to address the court. As it was very hot and depressingly sultry in Kuala Lumpur, I was concerned to discover whether or not the building had air conditioning. If it had not, my court dress of an English QC, thick tailcoat and waistcoat with a heavy silk gown would have been very uncomfortable. However, I was gratified to find, on entering the building from the sweltering heat of the street outside, that it was pleasantly cool and was well served by an efficient air conditioning system. I did not, therefore, take any special precautions by equipping myself with court clothing more suitable for tropical heat. The next day when I arrived to begin the case, I changed into my full English court dress. Just as I was about to start addressing the court, the air conditioning system broke down and the whole place soon became appallingly hot. I began to perspire freely and sweat streamed down from my forehead and down my back. I wondered if I would be able to go on. Fortunately, after a short period of extreme discomfort, the President said that he was getting uncomfortably hot and we would adjourn until the system was put right. So I was saved from a situation of some embarrassment. The fault was soon remedied and we got underway again. Wong Kim Fatt had decided to take a preliminary point so he began to address the court. This gave me an opportunity of judging whether or not the account of the judges I had been given earlier, was accurate. When Wong Kim Fatt made his submissions, he was given a very rough passage by Mr Justice Abdoolcadder and it appeared that what I had been told about this judge was a fair description. I wondered how he would treat me when my turn came. I decided to try and flatter him by referring to cases that he had decided and saying how helpful to a proper understanding of the difficult problem facing the court they were. He smiled. Thereafter, he was most friendly and I was heard with the utmost courtesy. Chelliah the Indian followed me. I wrote in my diary of him "Chelliah is an old Indian advocate who had been offered a judgeship which he had refused. He is a very dark Indian with a snow white imperial beard. He has a soft and most persuasive voice. He dealt with the case shortly and cogently. He was very good. Denning would have loved to have heard him." Fortunately, his charm did not lead the court astray and after all argument had ended, it indicated that it proposed to allow the appeal and would give its reasons later. This produced much rejoicing and Alauddin told me that the Chief Minister had been very worried about the outcome.

I will complete my account of this case by quoting a rather charming sentence from the judgement of the court that was given some time later.

"We should perhaps also add that acceding to the plea put forward for equitable relief against forfeiture and the exercise of the court's inherent jurisdiction on this matter would, quite apart from throwing statute to the winds, be no less than to signal a judicial imprimatur to a process of energising a renascence of the apparition of the length of the English Chancellor's foot as the criterion for meting out equity to reactivate itself in a modern context as that of our several judges' feet."

The other case which I had undertaken to do in Malaysia had in the meantime been settled so that I was free to set out for Sri Lanka to meet Elizabeth who was due to arrive there in about a week's time. My last two days in Kuala Lumpur were spent in seeing the sights of that town. Alauddin, who proved to be a well informed cicerone, shewed me the Sultan's palace, a fascinating museum shewing the history of the various states that made up Malaysia and the modern mosque, a magnificent cool building of polished white marble, spacious courtyards and gardens with fountains and canals running through them. Finally, he took me to the railway station which, rather surprisingly, is one of the city's finer buildings. Built by the British in a mixture of Victorian and Moorish styles it is a tribute to the British architects who so often in commonwealth countries managed to create fine buildings that captured the architectural atmosphere of both England and the country in which it was built.

I then flew to Colombo to await the arrival of Elizabeth who was due three days later. On landing at the airport, I learned that a day or two before, troubles had broken out between the Tamils in the north of the island and the Sinhalese who formed the majority of the country's population. The result of this was that I had to obtain a pass before I was allowed to travel by taxi to my hotel. The acquisition of the pass was a laborious business requiring a visit to the local police station and numerous interviews with clerks and officials. I was only able to leave the airport well after midnight, but it was as well, in view of what happened, that I got the pass.

The hotel at which I was booked in was a few miles down the coast on the road between the airport and Colombo. The road runs through plantations of coconut palms interspersed with a few small villages. It was a dark night when I set out in an elderly taxi with a determined looking taxi driver. As we drove under the arching palms we heard, from time to time, explosions and passed through a village in which several houses were on fire. Then suddenly in the rather feeble light of the taxi's headlights, I saw somebody in the middle of the road ahead waving a hurricane lamp. Whoever it was plainly wanted us to stop but my driver drove on, only slowing slightly until we reached the man with the lamp. I then saw that it was a soldier armed with a machine gun gesticulating to us to stop. There were other soldiers in the shadows to the side of the road. But we did not stop and it then became clear that the brakes of the taxi were of indifferent efficiency. Fortunately, the soldiers did not fire at us and when eventually we stopped some way down the road, they came running up and opened the door of the cab and asked who I was. Fortunately, the pass I had obtained did the trick and we were allowed to drive on. It had, however, been an unpleasant few minutes. The hotel, when I reached it, proved to be a modern and comfortable building built on the edge of an inlet running in from the sea. Small fishing boats were moored there and the activities of the men working them and many small children playing around them provided me with ready made subjects to sketch. I spent most of my time during the two days I was compelled to wait there, trying to catch the atmosphere of the place in sketches. Two days later, Elizabeth arrived at the airport and we set off at once in a car driven by a Sinhalese called David who I had found near the hotel. He proved to be an excellent driver and guide. He was a very devout Catholic and whenever we stopped in a town or village where there was a Catholic church, he would slip inside and offer up a few prayers before going on. We drove first to Kandy, the ancient city in the foothills of the mountain range in the centre of the island. We had hoped to be in time to see part of the celebrations, known as the Perahera, when Buddha's tooth is taken from the Temple of the Tooth in an elaborately decorated casket and paraded around the great lake in front of the temple on the back of a royal elephant suitably decked out in rich regalia. Unfortunately, due to Elizabeth's delayed arrival, we missed the main procession but saw several finely decorated elephants.

From Kandy we drove on to Anaradhapura, the old sacred city which covered at one time some 16 square miles. It is now in ruins but very fine ruins they are. The builders used remarkably advanced building methods. The roofs (now gone) of many buildings had been supported on huge square granite pillars which still stand. The baths had very fine examples of ashlar granite squares. One large pagoda was being restored with the help of funds from UNESCO and the archaeological department of the government was obviously making great efforts to preserve the large number of buildings in the old city. In the evening after a day spent seeing these sights, we walked down to a large lagoon where we saw a flock of egrets and other wading birds, beautiful in the setting sun. On our way, we passed a man who had a large wicked-looking cobra which danced as he played tunes on his pipe. Apparently, its poisoned fangs had been removed but it was no less a repulsive reptile for all that.

From Anaradhapura we motored across the island and north to the harbour at Trincomalee. During the war, Trinco had been an important harbour for the British fleet in the Indian Ocean and when I saw it then several allied warships were moored there and much of the activity associated with a busy harbour was visible. This time, it was very different. The harbour is hardly used and on the shore is a shanty town of huts and small shops. The old garrison buildings were still there now occupied by a small unit of the Sinhalese army. I talked to the sergeant major in charge of the Guard at the gate. He was a wonderful person, just like a British sergeant major of the Guards, complete with a fierce waxed moustache, a shining Sam Browne belt and a fine swagger stick. He stood erect and smart as he addressed me. He was obviously proud to carry on the British tradition of smart soldiering. He told me that he had joined the army in 1942 when he was sixteen. Later, I met a similar man from the Royal Navy, a chief petty officer who, too, was a mirror image of the typical British counterpart.

We spent three idyllic days at a small hotel on the coast south of the town. It was the time of year when the weather on the east coast of Ceylon is perfect, similar to that of a warm spring in Tuscany. We were taken by a fisherman to a small island, Pigeon Island, a mile or so off the coast where Elizabeth sunbathed and snorkelled reporting seeing lots of beautifully coloured fish. I wandered over the island which at its southern end has a small rocky hill where thousands of blue headed pigeons nest amongst the rocks. On another occasion, we visited an old Hindu temple built on the end of a promontory. It had been largely destroyed by the Portuguese settlers in the seventeenth century but had been handsomely restored. We were shewn round by, as I recorded in my diary, "a fat sanctimonious woman who was not very helpful or informative."

After this short but pleasant interlude, we started back to the south of the island. The country through which we drove was very dry and much of the paddy land was not producing any rice because of the lack of water. We were told that the drought was very serious and was causing much hardship in the villages. Our route took us through much of the jungle covered country where I had been with the East African Division during the war training for jungle warfare shortly before going on to Burma. Here and there, we passed hills which I could remember had been chosen as observation points for the guns and we also saw one of the extraordinary hatches of yellow butterflies which I remember so well. The side of the road becomes almost invisible through a cloud of insects all flying the same way. Then suddenly they disappear as suddenly as they had come. The water buffalo, the wading cattle and the coconut palm pushing its feathered head through the top of the smaller jungle scrub also brought back vivid memories. We paused for a day at Sigirya where there is now a very comfortable and pleasant hotel to house the tourists who come to see the remarkable rock which rises for several hundred feet above the jungle covered plain. Its sides are nearly vertical and on the top one of the Sinhalese kings built a fortress and palace largely carved out of the solid rock. Elizabeth stayed in the hotel swimming and sunbathing while I set off to climb the rock. I was given the wrong instructions for getting there and had a forty minute walk through forest. I enjoyed hearing the jungle fowl chuck chucking and the other odd noises that the many birds of the forest make. Eventually, I reached the rock where I was surrounded by a crowd of pedlars selling bright yellow lemonade and many beggars. I found a little boy who offered to be my guide. He proved to be a nice lad who looked after me well. I wrote in my diary:

"It is a good climb. 600 ft and very steep. Steps up are carved in the rock. It is a remarkable fortress. At the bottom is a moat walled with huge rectangular granite blocks. Climbing higher one reaches first an area consisting of the audience chamber and surrounding rooms, then a reverse slope under a bit of overhanging rock where frescoes of 'heavenly maidens' cover the rocks. They are more delicate and fresh than most oriental art that I have seen. Red and yellow ochre colouring rather similar to that of the wall paintings in the caves at Altimara. Then on past a 'mirror wall' which is a highly polished bit of vertical marble upon which, my guide was happy to tell me, graffiti is scratched which dates back to the 5th century AD. Halfway up is a great door leading to the last stretch of stairs, which is guarded by lions' feet on either side. These huge feet are shaped out of rock and brick. Originally, no doubt, plastered and painted. At the top of the rock there is a marvellous view of the hills around. The remains of the palace built on the top shew that it must have been a sizeable building. Fine stone baths and the site of wonderful gardens are clearly visible. From the top, one can see the shape of the considerable royal palace area at the bottom of the hill."

I rejoined Elizabeth in the hotel very hot and very thirsty, but I have rarely in recent years enjoyed a walk and a climb so much.

We completed our tour of Sri Lanka by returning to Colombo where we spent two days with Pamela and Vernon Wijetunge. He was by then the doyen of the Bar in Colombo having returned there after spending a number of years in England after Mrs Bandaranyika's government had confiscated almost all his property and made it very difficult for him to practise in his native country. I had got to know him when he lived in Abingdon where, quite coincidentally, Pamela had become the matron at the school. Vernon took me to the courts and introduced me to the President of the Court of Appeal,

Colin Thomé, who is a Burgher. He was writing a judgement even though it was the middle of his vacation. I then watched a case being tried by a Tamil judge. He seemed impressive and fair. Meanwhile, Pamela took Elizabeth to see a particularly lovely temple just outside Colombo. Our other day in Colombo was taken up with a trip down the coast to Bentota where I had been stationed during the war. It was then no more than a few huts and a temple in the palm groves. It has a wonderful long expanse of beach which in those days was totally deserted except for, perhaps, one or two fishermen. Now it is a prosperous tourist centre. Several large hotels line the beach. They are not ugly: indeed, I thought the architecture was pleasant and tasteful. They are rapidly becoming favourite tourist attractions and must bring some very welcome foreign money to the island. I gathered from one or two of the locals to whom I spoke that the German and Scandinavian visitors are very unpopular. They are arrogant and rude. It is surprising how popular the English now are. There is none of the suppressed hostility that was very noticeable in 1942 before the island had achieved independence. Quite a few of the Sinhalese with whom I spoke commented on how good things had been when the English ruled. There was plenty of work and it was better paid than now.

We arrived back in England on 26 August and on arriving at our flat in the Temple, found a message from my sister, Betty, to say that my father had died the day before. He was 94 and had been failing for some time, but even so, it came as a shock. On 28 August he was buried in a grave next to my mother in Chertsey where they had lived since 1928. It was a beautiful day, bright and clear. After the funeral, I wrote in my diary:

"Dad was, I think, a very unusual man. Always very quiet he never took a lead in conversation so that some might have thought he was insignificant. But his quietness overlay a character of remarkable strength and depth. He was totally devoid of ambition for himself and never allowed himself even the smallest luxury — except to smoke his pipe. He was a solicitor who took tremendous care with his work and would go to very great trouble to make sure his clients were given the best possible service. He never charged more than a very modest fee with the result that he made very little money and indeed much of his work must have been done totally uneconomically. He was kind and patient and I never heard him say a cross word. He and mother were devoted and lived together in what must have been quite unusual amity, I never heard them quarrel — ever. In the last year or two of his life, he thought a great deal about the troubled economic times through which England was passing. His cure for inflation was simple. It would be cured if we all acted without selfishness. He practised what he preached. He refused to consider increasing the rent of the builders yard next door to Curfew House from £250 p.a. at which it had been fixed many years ago even though the current value was about £4,000 p.a. He simply said if everyone did that sort of thing there would be no end to inflation. He was a good Greek scholar and until he went blind, he liked nothing better than to read in the original Greek the great Homeric stories and Greek plays. He always read the law reports in *The Times* and often when I called to see him he would ask me what I thought of a decision. His was a very conservative chancery mind and he knew the reasoning behind all the old rules of equity and conveyancing and was very critical of those who overlooked them or took short cuts."

His secretary, Eileen Buchan, who worked for him for twenty four years wrote to me after he had died and said she had very much enjoyed her years with him. "I find", she continued, "I get rather annoyed these days when people so often denounce solicitors as a class of money makers whose work is of little importance, no doubt because my ideas are based on the standard of your father's work which was so high whether he was to be paid a reasonable sum for it, or very little, or even nothing, but I suppose many people do not come up to his standards or give the time and care he did to find the right solutions to problems. We did not have plush carpets but the quality of work for clients was better than comes out of some grand offices."

Fortunately when I had gone to see my father shortly before I had left for Malaysia, I had known that I was to be made a judge and I had told him. I think it pleased him. When I first took up law, he rather hoped that I would follow him and become a solicitor, but I know that I had not the qualities that are necessary to make a good solicitor and so I was never tempted. He later became interested in the way my career developed and was always very wise and helpful with advice.

It had been estimated that the case that I was to have done in Malaysia and which was settled would take four weeks to try. This meant that there was a period of about a month after we returned to England before I was due to become a judge. Unfortunately, it proved impossible during this period, to go to Australia to see Drusilla as we had hoped, so I spent the last month of my life as a barrister doing two murder trials, one in Stafford and one in Birmingham. Then on 9 October 1981, I was sworn in before Lord Hailsham, the Lord Chancellor and my 34 years as a practising barrister came to an end.

CHAPTER TWENTY-SEVEN

Circuit Judge

The swearing in ceremony took place in the House of Lords. I had asked Jane and Lucy to bring the two eldest grandchildren, Muffy and Sophie and so they all accompanied Elizabeth and me in a large hired car from the Temple to Westminster where we were met by a member of the Lord Chancellor's staff who took us into the Victoria Gardens where photographs were taken. While this was going on, Lord Hailsham came into the garden with his little dog 'Mini' which wanted a run on the grass. The children got into conversation with the old man and were soon on excellent terms with him. We then all returned to Lord Hailsham's room where I was sworn in and he handed me the Letters Patent, the formal document, appointing me. Normally, it would have been signed by the Queen, but on this occasion, as she was out of the country, was signed by Princess Anne and Princess Margaret. Hailsham commented that I had two Royal signatures for the price of one. He apparently had thought I was only a tax specialist and had not realised that I had been a recorder trying crime for some seventeen years because he asked me how I thought I would enjoy doing criminal cases. He then told me that I should be made a Fellow of one of the colleges at Oxford as that was where I was going to sit. He laughed when I said that I had my eyes on Pembroke College. He had a few words with Elizabeth and Jane and Lucy and we were then taken on a short tour of the House of Lords before returning to chambers where the members had laid on drinks. Everyone was very kind. Thus began my life as a judge. A day or two later, I sat at Oxford for the first time in my new role. For a few weeks, I was given criminal cases to try and was doing substantially the same sort of work as I had done sitting as a recorder and the advocates appearing before me were, for the most part, on the Midland and Oxford Circuit and were well known to me. They welcomed me kindly and I found my immersion in the new waters of judicial life less alarming than I had feared. I had made it clear to the Circuit Administrator on my appointment that I hoped to be engaged in trying a wide variety of cases. I had always thought that to spend all one's time trying criminal cases would be very dull. I have always felt sure that it is best to have a varied diet. It was desirable, it seemed to me, that the problems coming before one should be varied and encourage flexibility of mind and approach. This I was able to achieve and was soon dealing with many different types of both civil and divorce cases as well as criminal ones. I remembered what Alan Orr had said to me many years before when I had been his pupil. He had said that he considered that far and away the most satisfying work that one could be asked to do during one's legal career was the work of a County Court judge. In those days a County Court judge was employed only to try civil and perhaps divorce cases and his jurisdiction usually covered a fairly limited area such as a large town or, in rural areas, a county. Most of the cases were of no great significance or importance, except to the parties involved. But to the parties even the most trivial case could seem a matter of major importance in their life. Alan Orr had said that if the humble litigants who came before you felt that their cases had been tried fairly and that the judge was understanding of their position and if he was courteous to the witnesses and explained carefully the conclusion to which he had come, they would be satisfied. There was much in the work of a County Court judge that was similar to the work of a parish priest. He was in contact with all sorts and conditions of men and women and saw much of life in its harsher manifestations. It was Alan's strong opinion that if a County Court judge got to know the problems of the less fortunate members of society in his areas and was able to deal with the cases coming before him, which often arose as a result of those problems, in a fair and understanding way, he was doing a worthwhile public service not unlike that of the pastor in a large parish. It was not long before I came to see the truth in what Alan had said and found myself trying to live up to the standards that he set.

Since 1947 when I had started there had been a number of developments which meant that the life of a Circuit judge was very different in the 1980s. The most significant was, perhaps, that there had been a very substantial increase in the number of criminal cases coming before the courts. This meant that the ordinary Circuit judge had to spend part of his time trying moderately serious criminal cases. The most serious were tried by the High Court judges who came round the Circuit at intervals. They tried murder and rape and other very serious cases. But all the rest were left to the Circuit judge. If a Circuit judge was certified by the Lord Chancellor as being capable of trying more serious cases, he might, too, be called upon to handle these cases if the High Court judge was not able to deal with them. I found myself trying rape cases from time to time in this way as well as the innumerable other types of crime ranging from robbery to shop lifting.

Another great change had taken place during my years in the law. There had been a staggering increase in the rate of divorce and a fundamental change in the law of divorce from that which prevailed in 1947. Nowadays, it is very rare for the question of whether the petitioner should be granted a divorce having to be decided. Before the law was reformed the divorce courts spent much time trying cases in which the issue was simply whether or not the petitioner was entitled to a decree of divorce on one of the grounds which the law then permitted, namely that the other party to the marriage had committed adultery, or treated the petitioner with cruelty, or had deserted the petitioner for upwards of three years. Arguing about these issues was a wasteful and distasteful exercise. It often involved the parties in enormous costs and almost invariably led to more and more bitterness and not infrequently, to perjury and aggravation. When the law was reformed, if it was clear that the marriage had irretrievably broken down, it was not usually necessary to go into the details of what it had been that had caused the breakdown. The courts were therefore, left to decide what should be the arrangements for the children and what should be the financial arrangements between the parties after the divorce. The arrangements for the children were, of course, matters of the utmost importance. Many parents are reasonable about this and reach an amicable and sensible settlement. But there are some parents who are unable to agree and so the decision is left to a judge. When I was doing divorce work, I often found myself starting the day by granting a decree nisi to some 25 couples whose marriages had plainly broken down. This I did twice a week so that in a single week, I often cut the bonds of marriage of a hundred men and women. When I had been doing this for some six or seven years, I felt that I must have divorced most of the married couples in Oxfordshire and some of them twice!

Cases in which I was called upon to decide the fate of children arose not only in divorce proceedings but also in cases where the local authority had taken children into care, or were contemplating doing so. These cases could be very difficult to decide as one was often faced with only two alternatives, both of which were in their own way undesirable. Either the child would have to live with an unsatisfactory family, or single parent or would be condemned to live in an institution or, perhaps, with foster parents.

The devoted work that is done by the vast majority of those who manage or work in the various homes in which children in care are often housed should never be forgotten. We all owe them an enormous debt. But the fact remains that the 'house mother' in charge of several children in a home is no substitute for a true parent. I think that most judges and indeed others like social workers and court welfare officers, who spend much of their time dealing with cases in which the welfare of children is in question find themselves wondering about the tremendous changes that have taken place in our society in the years since the Second World War. Does the relative ease of divorce make, on balance, for greater or less happiness in the children of the many more broken homes that exist nowadays? In the days shortly after the end of the war, it was often said that children suffered more and were more adversely affected if they were compelled to live in a family where the parents were continuously quarrelling, where perhaps violence was not infrequent, than they did after a divorce when they might be living with a single parent or in a household consisting of one of their own parents and a step parent and perhaps a number of step brothers and sisters. On the other hand, the present position where large numbers of children are separated from one of their true parents leads, in the view of many wise people, to great unhappiness. One thing that impressed me very much when I was trying a large number of cases about children was the attitude of the children when I was able to assess it with reasonable accuracy. In certain cases when the children were over about eight years old and were I thought old enough to have a sensible opinion, I would ask them what they wanted to happen. Almost always they would say they wanted mummy and daddy to stay together at home. That the home that they had always known should not be broken up was almost invariably their most deep desire. Though I never kept a record by which I could compare the numbers of children who expressed this sort of view with those, relatively few, who said from the start, that they did not wish to live with one of the parents, I have always had the impression that this latter category was very largely composed of those who had witnessed serious violence or terrible quarrelling between their parents. This experience, brought home to me over several years, made one wonder, as many have done before me, how society should regulate the relationship between men and women in the best interests both of the children and of the rest of society. It is a problem that has become more difficult to resolve in recent years because of at least two changes that have taken place. First, the life expectancy of both sexes has substantially increased so that many people marrying in their twenties can live to celebrate a golden wedding. During those years for some, their interests and their love may have brought them close to that perfect association which is the ideal of Christian marriage and their fiftieth wedding anniversary is indeed a golden occasion. For others, however, their interests, even their natures, may have changed from what they were in their early youthful days. Secondly, methods of contraception have enabled men and women living together to decide when and if they have children. This latter fact has led to many young people living together outside the bonds of marriage, a practice which a large part of society has come to accept. So long as each is working, or so long as each is in some way independently supported, no great harm comes if such liaisons are discontinued unless, of course, there are children.

In the light of these two changes that have taken place in our society in the past half century is there a case for altering the long held view of Christians that marriage should be for life and indissoluble? I think that there is. If it becomes generally acceptable for young people to live together before marriage, there is a greater chance of liaisons which prove unsatisfactory, either sexually or for any other reason, being brought to an end before the more solemn bond of marriage is tied. This should mean that fewer marriages take place that are likely to prove unhappy to the parties. This being so, the prospects of a marriage succeeding when once the parties have decided on it, should be greater than they are when the parties have not been able to assess whether or not they are truly suited to each other. Likewise at the other end of a marriage when the people have been married for such a length of time that all their children are mature then it seems to me that there really is little point in insisting that an elderly couple who have little left in common and whose natures and interests may have changed considerably over the years and who at best are living in a state of indifference to each other and at worst may be positively hostile to each other, should remain tied together. The interests of any children demand that while they are growing up they should do so in a family with both a father and mother playing an essential part. When once they are grown up and the parents are no longer of that crucial importance to them, then, if to require the parents to continue to live together will bring unhappiness, it seems cruel to require them to do so.

The conclusion to which I came after I had seen, as a result of my work at Oxford, a multitude of broken marriages and hundreds of desperately unhappy young children was one which I only recently realised was the solution put forward by Jack Simon my old friend from my early days at the Bar. He became the President of the Probate, Divorce and Admiralty Division of the High Court (as it was then) and expressed his view when the reforms that later came into effect in the 1967 Act were being considered. When I met him recently, he told me that he had tried to stop the Divorce Law Reform Act of 1967 from going through in its original form but was unable to persuade Gerald Gardiner, who was then the Labour Lord Chancellor. Had Jack been made a peer after being appointed to the Presidency, as had always been the practice in the past, he would have had a voice in the House of Lords and might perhaps have been able to affect the course of the Bill. But his peerage was held up until the Conservatives came into power in 1970 and Lord Hailsham became Lord Chancellor. Jack told me that he thought Gerald Gardiner had held it up on purpose to ensure that he could not press this view, which because of his position as President of the Divorce Court, would surely have carried considerable weight.

The solution that he wished to advocate was that until all children of a marriage had reached the age of sixteen, divorce of their parents should only be permitted in exceptional circumstances. Thereafter, divorce should be possible if in truth the marriage had broken down, though it was, of course, important that the financial position of the wife should be protected. The subject is, of course, a complicated one and I have only given a brief outline of his views because, quite independently, I had come to a similar conclusion as a result of the work I did in my early years as a judge. In a field which touches in the most profound way, the happiness of so many people what is required is a system of law which provides a framework in which people, children and grownups, are most likely to be able to lead their lives in contentment and happiness. A legal framework such as I have indicated would in my view, be the most likely to achieve this result. I feel sure that it would be an improvement on what, as a result of the reforms of the last quarter century, we have now got which is a system that results in many, many children being plunged into unhappiness early in life which not infrequently affects the whole of the rest of their lives. Equally, it would, I feel, be an improvement on what existed before the recent reforms, which often resulted in what A.P. Herbert called Holy Deadlock, whereby two essentially decent people were each condemned to be tied to someone with whom no common bonds of love or affection remained.

But that is a diversion. During my years sitting mainly at Oxford, I was not concerned only with children's cases. They occupied about one third of my workload. The rest of the time I was engaged in trying criminal and civil cases. When I was appointed, there was a shortage of High Court judges. An Act of Parliament lays down a limit to the number of High Court judges that may be appointed and at this time the limit had been reached but the existing number was unable to cope with the work and a backlog of High Court cases built up. To deal with this, some Circuit judges who were considered suitable were from time to time asked to sit as High Court judges in order to help reduce the backlog. I was asked to do this and went to Birmingham several times and to Lincoln. On these occasions, I stayed at the judge's lodgings where the other judges then sitting were also staying. On my first visit to Birmingham, I put up an awful gaffe. I had been told that the housekeeper there was a lady of pale complexion and humourless disposition who always dressed in black. She was irreverently known to the local Bar as Mrs Danvers after the housekeeper at Manderley in Daphne du Maurier's novel Rebecca. When I arrived at the lodgings one Sunday evening, I entered the hall and coming down the stairs was a stoutish lady of pale complexion dressed in black and I assumed that she was the housekeeper and treated her accordingly. At dinner that night, I realised to my horror that she was Lady Bush, the wife of the senior High Court judge present. It soon became apparent that she was not of a humourless disposition and I do not think that she bore me any ill will. At Lincoln where I was sent with Desmond Fennell, who later became a High Court judge, but at that time was Leader of the Midland and Oxford Circuit, the lodgings are in a fine Georgian house half way along the ridge that is dominated by the Cathedral at one end and by the Castle (in which the crown courts were situated) at the other. We were looked after by a housekeeper and butler in great comfort. It was July and the weather was very hot and it always seemed to me ridiculous that we were not allowed to walk the short distance from the lodgings to the courts but had to be transported in a huge black hired car. We were told that this was for reasons of security and to ensure proper respect for Her Majesty's judges. When I inquired how much the hire car cost was, I was told £500 per week. £500 per week would have comfortably paid for a good typist at Oxford where one was desperately needed and where we were told that there was not enough money to pay for one. It has for some time seemed to me that now that the old circuit system that prevailed when I started has been completely altered, the old practices of housing the High Court judge, as he proceeded from county to county, in large expensive houses, manned by cook and butler should be abandoned. A system that would cost the taxpayer a great deal less and which would not detract from the respect in which the judiciary should be held would not be difficult to arrange. For each big city, Birmingham, Leeds, Manchester, Bristol and the like, two High Court judges who had roots in the area and who lived nearby could be appointed to sit in that city and if necessary in local towns. They could find their way to court without the aid of an expensive hired car, just as High Court judges sitting in London find their way to the courts in the Strand by tube or bus like any other commuter. It is probably desirable that High Court judges spend part of their life in London so that they can keep in touch with their colleagues there and with the latest developments in the law and practice. This could, however, be arranged by having two High Court judges allocated to each large city and requiring each of them to sit there for six months in the year and for six months in London.

The days when the Queen's judge sent to a county town in order to hold an assize arrived in a coach and six to impress the locals with the majesty of the law have long passed. The judges should be respected by the man in the street because they are seen to be people deserving respect for the way they do their difficult job.

But only a small part of my time was spent doing the work of a High Court judge in these posh surroundings. Usually I was in Oxford dealing with the normal run of criminal and civil cases. They varied greatly in their importance and their difficulty. When I came into my room in the morning, I might find that I was going to be faced with a case of petty theft or, at the other extreme, a case of serious violence or fraud or even rape. Civil cases were equally varied. One might be trying a case where a landlord was seeking to evict a tenant for non-payment of rent or where two neighbours were arguing about the boundary between their houses or one where a plaintiff who had suffered a serious accident in a car or at work in a factory was claiming against the person who he said was responsible. All these cases were of great importance to the people involved in them and the views that Alan Orr had expressed to me were never far from my mind. It was of paramount importance that everyone who was involved in the case should feel that they had been treated fairly and that the proceedings had, throughout, been conducted in a dignified but friendly manner. Whether I succeeded in doing that is for others to judge. It is rare for a judge to learn what those in front of him think about the way he has treated them but just occasionally, one has one's eyes opened. Once when I was sitting in Oxford, I slipped out of the court buildings during the lunch hour to go to the shops. I was walking along the High Street which was very crowded when suddenly, a hand was slapped onto my shoulder from behind. I looked round and saw a very large West Indian, at least six foot six tall and broad in proportion. My first thought was that I was about to be mugged and said to myself "Medd, you must be brave" But I need not have worried. He was a delightful chap. He said, "You are Judge Medd aren't you?" I said "Yes". He then said "Thank you so much for putting me on probation the other day. I am so grateful!" I am afraid that I could not remember him coming up in court and had no idea of what it was he had done. But I got the impression that he had genuinely learned his lesson.

After I had been at Oxford for a year or so, I was invited to become a part-time Special Commissioner of Income Tax. This was an offer I accepted with pleasure as it meant that from time to time, I would have to try tax cases in London and elsewhere. Not only did this mean that once again, I would have to tackle work of a sort that I would enjoy, but also it meant that my work would be more varied. Shortly after agreeing to take this on, I was called upon to hear a tax appeal by one of the big oil companies that had been boring for oil on the bed of the North Sea. The case concerned the precautions that the oil companies were required to take to ensure that the sea was not polluted with oil after they had drilled into the sea bed and then decided that it was not economic to extract oil from that area. So they took away all their equipment and left a hole in the sea bed. They were required to plug this hole on the floor of the sea. The plugs were large metal contraptions. The question raised by the case was, as far as I can remember, whether or not these large plugs were part of the 'plant and machinery' used by the companies in carrying on their business. It may sound a dull enough question but there was a large amount of money at stake and the outcome was important for both the oil company and for the Inland Revenue. But what I found fascinating was how the drilling from rigs was carried out and understanding the scientific and engineering problems that have to be overcome. It was this aspect of tax cases that always intrigued me. One learned so much about so many different aspects of life which would never have otherwise come one's way.

For the six years from 1981 to 1987, my life proceeded on a fairly uneventful course and it looked to me as if my career would continue that way until I was due to retire in some four years time. It was a pleasant life. I was spared the hassle of London and the travelling and staying away from home in hotels in provincial towns that my circuit work involved but best of all was the relief of not having to work late into the night, night after night, preparing for the following day's work. I was always a slow worker and I swore early on in my career that I would never go into court without having prepared the case as completely as I possibly could. Moreover, the change to judicial work meant that I was able to see much more of Elizabeth and enjoy family life as I had not done for some years. For me too, a great advantage was that I was able to spend more time in our garden. I had always thought that the garden at Little Place had great possibilities. On a protected south facing slope the lower part of the garden was obviously capable of being improved, while at the top of the rising ground there was an old walled area which could be turned into a pleasant orchard and croquet lawn. So during those six happy years, the garden was gradually developed until eventually we were persuaded to open it to the public once or twice a year in order to help raise money for charity. To our amazement when we did this, we were able to raise sums in the order of £500 each time we opened which meant that we found ourselves able to give to charity sums far in excess of what we could have otherwise afforded. In recent years, it has become quite a habit for people to spend a warm Saturday or Sunday afternoon in the summer visiting local gardens. It is not only the grand gardens that receive this attention but many modest ones, such as ours, are popular with people who often come, I think, to see how other people manage their little bit of land. All this was most enjoyable and made more so by the fact that, during these years, three of Elizabeth's children settled with their families within a short distance of our home. So Elizabeth was able to be a caring and helpful grandmother – a role that she plays to perfection. But this enjoyable existence was not to last for ever. I was in my bath, before going to bed one day in November 1987 when Elizabeth came and said that there was a Mr Hanratty on the telephone who wanted to speak to me. I knew no-one called Hanratty. The only Hanratty I had ever heard of was a man who many years before had been convicted of a sensational murder on a motorway. His name had remained in the news because for some years, a campaign had been carried on to establish that he had been wrongly convicted. But I did not think that my caller could have been connected with him. So I got out of my bath and wrapping a towel around my tummy, I went to the telephone. My caller was James Hanratty who told me he was employed by the Lord Chancellor's office. He told me that Lord Grantchester, the President of the VAT Tribunals, was retiring a the end of the year and asked me whether or not I would like to take on the job. He said that the Lord Chancellor, Lord Mackay would be very pleased if I would. This came as a great surprise to me, but was a proposal that had certain attractions. It was arranged that Hanratty would come down to Oxford the next day and explain what was involved. Ever since I had first been concerned closely with taxation, I had felt that there was a great need for reform of the system by which the appeals of taxpayers were dealt with. Some years before I had been a member of a committee set up by the then Chancellor of the Exchequer, Geoffrey Howe, which had been charged with suggesting solutions to this problem. The committee had made various recommendations which appeared to have gained the approval of the two Government departments primarily concerned with administering the country's taxation. The Inland Revenue was responsible for income tax, capital gains tax, corporation tax and inheritance tax whereas the Customs and Excise had charge of VAT. But nothing had been done about it in the several years that had passed since we had reported. It seemed to me that if I became the President of the VAT Tribunals, I might be in a position to stimulate some action in this field. So when James Hanratty arrived, I was able to discuss this with him. He told me, as I already knew, that the Lord Chancellor (who when at the Bar in Scotland had had considerable experience in tax) was in favour of some at least of the reforms we had proposed. He told me that there was a good prospect of combining the VAT Tribunals and the Special Commissioners of Income Tax so that they were administered by a single staff in one building. This was obviously a step towards creating a single tax court where appeals relating to all sorts of tax could be heard. If this were achieved, it would effect a considerable saving in the total cost of the two tribunals as well as making for greater efficiency in the case of judicial manpower. There were other reforms which I would have liked to see, in particular, a reduction in the number of steps in the appeal system which at present is, in my view, absurdly extended. In some cases, there are no less than five possible steps on the ladder of appeals. As it often takes up to a year for an appeal from one court to be heard in the next court up, it is not unusual for the case to take four or five years before finality is achieved. This can mean that taxpayers and the Inland Revenue are left in doubt as to what the law is on a particular point for several years. This is very unsatisfactory for businessmen and traders for whom the need to know for certain the law that affects them is of great importance.

I discussed all these points with Hanratty and although he could give me no certain answers, I felt that if I were to accept and take on this new commitment, I might be able to effect a modest improvement in the justice system so far as it relates to matters of taxation.

After I had discussed the matter with Elizabeth and I decided to accept, I wrote in my diary that day:

"I will be sorry to leave the courts here where I have got to know so many people and feel I am a part of Oxfordshire life — but I will move to an interesting job that will stretch me and keep my brain ticking over — I hope".

And so, once again, I moved into a new life.

CHAPTER TWENTY-EIGHT

Tax Judge

I took over as President of the VAT Tribunals in January, 1988. My predecessor, Lord Grantchester, had held the post since VAT had been introduced in 1973. Because it was a new form of tax, unfamiliar to the British, there had been many teething problems relating to the interpretation of both the UK statutes and regulations which laid down how the tax was to be administered and of the European law from which the UK statutes were derived. These problems had in large part been resolved and he had built up a good working relationship between the Tribunal and the Customs and Excise, the Government department responsible for the collection of the tax. But the early years had shewn up one area in which the legislation had not achieved the efficiency hoped for. The tax was a tax on trading transactions and the idea underlying it was that the tax should ultimately be borne by the consumer, the member of the public who ultimately bought the goods or made use of the services upon which the tax was charged. But it was not he who paid the tax to the Government. It was the trader who sold the goods or services who had to pay the tax to the Government, although he was entitled to recover it from the person to whom he sold the goods or services. Thus it is that when we, as members of the public, pay for goods or services, we receive a bill which includes a sum specified as VAT which we pay to the trader — not to the Government. The scheme of the tax is that the trader has to pay over to the Government, the tax that is paid to him by his customers. In order to achieve this, each trader is required to make a return to the Customs and Excise at regular intervals in which he sets out all the goods or services he has provided in that period and the VAT he has charged to his customers on these transactions. He is required, at the same time, to send to the Customs and Excise, the tax he has charged to his customers. During the early years of the tax it was found that a high proportion of traders consistently sent in their returns, and the tax owing to the Government, very late. The result of this was that the traders might have the use of quite a sizeable amount of money that rightly should have been paid to the Government. They often held on to it for several months. The provisions in the original Act which were intended to prevent this occurring proved unsatisfactory. They were expensive to operate and often did not succeed in effecting an improvement in a trader's compliance with the time limits for rendering his returns. To overcome this difficulty, a committee under the chairmanship of Lord Keith, a Scottish Law Lord, was invited to suggest ways of remedying the problem. The committee came up with the proposal that was passed into law in the Finance Act 1985, that traders who were late in rendering their returns or in paying their tax on more than two occasions, should be liable to pay an automatic penalty calculated on a sliding scale depending on the number of times he had been late in paying his tax or rendering his return or had sent in an inaccurate return. When the legislation was first drafted, there was no provision that enabled a trader to be excused from paying the full amount of the penalty even if his return was only late by a day, or even if the circumstances were such that in common fairness, the penalty should not be imposed. Lord Keith told me once when I found myself sitting next to him at dinner, that when he saw this proposed legislation he had protested strongly to the Customs and Excise and said that the penalty should not apply if the trader had a reasonable excuse. As a result of his intervention, the legislation was amended as it went through Parliament to provide that the penalty should not apply if the trader had a reasonable excuse. The Government, however, came near to nullifying this alteration by causing a sub section to be inserted into the interpretation section of the act which provided that:

(a) "an insufficiency of funds to pay any tax due is not a reasonable excuse and;

(b) where reliance is placed on any other person to perform any task, neither the fact of that reliance, nor any dilatoriness or inaccuracy on the part of the person relied upon is a reasonable excuse".

This later provision was inserted to ensure that the excuse that earlier traders often put forward to explain why their return was late or inaccurate, namely that they had entrusted the preparation of their returns to their accountants or their book-keepers, should not avail them.

When I arrived at the VAT Tribunal, the first appeals against the imposition of these penalties were coming before the tribunal in large numbers. After we had a little experience of trying them, it was borne in on us, as indeed had been obvious from the start, that the cases varied widely in their gravity. At one end of the scale was the trader who made no real effort to render his returns in time, whose book-keeping was slack and often inaccurate. There was no injustice in imposing a penalty in such cases and indeed, usually, when this sort of trader had had a penalty imposed once or twice, he learnt a lesson and was careful in future. In other words the system had a salutary effect on the way in which the records of many businesses were kept. But there was a down side. In the nine years that had elapsed since the Conservatives had come to power under Margaret Thatcher, great changes had taken place in the economy. One result of the shake-up was that many thousands of people who had found themselves unemployed as a result of large companies shedding labour set themselves up as small businesses. All over the country, husbands and wives helped perhaps by a redundancy payment or small grant began small ventures. Such people often had little or no experience of keeping books and in their early days they were almost always working on a very small margin of profit. If they were a day or two late with their return, or made some mistake through a lack of knowledge, they would find themselves saddled with a fixed penalty sufficiently large to swallow up all their profits of the previous period. It was a time when the recession was beginning to bite and not a few of these new businesses were driven into liquidation or bankruptcy as a result. Although the scheme of the tax was intended to be broadly fair in that the trader was to pay over to the Government, the tax which he had charged to his customers, there were occasions when it worked harshly. Thus, if as not infrequently occurred, a newly established family business did a lot of work for some large company or institution, for example a local Government authority, it would often find that its customer insisted on being given a long period, perhaps three months, credit and if it did not get the long credit, it would take its business elsewhere. This would mean that when its VAT return was due, the small trader would find that he had done the work for his customer for three months and had charged him for all that work so that he was liable to pay over to the Government, all the VAT he had charged, but, because his customer insisted on three months credit, he had received none of what he was owed for the goods or services he had provided and none of the VAT he had charged. This frequently meant that he had no money with which to pay the VAT which he was liable to pay to the Government. When he was assessed for a penalty because of his failure to pay the VAT, the Customs argued that he could not be excused, despite the manifest unjustness of the situation, because the Act laid down that 'an insufficiency of funds' was not a reasonable excuse. This seemed to me monstrously unfair. The small traders, of whom there were many, who suffered in this way justifiably felt very aggrieved. I set about trying to persuade the Government to change the law by giving the tribunal the power to mitigate the amount of the penalty in suitable cases. But, as I learned, the Civil Service is very hard to persuade. In the Government, the practice had grown up of making a junior minister at the Treasury responsible for matters relating to VAT. The minister concerned had at one time been Peter Brooke, the brother of Henry Brooke in my old chambers, but he had moved on and when I arrived, it was Lord Caithness. He came to the tribunal and we had a discussion on this question, but I formed the impression that it was a subject on which he was not interested. To every suggestion I made, he gave the reply that was fed to him by the civil servant who had accompanied him. During his time in office, we made no progress. But two years later, his successor Mrs Gillian Sheppard came and discussed the problems again and this time our arguments went home.

She had come well prepared and knew the subject so that it was easy to explain to her where the system seemed to produce unjust results and should be reformed. By the time she came, fixed penalties had been introduced for what came to be known as serious misdeclarations in traders' returns. These penalties were even more draconian in their effect. The penalty was an automatic 30% of the amount of tax that would have been lost if the misdeclaration had not been discovered. In the case of companies that had a large turnover, 30% of the tax was often a very large sum. It could easily be in six or more figures. The unfairness of this type of penalty was particularly apparent when one realised that the misdeclaration that resulted in the penalty being imposed could arise from a book-keeper making a simple accidental error. An example would be if a supply of goods or services was shewn in the books as having been made a day or two after it was, in fact, made with the result that it fell into the period after the one in which it should have been shewn. The tax would not have been shewn as due in the earlier period, but as due in the later period. When this happened, the Government did not receive the tax at the end of the period in which it should have recovered it but at the end of the next period. It was kept out of its money for the period and could fairly be said to have lost the interest on the amount of tax, but to add to that, a penalty of 30% of the amount of the tax which in one case that came before me resulted in a penalty of approximately £100,000, was very unfair, when the misdeclaration was the result of an innocent mistake. So for these cases too, I pressed for the tribunal to be given a power to mitigate the penalty in appropriate cases. Eventually, after much pressure had been applied both by the member of the tribunal and others, a power to mitigate was granted and a much fairer system has resulted. But it took several years to achieve.

During the time that passed before this reform was brought about, I did my best to soften the impact of the legislation, where this was possible, without flying in the face of what Parliament had laid down in the Act. It has always seemed to me that it is legitimate to presume that Parliament when legislating did not intend to treat anyone unjustly. If therefore, a statute can be interpreted in more than one way, one of which produces an injustice and the other does not, it is not only permissible but it is right to give it the meaning that produces less injustice. In this way, I was able to soften the impact of the provision that said that 'an insufficiency of funds to pay any tax is not a reasonable excuse'. The word 'excuse' when given its ordinary meaning means a reason why someone should be excused. Now it quite often happened that a trader found himself unable to pay his VAT because he simply had not the funds with which to pay it. The Customs and Excise in case after case where this was the position, said that the taxpayer could not plead that he had a reasonable excuse and that was the end of the matter. But every now and then, a case came up where the reason the taxpayer was short of money was because something quite unexpected or unusual had cropped up. It seemed to me that the reason why, in such cases, he was asking to be excused was because this unusual event had occurred and not because he was short of money. So I held in one case that a trader who was unable to pay for lack of funds, nevertheless, had a reasonable excuse for not having paid the tax on time because he was saying that the reason why he should be excused was because the underlying cause of his having failed to pay was that the unusual and unexpected event had occurred — in the particular case the taxpayer had been deceived by the person who sold him a business into thinking that all outstanding VAT had been paid whereas the truth was that it had not. The Customs appealed but the Court of Appeal upheld my view so that a small dent had been made in what at first appeared to be an impregnable statutory provision. There were two or three other cases where a similar opportunity arose to allow a little humanity and indeed common sense, into the working of the very stringent provisions of the Act.

Another interesting aspect of my work at this time arose from the fact that the law relating to VAT derives ultimately from legislation issued by the European Community. In the early years, when the tax had only recently been introduced, English practitioners were slow to realise the extent of the impact of the European legislation on the British code. The courts of our country really became alive to this after Lord Denning in a well-known case pointed out in typically graphic phrases what was happening. He said that:

> "When we come to matters with a European element, the Treaty is like an incoming tide. It flows into the estuaries and up the rivers. It cannot be held back. Parliament had decided that the treaty is henceforward to be part of our law. It is equal in force to any statute".[1]

---

[1] *See H P Bulmer Ltd v Bollinger S A (1974) 2 ALLER 1226 at p.1231.*

Thereafter, as the courts realised that the effects of European law permeated many corners of our own law, it became more and more common to have to consider whether or not a British statute relating to a particular subject was consistent with the European legislation from which it was derived. Not long before I started at the tribunal, the European Commission had issued an important directive (the 6th Directive) which laid down in a comprehensive code what a member state should, or could, do in its own legislation by which it defined the way the tax was to work in its area. This meant that I was frequently having to decide appeals in which the taxpayer contended that the British Parliament had enacted a provision that was incompatible with the European law on the point. This was interesting work. It involved learning to look at European legislation as Europeans looked at it and not as an English lawyer tends to look at our statutes. It has always been a basic principle of our system that when called to decide what a statute meant, the court was bound, if it could, to give it the precise meaning that the words of the statute held. But a European lawyer is permitted to approach the problem in what has come to be called a more 'purposive' way. That is, one is permitted to try and see what was the purpose that the legislation was trying to achieve and then give to the disputed words, a meaning that is consistent with that purpose. On a number of occasions, cases came up which raised this problem and occasionally the conclusion to which the tribunal came was that the Customs and Excise had persuaded Parliament to enact provisions that ran counter to the European directives which were binding on the British courts. If a judge did not feel sure of the answer, he was permitted to refer the question to the European Court of Justice which would give an answer to the question which would enable him to decide the case. Usually, when I was faced with this sort of problem, I tried not to refer the question to Europe as to do so added greatly, at that time by as much as two years, to the time that it took to finally decide the appeal. Where, however, in one case the issue raised by the appeal was one which turned on land law, which is very different in European countries from the English law, I felt bound to send the case to Europe for a definitive view. This was because it is obviously desirable that all countries in the Community should apply the European law in the same way and it was very possible that a judge brought up on the English land law would interpret a particular provision in a different way from a continental lawyer familiar with the continental system. I was gratified that when the answer came back from the European Court of Justice, the court agreed with the view that I had tentatively indicated that I had reached, which was that the United Kingdom legislation did not accord with the European law and was therefore void. This was a case which concerned a well known firm of accountants, Lubbock Fine & Co, who had surrendered a lease of an office block in the West End of London which they had occupied. They had been paid a large sum, I think it was £850,000 by their landlords to persuade them to go. The United Kingdom legislation decreed that VAT should be paid on that sum. This provision was held to be invalid so the accountants did not have to pay VAT, which at 15% was itself a substantial sum.

Another attractive feature of my job was that unlike almost all other judges in England, I had jurisdiction to try cases in Scotland and Northern Ireland which involved me in travelling across the border, or the Irish Sea, to hear appeals in Edinburgh or Belfast. These visits were particularly enjoyable. I usually took Elizabeth with me and she enjoyed the experience. The members of the Scottish and Northern Irish Bar and judiciary were always immensely hospitable and we got to know well and became good friends of the men responsible for doing the VAT work in these countries. Ronnie Bennett, a charming and wise Scot, looked after the tribunals in Scotland and was a good example of the best type of Scottish lawyer. Learned, fair and brief and concise in his judgements. He is married to a delightful Icelandic lady and on the first occasion I went to Edinburgh, they gave me a sumptuous dinner in their home at which I had sitting on one side of me, his wife and on the other, her sister, also married to a Scottish judge. As the dinner progressed, I learned that they were both sisters of Magnus Magnusson who ran the highly popular TV programme 'Mastermind'. They were both every bit as astute at asking difficult questions as their brother and I realised, not for the first time, how high is the quality of the best brains north of the border.

In Northern Ireland, which was still suffering from the terrorism of the IRA, I was always guarded by two members of the Ulster security services. They were very calm and seemed immensely efficient. No one ever tried to shoot me and it always seemed faintly ridiculous that I should be protected in this way. I do not believe the IRA were interested in a judge from England who came to try VAT cases! But it was different for the Northern Ireland judges who tried VAT cases. They only tried VAT cases at intervals and other parts of their time was taken up with trying criminal cases which necessarily, from time to time, involved trials of IRA defendants. These judges were always on the IRA hit list and had to submit to having two security men shadow them day and night for years on end. This imposed a great strain on their wives and families but they refused to be perturbed by the conditions in which they were forced to live and work. When I first went to Belfast, the courts had recently been the target of an IRA bomb and one side of the court room was composed of sandbags which filled the gap blown in the wall. On one occasion, when Elizabeth and I had been over to Belfast for a week, we were taken to the airport for our return journey by our faithful 'minders'. When we arrived, there were still twenty minutes before we were due to board the aeroplane so we went into the lounge and I thanked the senior officer looking after us for his trouble and said that he was free to go. But he refused, saying that their orders were to remain with us until we were safely on the plane. So we sat and talked for another twenty minutes until we were summoned onto the aircraft. We then said goodbye and thanked them again. At that point, they told us that before we had arrived at the beginning of the week, the security police had received information that the IRA had said that they were going to 'get' a judge that week! I am glad that we had not been told and that the IRA never got their judge.

Shortly before one of my visits to Edinburgh, Elizabeth had been involved in a motor accident as a result of which her leg, which had been broken, was encased in plaster. To give her a bit of a change, I took her with me. One day the case I was hearing ended unexpectedly before lunch and I was free for the afternoon. So we decided to take a bus to Dalmeny, the home of Lord Rosebery. I had a recollection that the Rosebery who had been the Liberal Prime Minister and had written of Napoleon, had a considerable collection of Napoleonic relics which might be interesting. So we took a bus and I asked the conductor to tell us when we got to Dalmeny. Stupidly, I had not realised that there was a village of that name as well as the great house. The conductor stopped at the village and then we realised that we had passed the house some two miles back. The conductor said that we could stay in the bus while it went on to the Forth Bridge and turned round and he would put us off at the house. "We stop right at the entrance" he said. So we went on and were eventually put down at the gates of a park. When the bus left us I realised that beyond the gates was not, as it seemed from the road, a short drive to the house, but a long one which, after a bend by the gates, disappeared over the hills. It meant a walk of at least half a mile — out of the question for poor Elizabeth. So we were left on the deserted road. It was November and it soon began to rain and as it was about four o'clock, the light was beginning to fade. No cars came from which I could beg a lift. It was a most desolate picture and, not surprisingly, Elizabeth began to show signs of irritation. I was racking my brain to think of a way out of our difficulty when eventually, a small car drove up and stopped by me. The driver wound down the window and a head came out. "What are you doing here Patrick?", it said. The driver was Peter Gibson who had been a chancery barrister but was by then a High Court judge. I knew him well and had many times led him in cases when I was myself still practising. It turned out that his wife, Katy, was writing a book about a particular type of political cartoon prevalent at the end of the seventeenth century and of which there was a good collection in Dalmeny House. So they took us in their car to the house where we were given most royal treatment by the curator and shewn much of interest. They then took us back to Edinburgh. Rarely can a husband, who was on the verge of incurring great and justifiable wrath from his wife, have been saved by so lucky a coincidence. We were both some 400 miles from our normal haunts. Since that occasion, Peter has been promoted to the Court of Appeal and there, not so long ago, he gave a judgement overturning a decision of mine which had been upheld by a High Court judge. One member of the Court of Appeal dissented and as I write this, the case is on its way to the House of Lords. All of which perhaps shows that nothing is so strange as chance.

As well as trying the cases that came to the tribunal (as President, I was usually expected to try the most difficult or sensitive ones) there was a fair amount of humdrum administration to be done. It was important that the tribunal disposed of appeals that taxpayers brought to it as quickly as possible, otherwise, inevitably, a backlog built up and appellants had to wait longer and longer before they could be heard. This meant keeping a close watch on the number of cases being set down and estimating how long they would be likely to take to try and what was the prospect of the parties settling their differences before the day for trial arrived making it unnecessary to hear the appeal. During nearly all the period I was President, the number of appeals coming to the Tribunal steadily increased so that it became necessary to have available more legal chairmen to preside at the trials and furthermore, it soon became clear that we would need more court rooms than were available in the premises in Marlborough Street where the tribunal was originally situated. This situation enabled me to press the Lord Chancellor's Department to take the first step towards reforming the tax appeal system in the way that I and others had for some years thought was desirable. The Special Commissioners who heard income tax and corporation tax appeals were a separate body, administered by a different Government department from VAT Tribunals. The judicial members of both tribunals were men and women who, for the most part, were perfectly capable of handling cases raising either problems of VAT or of the other taxes. They were, however, only permitted to deal with the type of case coming before the tribunal to which they had been appointed. It so happened that at the time, the workload coming before the

Special Commissioners was light and they were underemployed while, as I have said, the burden falling on the VAT Tribunal was steadily increasing. It seemed sensible, therefore, to allow the special commissioners to try VAT cases and vice versa. This would make better use of the judicial manpower available. Another criticism that is often made was that the Special Commissioners were administered by the Inland Revenue and the VAT Tribunals by the Customs and Excise. Though the two Government departments did not try to influence the decisions of the tribunals under their control, the fact that they were in technical control gave the impression to taxpayers that they were not independent. For this reason, there were many who thought that it would be more appropriate for both to be administered by the Lord Chancellor in the same way that he administered the criminal and civil courts in the country. It was fortunate for us that Lord Mackay, the Lord Chancellor, had when practising as an advocate in his native Scotland, been involved in many tax cases and therefore understood the position. Shortly after I had been appointed President of the VAT Tribunal, I had submitted a paper to the Lord Chancellor which I entitled *A Combined Tax Tribunal or Court* and in which I suggested the need for these and various other reforms. When he had visited the tribunal he had indicated that he was broadly in favour of my ideas.

The circumstance that brought these matters to a head was the fact that the lease of the premises occupied by the Special Commissioners in High Holborn was due to run out shortly. New premises would have to be found for them and as we at the VAT Tribunal, were outgrowing the building in which we were housed, efforts were made to find a building where both the Special Commissioners and the VAT Tribunals could be brought together under one roof. At this time, too, the Lord Chancellor's Department took over the administration of both the Special Commissioners and the VAT Tribunal. Eventually, three houses in Bedford Square were chosen and it was decided to adapt them for our accommodation. I believe the houses had been bought by an advertising company which had restored them fairly lavishly but had gone into liquidation before being able to occupy them. The essential work that was necessary to enable us to use them was the preparation of court rooms. This took time and while it was in train, Roland Widdows who was the Presiding Special Commissioner retired. Not long after that, I was invited to take over his job as well as President of the VAT Tribunal. This was more than I had ever expected. When, therefore, the Special Commissioners and the VAT Tribunal moved into the new premises in Bedford Square and became known as the Combined Tax Tribunal, I found myself presiding over the new arrangements.

The three houses in the square into which we moved were all built in 1777 and are excellent examples of Georgian town house architecture. Andrew Byrne, the author of an architectural study of the square published in 1990 says of No 44:

"There is some good detailing inside this house. The entrance and staircase halls are divided by a screen with an excellent fanlight and carved softwood transom of anthemion and palmette. Both halls have a standard ornamental plaster frieze of alternating bucranea and anthemion in a guilloche band. The staircase rises to the second floor and has an apsed rear wall and a splendid lantern light which has a decorative lining of swags and rosettes. The decorative plaster ceiling in the front room on the first floor is a fine example of its type. There are also good consoled doorcases on this floor with carved friezes of flute and palmette."

It was the front room in No 44 referred to in that quotation that I had as my chambers for the rest of my judicial life. Fortunately, the building was listed and the planning authority would not allow the room to be altered or subdivided into smaller offices as often happens when old domestic buildings are converted for business use. This room thus remained in much the same condition as when it had been the principal reception room of the various private tenants who had lived there. They had included a number of distinguished people. From 1827 to 1846 Sir Nicholas Conyngham Tindal who became Solicitor General in 1826 and Chief Justice of the Common Pleas in 1829 was the tenant. More recently between 1906 and 1913 Lady Ottoline Morrell, the socialite hostess usually associated with the Bloomsbury set lived there with her husband, an MP and used the fine drawing room for, as has been said, "spectacular if unorthodox entertaining".[1] In this room she entertained such writers and artists as W B Yeats, D H Lawrence, Virginia Woolf, and Augustus John. But what delighted me most was that from 1921 until his death in 1928, No 44 had been the London house of H H Asquith, the great Liberal statesman whom I had always admired. He had been forced to abandon his larger and more expensive house in Cavendish Square for the cheaper one in Bedford Square.

On 15 May 1991, Lord Mackay, the Lord Chancellor, visited the premises and performed the official opening of the building. When he saw the splendid room in which I was housed, he said that he would willingly swap it for his less commodious room in the House of Lords! I think it is probably true to say that no member of the judiciary in England has chambers that are more elegant or spacious than my room in No 44.

During the time that I presided at the Combined Tax Tribunal, it was necessary to recruit several new judicial members to cope with the steadily increasing burden of work. Most of these were practising barristers or solicitors who did their judicial work part time in the interstices of their practices, others were either retired or people who were working part time on other tribunals. It was my hope that it would be possible to build up a team of really good lawyers who could handle the sometimes difficult legal problems that arise in tax cases and at the same time deal speedily, effectively and humanely with the many small cases that came up. In all this we were lucky and eventually a team was got together that worked happily with each other and proved of high quality. On one of my visits to Northern Ireland, Elizabeth and I had been asked to dinner by Sir Barry and Lady Shaw. He was a Bencher of the Middle Temple and I had met him there. He told me that he had just retired from his post as Director of Public Prosecutions in Northern Ireland and was looking for something else to do. Unfortunately, he could not be given a judicial post in Ulster as it was thought that having been DPP, the Republicans would not believe that he would be independent. I suggested that he might try VAT and happily he agreed and was a wonderful accretion to our team. In a rather similar way I came across Paul Heim. Elizabeth and I had been in Maastricht where I attended a short course designed to try and teach judges how the European Commission worked. Paul was one of the lecturers and his great knowledge of European law mixed with a strong and comic sense of humour appealed to me. He had been, for six years, the Registrar of the European Court of Justice, but had not been re-appointed because the Germans persuaded the other member states that they were under-represented in the legal hierarchy and so a German was appointed

---

[1] See Roy Jenkins 'Asquith' p493n.

in Paul's place. Paul was, therefore, looking for work to do. He was ideal for us as we needed someone with a good knowledge of Community law which was steadily becoming a more and more important part of VAT law. John Avery-Jones, who was the senior partner of one of London's leading firms of solicitors and who had made a special study of VAT legislation and written a good deal about it, also came to us and was a very valuable addition to our number. Ron Miller was also a solicitor who had just retired as the solicitor of Inland Revenue. He was an old friend who had briefed me in my days as standing counsel and whose acute brain and modest ways made him an ideal chairman. He had to sit for some time only as a VAT chairman as he was required by the Lord Chancellor's Department to have a period in 'quarantine' before he could be let loose on work as a Special Commissioner, for which, of course, he was particularly well qualified. Nor were the people joining us all men. Gill Gort, who had been a pupil of Lord Woolf when he was the treasury devil and had had to give up practice at the Bar because of a bad back, was ideally qualified and proved to be an excellent judge. Jane Plumptre was a partner in another of London's best firms of commercial solicitors. She had done a lot of work for the Customs and Excise and was, too, admirably qualified. She proved to be first class when sitting in a judicial capacity: quick and having the invaluable quality of being able to ensure that the repetitive verbosity of advocates is kept on a tight rein — and yet always courteous and totally fair.

It was with people such as these that I worked and I could not have asked for a better team. They were backed up by a number of civil servants led by the former Clerk to the Special Commissioners, Dick Lester, who, when we moved to 44 Bedford Square became Registrar of the VAT Tribunal as well. He was a very tolerant man who put up with the foibles and occasional prima donnaism, of the judicial members. All things considered, when I left, I was able to hand over to my successor, Stephen Oliver, a happy, well run and efficient ship.

In the two years that have now passed since I left, Stephen Oliver has proved both popular and efficient. A considerably increased jurisdiction has now been put upon the VAT Tribunal in connection with various Customs duties and insurance premium tax. As a result, it has become even more imperative than it was in my time (and God knows it was imperative enough then), to rationalise, simplify and reform the tax appeal system. In November 1994, Stephen gave a lecture at Kings College, London, in which he set out his ideas on how this should be done in order to create a system that is suitable for the present age. He reiterated some views that I expressed in a talk to the Institute of Taxation and has greatly improved on them. Let us hope that before long, in his time, his suggestions will be implemented. The twenty years that must elapse before the reforms advocated by a Tory reactionary can be implemented have nearly passed now.

CHAPTER TWENTY-NINE

Final Assesment

It is provided in the Act under which the VAT Tribunal was set up that the President must retire at the end of his year of service following his 72nd birthday unless the Lord Chancellor considers that it is in the public interest he should continue. I was 72 in 1991 but the Lord Chancellor extended my time by a year so that I retired from full time work in 1992. Shortly before my final day at the Combined Tax Centre, the members gave me a splendid dinner at the Garrick Club and presented me with a very handsome cheque with which I was able to buy myself a small greenhouse which I badly needed for the garden at Little Place. I was rather ashamed later when I learned how it came about that they knew I wanted a greenhouse. Apparently one day, unbeknown to me, my secretary rang up Elizabeth and asked her if she knew what I would like and she apparently said that she did not really know but that I had mentioned the need for a greenhouse. It would have been more appropriate if she had said that I would greatly appreciate a garden trowel, or a book on how to take cuttings. To ask for a greenhouse did seem very greedy. But such was the kindness and generosity of my colleagues that I have ever since had a greenhouse in which I can house tender plants through the winter. My old friend Michael Nolan, then a Lord Justice of Appeal, made an embarrassingly flattering speech about me and I, in reply, said a few haltingly modest (I hope) words of the sort that are usually said on such occasions. Although that was the end of my full time career, I was called upon from time to time to help out both on circuit and with tax cases during the next eighteen months. At that point, I had to go into hospital to have a peptic ulcer dealt with and thereafter, I retired completely. So ended my legal career which had lasted forty six and a half years. It would be surprising if when the moment comes for a person to stop work in the calling he has followed for many years, he did not feel apprehensive. When that moment arrived for me, I certainly felt butterflies in my tummy. But I had, for some time, been giving thought to how I would spend my time. I felt that it was important to have a plan so that I did not spend all my time busily doing nothing. I remembered one person I met shortly after he had retired saying to me that what he had learned in his new life was how very long it took to do nothing. I was lucky though, I still had two things I wanted to achieve. I wanted to be able to give more time to the garden. Over the years that had passed since we moved into Little Place, I had created a garden of which I was proud, but there was room for much improvement. I wanted to make it a garden that would give real pleasure to whoever lived in the house and to those who might visit it. So I decided that I would spend my afternoons working in the garden. In the mornings, I decided on a different activity. During the years that I had been practising as a barrister and acting as a judge, there were in England a number of exceptionally able judges and I had had the good fortune to know several of them and to practise before others. It so happened that during these years, many of the great judges were members of the Middle Temple and I got to know them as fellow Benchers of the Inn. At one point, five of the eleven Law Lords were members of the Middle Temple. In the first part of the nineteenth century, there had been a flowering of great men in Edinburgh and Lord Cockburn in a collection of biographical sketches contained in 'Memorials of his time' painted an entrancing picture of them. Walter Scott, Adam Smith, Erskine, Dugald Stewart and many judges and other pillars of Edinburgh society of his times are depicted in Cockburn's inimitable style. I determined to write of some of the great judges I knew and embarked on a book that I intended to call 'Seven Pillars of Justice' which was to be a series of brief sketches of seven great judges of my time with an appreciation of each one's particular contribution to our English legal system. This would occupy my mornings. This plan of action, writing in the morning, working in the garden in the afternoon, appealed to me as it would ensure that a certain amount of mental effort would be required in the morning while fresh air and the modicum of exercise required for working in the garden would help to keep me fit and ensure that I did not — as so many elderly men do — fall asleep in front of the television or over a book. But all the plans of mice and men are liable to gang awry. I had hardly embarked on this regime when I had to go into hospital for the removal of part of my colon. I made a good recovery from that and was once again beginning to get back into my planned routine when Elizabeth was involved in a serious motor accident, as a result of which she was in hospital for three weeks and on her return home was confined to bed for a long period. Even now, as I write, some three months after the accident, she has only just begun to be able to hobble about. It may well be several months yet before we know to what extent she will recover from her injuries. It looks as if she may end up lame and with a painful right foot. This further misfortune has meant that the time when I will be able to divide my life between writing and gardening has been further delayed. So, as I draw to an end this record of what I have done with my life, I offer up a prayer that Elizabeth may fully recover and that I may be allowed, in such further time as is granted to me, to improve my garden and write my book in praise of seven judges who I have admired and with whom I have had the good fortune to be acquainted.

As I look back over my life, I am amazed at my good fortune. I have lived in England and for much of my life in some of the most beautiful parts of England and have lived and worked amongst kind, intelligent and understanding people. And yet, in my lifetime that has extended for three quarters of a century, from just after the end of the First World War to fifty years after the end of the second, the England that I know has seen more change in almost every aspect of life and human affairs than in any other similar period in its history. The changes in the material things which surround us have been dramatic.

The horse and cart that I used to hear clip clopping along the roads of Battersea has disappeared, to be replaced by the omni-present, high speed motor car. In the countryside, too, which I knew as a child on visits to my grandmother, heavy shire horses no longer pull the plough and labourers no longer make stooks of bundles of harvested corn. Tractors or huge combine harvesters do the work formerly done by many men and horses. The magnificent trains hauled by great steam locomotives in which we travelled to the coast or to the country for our holidays have given way to jumbo jets which hurtle loads of 300 or so people cheek by jowl through the air to destinations all over the world. Nowadays, many young people by the time they are in their twenties have visited several countries and become accomplished proper globe trotters. In the home, the chores of washing up or of laundering the household dirty linen that was carried out by my mother or a maid in tubs of soap suds and soda are for the most part no longer performed by humans. Dishwashers, washing machines, spin dryers and endless gadgets have reduced the drudgery of domestic life and have resulted in other forms of mechanical or monotonous activity. Partly as a result of this and partly through advances in education, women form a large part of the country's workforce and a high and ever increasing proportion of the majority of the professions. Television and videos have created a situation in which entertainment is available at all times of the day in one's own home at the flick of a switch. No longer does one have to go to a cinema, theatre or village hall to be entertained by others. The entertainers can be summoned into one's sitting room as required.

But dramatic as the changes have been in the physical conditions in which we live, they are less fundamental than the changes that have taken place in the same period in many of the intangible ideas and precepts by which we try to fashion our lives. To one whose parents grew up in middle class homes where the virtues of the Victorians seemed to circumscribe the sort of life that those parents would have wished their children to lead and to one who as he grew to maturity, was himself constantly made aware of those virtues, it sometimes seems that the solid foundations upon which he hoped his children would build seem no longer to be there. Wherever they tread, they feel beneath their feet only shifting sands. And yet when I consider my children and my stepchildren, now all grown up, and my grandchildren, the eldest of whom are approaching maturity, I realise that they have managed somehow to stand up straight despite the shifting sands. Their aims may be different from those of an earlier generation and their moral foundations may be differently expressed but their standards are, I am sure, as high or higher than those of the Victorians. I am proud of them all and can truly say in the words of Charles Churchill:

> "Be England what she will,
> with all her faults, she is my country still."

Index

Abberley Hall Preparatory School, 9–12
Abingdon, 155
–, appointment as Recorder of, 144
–, court room, 145
Ackner, Desmond, 164
adoption as Tory candidate for Swindon, 121, 126
alcohol, first taste, 18
Aldenham, Lord, and Keble College, 162
Allen family, Kenya, 58
–, –, offer of land, 58, 97–98
Ambatolampy, 67–68
ammunition dumps, 42
Anderson, John, 67–68, 72
Antananarivo, 65–67
apprentice shipwright, 20–21
architecture, interest in, 17
Ashton, Gilbert, 9, 24
Ashton family, 9
Asquith, Lord Oxford and, 183
–, Raymond, 149
atomic bombs, dropped on Japan, 96
attacked by witness, 139–140
Avery-Jones, John, 210

Bagnall, Arthur, 99
Baker, Michael, 147
Baldwin, Stanley, 138
Baldwin of Bewdley, Lord, 138
Bar exams, exemptions from some papers, 99
–, pass, 100
Barker, John, 23, 37, 38
Barnard, Alec, 72, 91
barrister's Clerk, duties of, 165
Barristers' Clerks Association, 165
barristers, disciplining, Royal Commission, 163
–, education of, Royal Commission, 163
–, increase in numbers wanting to practise, 163–164
barristers and solicitors, professions to remain separate, 163
Basingstoke, 134, 135
Batchelor, Cyril, 165, 166
Bathurst, Christopher, 164
Battersea, 3
Bedstone, 43, 44
Beeching, Lord, 144
Belk, Toby, 15
Bellerby Camp, infantry officers' course, 46–47
Bencher, election, 162
Bennett, Ronnie, 206
Benson, Lord, 163
Bentley, Stokes and Lowless v Beeson, 174, 175
Bentota, 71, 72, 75, 190
Best, Emily (née de Horne), 107
Beyfus, Gilbert, 115–116
Bingham, Tom, 102, 170, 171
Blackwood, Michael, 73
Bletchley Hall, 100
boat designing, 155

Bosanquet, David, 24
Bourne, Wilfrid, 102, 114, 169, 170, 171
Brightman, Mr Justice, 175, 176
Brooke, Henry, 102, 203
–, Peter, 203
Brown, Ivor, 82
Browne, Lord Justice, 173
Buckley, Denys, 171
Budapest, 32–33
Bunton, George, 37
Burke, Edmund, 133
Burma, 76–92
–, Allied advance, 81–92
–, invasion by Japanese, 76–77
–, leave, 92–95
–, topography, 76
Bush, Lady, mistaken identity, 196
Butler, Paddy, 24
–, R.A., 119

Caithness, Lord, 203
call up papers, 39
Cambridge Union, 24–25
capital punishment, 121–123
car ferry, 1939, 27, 109
Carr, Mike, 11
cases, other than murder, 145–146
Cassells, Mr Justice, 100, 101
censoring, of soldiers' letters, 50
Ceylon, 71–75 see also Sri Lanka
champagne, introduction to, 12
Chertsey, coronation procession, 109
Cheshire, Leonard, 155
Cheshire Home, 155, 171
Childrens Home, inquiry into, 167–168
Chorley, Lord, 168
Christmas dinner 1944, 90
Churchill, Winston, 133
circuit judge, 192–200
–, application for appointment as, 170
–, Oxford, appointment as, 184
citizen's rights, ICCUS report, 120–121
Citizens Advice Bureau, 114
Clark, Sir Andrew, 115
Clifton Hampden, 156, 162
Cockburn, Lord, 212
Colombo, Sri Lanka, local troubles, 187
Colville, John, 49
Combined Tax Tribunal, 208–218
–, President's room, 183
commandos, role of, 47
'Compiegne', boarding, 53
Conservative Party, meeting to enlist support of members of the Bar, 118
Control Commission for Germany, 99
convoy, tactics of, 49–50
Council of Legal Education, 163
counsel, choice of by prisoner, 116
Court of Appeal, 154
Courts Act 1971, 144
Couse, Philip, 168
Crichel Down inquiry, 119–120
Cross, Richard, 51
Curfew House, Chertsey, 6, 7, 8, 109

Customs and Excise, 149
cyclone warnings, 65

Dalmeny, 206–207
Daly, Laurance, 147, 148
Davenport, Brian, 176
Dayrell, William, first Recorder of Abingdon, 144, 145
Dean, Terence, 113
Deepwell Cottage, Oakley, 112
Dehn, Conrad, 102
Denby, Phil, and wild boar, 57
Denning, Lord, 151, 173, 204
Dilhorne, Lord, 152
diminished responsibility, defence in murder cases, 122
Diplock, Lord, 152, 170, 175, 176
dividend stripping, 150–151
divorce, thoughts on, 193–196
dock briefs, 116, 117
Donaldson, Lord, 175
Donner, Sir Patrick, 135
Dunboyne, Lord, see Butler, Paddy
Durban, 49, 51–53

East Africa Division, 189
East African Artillery, creation of, 54
–, loss of 301 Field Regt at sea, 73–74
East African Artillery (Tanganyika) Field Battery, 55 et seq.
11th East African Division, 80, 81, 82, 87, 90
Eastbourne, study at, 99
Eden, Anthony, 133
Egypt, 71
Elephant Bill, see Williams, J.H.
elephants, recovery of from wild, 85–86
'Ellsea', cabin cruiser, 113, 155
Elwyn-Jones, Lord, 149, 150, 175, 177
embarkation, for Middle East, 48
England, return to, 98
Equitable Life Assurance Co., member of Board, 137–138
Europe, 1939 tour of, 26, 27–35
Evans, Dudley, 155
–, Dudley Murray and Olga, 72
Executive Committee of the Inn, member of, 163

Fairfield's shipyard, Govan, 20–21
family casualties, 94
father, death of, 190–191
Fennell, Desmond, 196
Ferguson, Bernard, 70
–, Ken, 18
Fetcham, 3
Fife, Ian, 99, 100
Finance Act 1960, 151
first case, 116
Fletcher-Cooke, Charles, 134
Foot, Sir Dingle, 186
Forbes, Bill, 102
forced landing, at Mersa Matruh, 93
Fowkes, 'Fluffy', 96

INDEX

Fox, Mr Justice, 173
Franks Committee, 121

Garden Court, London flat, 162
Gardiner, Gerald, 115, 195
Gardner, Micky, 8
Gasser, Joe, shipwright, 20
Geddes, Duncan, 90
General Commissioner of Income Tax, 174
General Election 1955, 128–130
General Medical Council, legal adviser to, 169
Germany, pre-war experiences, 28–29
Ghurkas, 81
Gibson, Peter, 207
Gill, Ernest, 102
Glasgow University, 19
Gormley, Joe, 147, 148
Gort, Gill, 210
Gould, Sir Charles, Equitable Life Assurance Co., 137
Grantchester, Lord, 199, 201
Grey, Edward, 126
Griffiths, John, 146
Griffiths v Harrison, 151

Hailsham of St Marylebone, Lord, 170, 171, 191, 192, 195
Hambantota, 73
Hamilton, Ronnie, 89
Hampshire County Council, bird expert, 136
–, building of new court, 136–137
–, bye law on swans, 136
–, committees, 136
–, election defeat, 137
–, election to, 135–136
Hart, Jerry, 39
Head, Adrian, 74
–, Henry, 74
head of chambers, 164, 165
Healey, Dennis, 152
Heidsieck, Charles, 27–28
Heim, Paul, 209
Hemley, David, 166, 170, 184
Henry, Denis, 102
Heyworth-Talbot, Frank, 173
High Court Bench, hopes of invitation, 169–170
High Court judges, transport for, 196–197
Hills, Sir Reginald, 149
Hodge, Edward Vere, 37, 38
Holland, Milner, 115
Holy Land, 70–71
Homicide Act 1957, 122
House of Lords, 151, 154
Howe, Geoffrey, 131, 199
Hulett, Guy, 140, 141
Hungary, 32–33

ICCUS, secretary of, 118–119
–, report on human rights, 120–121
Imphal, 76, 77, 79, 80, 81
5th Indian Division, 82
23rd Indian Division, 80, 81
Inland Revenue, appointment as Standing Counsel to, 149–150

–, cases, 172–179
Inns of Court Conservative and Unionist Society, see ICCUS
inquiries, 167–168
Intelligence Officer, appointment, 63
invasion alert, 40–41

Jackson, R.M., St. John's College Cambridge, 25
James, Ewart, 137
–, Basil, 182
Japanese surrender, 96
Jekyll, Gertrude, 156
Jenkins, Patrick, 132
judge, swearing in, 191, 192
judicial review, procedure for, 121
Junior Staff College, Middle East, 68, 69

Kalewa, 85, 111
Karachi, 93
Keble College, Oxford, 162
–, –, grandfather's part in foundation, 1
Keith, Lord, 201
Keuneman, Pieter, President of Cambridge Union, 24–25
Kijabe, Kenya, 54, 110
kindergarten, Mrs Spencer's, 5
King's African Rifles, 89, 90
Kuala Lumpur, sightseeing, 187
Kumarangalam, President of Cambridge Union, 24

Labour Party, disillusionment with, 118
–, early interest in, 24
Lake Vyrnwy, guard duties, 44
–, honeymoon at, 94
Larkhill Camp, Kijabe, Kenya, 54, 110
leave, in England, 92–95
lecturing, to augment income, 114
legal appointments, part-time, 147
Lester, Dick, 210
lifestyles, changes in, 212–213
Lindley, Lord Justice, 173
lion hunt, 59
Little Place, Clifton Hampden, development of garden, 156, 157–161, 198, 211–212
Llewellyn-Davies, Lord and Lady, 177, 179
Lloyd, Selwyn, 118, 119

MacCarthy, Justin, 55, 56
Machek, meeting with Croat leader, 33
Mackay, Lord, 199, 182, 208, 209
Macleod, Iain, 119
Madagascar, securing of, 61–63, 64–65
–, strategic importance of, 61
Maenan, Lord, 146
Major, John, 132
malaria, 95
Malaysian cases, 184–187
Malaysian Government, instruction from, 154
Mallalieu, Ann, 174, 175
marriage, to Jeananne Powell, 94

–, –, end of, 148
Maudling, Reginald, 119
Mayhew, Patrick, 132
McKenna, Brian, 141
McNeile, Rev Fergus, 13
Medd, Agnes E.G., née Parsons, mother, 3, 105, 108, 113
–, Alfred, 3
–, Betty, 6, 94, 113
–, Drusilla, 100, 103, 112, 180
–, Elizabeth, 161, 180, 206, 212
–, E.N., father, 105, 108, 113
–, family photograph, 113
–, Fred, 2–3
–, Henry, visit to in New Delhi, 91
–, – and Marjorie, 113
–, Jane, 103, 192
–, Jo, 94
–, Jocelyn, 8
–, Louisa, grandmother, 1, 2, 3, 104
–, Marjorie, 3, 108
–, Patrick, 111, 180, 181, 182
–, Peter Goldsmith, Canon, grandfather, 1–2, 104, 106, 108
–, Robin, 2, 113
–, Sarah Louisa, 113
–, Thomas, 3, 103
Mepacrin, malaria protection, 95
Mersa Matruh, forced landing, 93
Micklethwaite, Sir Robin, 170
Middle East, embarkation, 48
Middle Temple, new hall, 131
Mildon, Arthur, 132
Miller, Norman, 42, 43
–, Ron, 210
Ministry of Health, inquiry for, 168
Monkton, Walter, 133
Monroe, Hubert, 175
–, John, 174
Morrell, Lady Ottoline, 156, 183, 209
Morris of Borth-y-Gest, Lord, 147
Moses, Eric, 174
Mountbatten, Lord Louis, 81–82, 90
mumps, 95
Munby, James, 173
Murder (Abolition of Death Penalty) Act 1965, 123
murder cases, 142–144
Murison, Mac, 137

Nairobi, 53
National Insurance Commissioner, invitation declined, 170
naval architecture, 16, 18
Neave, Airey, 134, 171
Nesbitt, Alexander, gt.-grandfather, 2
new chambers, 164
Newcastle, Co. Down, 47
Nice, 34
Noel-Baker, Francis, 127–128
Nolan, (Lord) Michael, 176, 182, 211
North Cerney, Glos., 1
Northern Ireland, posting to, 47

Oliver, Stephen, 210
Ombudsman, 121
Orr, Alan, 101, 102, 116, 149, 169, 192, 193, 197

INDEX

Owen, Rev Reggie, Headmaster of Uppingham, later Archbishop of NZ, 14, 15
Oxford Circuit, 116

Parents, honeymoon at Clifton Hampden, 163
Parliament, end of ambition to become MP, 135
Parsons, Bertha, 105, 107
—, Muriel, 4
—, Rt Rev Richard G., 4, 21, 107
—, William, 105, 107
Parsons family, 3–4
Patch, Catherine, 37, 38, 45
Paul, Gilbert, 115
Payton, Roger, 168
Pennycuick, Lord Justice, 173, 174
Percival, Ian, 134
Philips, Raymond, 102, 149, 164, 169
Pioneer Corps, 39–45
Plowden, Edmund, treasurer of Middle Temple, C16, 131
Plumptre, Dr, 1
Plumptre, Jane, 210
Poland, hospitality, 31
Politics, introduction to, 16, 24
'Pookie', see Powell, Jeananne
Potter, Mark, 102, 171
Powell, Enoch, 119, 132
—, Jack, 43
—, Jeananne, conversion to Roman Catholicism, 155
—, —, death of, 155
—, —, end of marriage to, 155
—, —, first meeting, 43
—, —, marriage to, 94
Powys, Lord, 146
President of VAT Tribunals, ability to try cases in Scotland and N. Ireland, 205–207
—, security measures in N. Ireland, 206
Price, Richard, Equitable Life Assurance Co., 137–138
Prince Paul, of Yugoslavia, 60
Princess Olga, of Yugoslavia, 60
Privy Council, 154
promotion, to major, 96
Prudhoe, 45

QC, appointment as, 154
Queen Mother's Fund, 164

Raeburn, Edward, 14
'Ramillies', torpedo attack, 64
Rawlinson, Peter, 169, 170
Ray, Eddy, 168, 178, 179
Reading goal, inquiry into riot at, 167
Red Mini Murder, 142–143
Rees-Mogg, William, 133–134
Reid, Lord, 151
rejection, by constituencies, 132
Rentokil, 175
Renton, David, 134
retirement, 211
return to England, 98
Richard Thomas and Baldwin, steel makers, 43
Rippon, Geoffrey, 118
'RMS Otranto', conditions aboard, 49

Rowlatt, Mr Justice, 173
Russell of Killowen, Lord, 170

Sacred crocodile, 64
Sainsbury, Capt, 41–42, 43
Sarafand, 69
Saunders, V.T., 15
Scargill, Arthur, 148
Scarman, Leslie, 101, 116, 140
scholarship funds, attempts to increase, 164–165
Scott, Peter, 38
Sedley, Stephen, 148
selection committee, Basingstoke, 134
—, Bristol, 133
—, Hemel Hempstead, 134
—, Isle of Wight, 133–134
—, SE Leicester, 134
—, Southport, 134
—, Tavistock, 134
Selwyn College, Cambridge, change to law studies, 21, 23, 25, 37
Shaw, Sir Barry, 209
Sheppard, Gillian, 203
Shropshire County Council, inquiry for, 167–168
Shropshire Quarter Sessions, appointment as deputy chairman, 146
silk, decision to apply for, 148, 150
—, grant of, 154
—, risks in taking, 154
Simon, Jack, 61, 119, 126, 134, 171, 195–196
—, Sir John, 135
'Skipper', see Sainsbury, Capt
Slade, Mr Justice, 174, 175
Slough Estates Ltd., 146
Smith, Derek Walker, 134
Snow, C.P., 142–143
solicitors, greater rights of audience in courts, 164
solicitors and barristers, professions to remain separate, 163
South Staffordshire Regt, 5th Battn, posting to, 45
Special Commissioner of Income Tax, part-time appointment, 198
Spencer, Elizabeth, marriage to, 155
Sri Lanka, sightseeing, 187–190
Stable, Sir Wintringham, 146
Stanley, Oliver, 133
Stevens, Cleveland, 99
—, Lt-Col, 73
Stevenson, Hugh, 168
—, Melford, 101, 102, 114–115, 115–116, 165
student scholarship, 28
sugar, case in Tanzania, 140–142
Suter, Martin, 72, 96
Swahili, learning, 56
Swindon, Tory candidate for, 121, 126

Talbot, Michael, 146, 147
Tamu, 83, 84
Tanzania, punishment for theft in, 141
—, sugar case in, 140–142
Taverne, Dick, 132
tax avoidance, 151–153

tax consultants, 150
Temple, Sir Rawdon, 170
Templeman, Mr Justice, 172
Thatcher, Margaret, 128, 132, 177, 202
Thesiger, Frederick, 145
—, Mr Justice, 145
Thomas, Richard, 43
—, Ruby, 43
Thompson, John, 51
—, Treffry, 95
Thorn, Robin, 70
Thorndyke, Sybil, 5
Tindal, Frank, 27, 28, 32, 33, 34, 109
tinnitus, cause of, 63
Tixal Lodge, 2
Tomlin, Lord, 150, 151
Town and Country Planning Act, 139
trades unions, pamphlet on legal position of, 123–125
transit camp, 52–53
trials, last as barrister, 191
tribunal, tax avoidance, chairman of, 168–169
Trieste, 34
Tubbs, Raymond, 55, 56
Tumim, Stephen, 132
Tutt, Nigel, 152
Tyrer v Smart, 175–177

University College, Oxford, mastership of, 1
Uppingham, scholarship to, 11–12

VAT, difficulties for small traders, 202–203
—, effect of European legislation, 204–205
—, explanation of, 201–202
—, reform of, 203–204
VAT Tribunals, President of, 199–200
—, reforming appeal system, 207–208
Vaughn-Jones, Freddy, 36
Venice, 34
Verona, 34

Walton on the Naze, pier demolition, 40
war injury, 63
Warner, Mr Justice, 179
Warsaw ghetto, 30
Wavell, Lord, dinner with, 91
Webster, Peter, 102, 163, 170, 171
Weldon, Huw, 47
wellington boots, missing from store, 44–45
81st West African Division, 80
Widdows, Roland, 208
Wijetunge, Pamela and Vernon, 189–190
Williams, J.H., 85, 86, 87
Wolfenden, John, 15
Woolf, Harry, 149
World War II, approach of, 22–23
—, first months, 36–38
Wright, 'Cud', 17

Yugoslavia, 33–34

Zagreb, 33
Ziegler, Prof, Pembroke College Cambridge, 25